Crisis and Criticism

Historical Materialism Book Series

The Historical Materialism Book Series is a major publishing initiative of the radical left. The capitalist crisis of the twenty-first century has been met by a resurgence of interest in critical Marxist theory. At the same time, the publishing institutions committed to Marxism have contracted markedly since the high point of the 1970s. The Historical Materialism Book Series is dedicated to addressing this situation by making available important works of Marxist theory. The aim of the series is to publish important theoretical contributions as the basis for vigorous intellectual debate and exchange on the left.

The peer-reviewed series publishes original monographs, translated texts, and reprints of classics across the bounds of academic disciplinary agendas and across the divisions of the left. The series is particularly concerned to encourage the internationalization of Marxist debate and aims to translate significant studies from beyond the English-speaking world.

For a full list of titles in the Historical Materialism Book Series available in paperback from Haymarket Books, visit: www.haymarketbooks.org/series_collections/1-historical-materialism.

Crisis and Criticism

Literary, Cultural and Political Essays
2009–2021

Benjamin Noys

Haymarket Books
Chicago, IL

First published in 2023 by Brill Academic Publishers, The Netherlands
© 2023 Koninklijke Brill NV, Leiden, The Netherlands

Published in paperback in 2024 by
Haymarket Books
P.O. Box 180165
Chicago, IL 60618
773-583-7884
www.haymarketbooks.org

ISBN: 979-8-88890-347-6

Distributed to the trade in the US through Consortium Book Sales and
Distribution (www.cbsd.com) and internationally through Ingram
Publisher Services International (www.ingramcontent.com).

This book was published with the generous support of Lannan
Foundation, Wallace Action Fund, and the Marguerite Casey Foundation.

Special discounts are available for bulk purchases by organizations and
institutions. Please call 773-583-7884 or email info@haymarketbooks.org
for more information.

Cover art and design by David Mabb. Cover art is an adaption of *Variant
6, Morris, Chrysanthemum / Stepanova, Untitled textile design*, paint and
wallpaper on canvas (2006).

Printed in the United States.

Library of Congress Cataloging-in-Publication data is available.

Contents

PART 4

Critical Figures

Acknowledgements

This collection was brought together at the suggestion of Sebastian Budgen, and many of the essays on contemporary critics appeared under the auspices of the journal *Historical Materialism*. Among my friends, Jason Adams, Sean Bonney, Sarah Brouillette, Nathan Brown, Joshua Clover, James Corby, Gail Day, Jodi Dean, Steve Edwards, Endnotes, Mark Fisher, Mark Francis Johnson, Agon Hamza, Johanna Isaacson, Joe Kennedy, Dean Kenning, Jaleh Mansoor, Daniel Marcus, Rodrigo Nunes, Corina Oprea, Nina Power, Evan Calder Williams, Goran Sergej Pristas, John Roberts, Frank Ruda, Steve Shaviro, Daniel Spaulding, and Gavin Walker have all offered critical support for this project. In particular I would like to thank Alberto Toscano and Harrison Fluss, who have both been companion critics and friends. Finally, this work would not have been possible without the intellectual and moral support of my family and of Fiona Price.

This book involves the following work that has been revised and reworked. I would like to thank the publishers for permission to reuse this material:

Chapter 1
'Skimming the surface: Critiquing anti-critique', 'Critical Distance: Reclusiveness, Secession, Indifference' special issue, ed. James Corby, *Journal for Cultural Research*, 21, 4 (2017): 295–308. DOI: 10.1080/14797585.2017.1370483 https://www.tandfonline.com/toc/rcuv20/current

Chapter 2
'Matter against Materialism: Bruno Latour and the Turn to Objects', in *Theory Matters: The Place of Theory in Literary and Cultural Studies Today*, ed. Martin Middeke and Christoph Reinfandt (London: Palgrave Macmillan, 2016), pp. 81–93.

Chapter 3
Apocalypse, Tendency, Crisis', *Mute: Culture and Politics After the Net*, 2, 15 (April 2010): 44–59.

Chapter 4
'Estetika krize: forme romana in forme vrednosti', trans. into Slovenian by Rok Benčin, *Borec* LXVI, 706–708 (2014): 178–91.

Chapter 5
'Epic Fails: Scale, Commodity, Totality', in *The Idea of the Avant Garde And What It Means Today, Volume 2*, ed. Marc James Léger (Bristol: Intellect Books, 2019), pp. 351–62.

Chapter 6
'Europe Endless: Crisis, Spirit and the End of Europe', *Crisis and Critique* 7, 1 (2020): 163–80.

Chapter 7
'Introduction: The Fabric of Struggles', in *Communization and its Discontents: Contestation, Critique, and Contemporary Struggles* (Brooklyn, NY: Autonomedia / Minor Compositions, 2011), pp. 7–17.

Chapter 8
'Communisation and the End(s) of Art', in *Time and (In)completion: Images and Performances of Time in Late Capitalism*, ed. Goran Sergej Pristas (Zagreb: BADco, 2014), pp. 59–70.

Chapter 9
'The War of Time: Occupation, Resistance, Communization', *Identities: Journal for Politics, Gender and Culture*, 10, 1–2 (2013): 83–92.

Chapter 10
''The Masses Make History': On Jameson's *Allegory and Ideology*', *Historical Materialism* 29, 1 (2021): 134–50.

Chapter 11
Review of Gregory Elliott, *Ends in Sight* (Pluto 2008), *Historical Materialism*, 17, 4 (2009): 157–63.

Chapter 12
'The Peculiarities of English Culture: A Review of *Figures of Catastrophe: The Condition of Culture Novel* by Francis Mulhern', *Historical Materialism*, 26, 1 (2018): 165–74.

Chapter 13
'The Breakdown of Capitalist Realism', *Mediations* 33 (1–2) (2020), available at: https://mediationsjournal.org/articles/breakdown.

Introduction

This book is a collection of essays originally published between 2009 and 2021. The dating is important as all the essays respond in various ways to the global capitalist crisis of 2007–8, the resulting regimes of austerity, and the emergent reactionary politics following that crisis. While the essays have been thoroughly revised, I have also attempted to preserve the punctual sense of a response to a particular crisis. To the apologists of capital, crisis can only appear as contingent, but crisis is, according to Marx, a recurrent and typical feature of the capitalist mode of production.[1] Walter Benjamin gave a resonant formulation of this situation when he wrote that 'the tradition of the oppressed teaches us that the "state of emergency" in which we live is not the exception but the rule'.[2] Of course, this state of permanent crisis or emergency must not blind us to particular and severe moments of crisis. The 2007–8 global financial crisis, which has converged and exacerbated the ongoing climate crisis and, most recently, overlapped with the global pandemic of Covid-19 that began in 2020, was such a severe crisis. It would be worthwhile to tease out and assess the interrelations of these complex forms of crisis. This is not my particular aim. Instead, the goal here is to assess how crisis should shape our moment of criticism and, more broadly, how contemporary culture is impacted by crisis and how that shapes our critical understanding of crisis.

The crisis of 2007–8 was not simply a punctual moment of crisis, but has been an ongoing experience. It was not a crisis left to go to waste,[3] but was used to intensify neoliberal capitalism. A central part of the shock and awe of the global financial crisis was that, contrary to expectations, it did not significantly rebound to the benefit of the global left.[4] Instead, fractures have emerged in the capitalist order, as have significant moments of protest and rupture from the left, but so too from the extreme and reactionary right. The moment of crisis and its ongoing shock waves have not simply equated to a resurgent and confident left or a resurgent and confident left culture. In both cultural and political terms, insurgent forms of reactionary and fascist thought stalk the cultural landscape, although, of course, they never really went away. This development has been evident at the level of capitalist culture and this book, largely

---

1   Marx 1990, p. 103.
2   Benjamin 1968, p. 257.
3   Mirowski 2014.
4   Clark 2012, p. 55.

by looking to the recent past, especially the recent literary past, tries to scry and discern the ideological elements that compose our present.

Certainly, as this book attests to, significant work has been done in rearticulating a left cultural work. While the difficulties should not be underestimated, a number of critical projects have not only tried to sustain but also critically to develop a left thought and culture that could address our moment of crisis. This is what I would call the necessity of criticism – the imperative of Marx's well-known call, in a letter to Arnold Ruge, for 'the *ruthless criticism of the existing order*'.[5] Crisis does not do the work of criticism for us. This is what we have learned. Instead, crisis demands that we continue and intensify the work of ruthless criticism, especially in the face of all the affirmations of what William Godwin called 'things as they are'.[6] The work of criticism is one that must clarify the stakes of crisis, engage crisis as a crisis of the existing order, and indicate the possibilities that this existing order excludes, including the possibility of overturning that order. This is what we could call the revolutionary orientation of criticism.

In the case of the literary humanities, one particular focus of this collection, we have witnessed a fragmented state, similar to the wider cultural divisions I have indicated. Fascist and neo-reactionary forces remain a largely fringe phenomenon, although growing in confidence, while the bloated centre is seemingly content with disavowing the demands of criticism and critique in exchange for an explicitly affirmative relation to the world.[7] It is true, as we will see, that this affirmation is still intended to do critical work, but the claim to ruthless criticism is largely ruled out from the start. We could say that in addition to capitalist crisis as a global phenomenon, we also have the other crisis of the teaching of literature and the humanities within the academy. This is the discipline, English Literature specifically, to which I belong. Certainly, it has been a discipline that has thrived on crisis. The proclaiming of the crisis of the humanities seems to have accompanied this mode of pedagogy and analysis since its beginning. This might well be due to the close relation between the discipline and capitalist crisis, and to how the discipline legitimates the cultural order in response to crisis.

The particular emergence of English Literature as an institutional form in the wake of the Russian Revolution, although also before that, indicates how the discipline might have been a disciplining of crisis.[8] The project of literary

---

5   Marx 1975, p. 207; Tally 2022.
6   Godwin 2009.
7   Noys 2010.
8   Hawkes 1986, pp. 120–7.

studies has, in part, been founded on the notion of a secularised priesthood, dating back to various formulations in the nineteenth century.[9] It has also been founded as a collective project of cultural mediation, especially the mediation of crisis and of the damage capitalism has caused to the social fabric. It is, in the words of Althusser, an exemplary ideological state apparatus.[10] At least this has been clearly evident in Britain and, thanks to Britain's imperial dominance, it has also been a model widely exported or imposed. This global dimension of English Literature, already parodied in David Lodge's 1984 novel *Small World: An Academic Romance*, has only become more evident since.

And yet, the many crises to which the discipline has been subject have often felt like internal affairs. Most recently we could say the long crisis over theory, itself now defeated and absorbed into a largely historicist mode, has felt like a debate dependent on the luxury of assuming the future of the profession. It seems like the current disciplinary crisis of English Literature is one that erodes the basis of the discipline in more profound ways: a demographic crisis, the financialisation of education in Britain, the intensifying ideological war against left ideas, a particularly British anti-intellectualism, the way in which contemporary capitalism erodes the necessity for the literacy of fiction reading – the brew is toxic. It is not just local, as variants of these forces are operating globally.[11] This might all appear irrelevant. After all, disciplines rise and fall, and who would care if English Literature went the way of Classics? My aim in this collection is not to respond at this level. This book is not meant, at least in an overt way, as a defence of English Literature or the Humanities. I will, however, assert the necessity of criticism against the turn against the critical that has marked the humanities in the twenty-first century and suggest that the future of criticism lies with the critical. Such a future is posed against the current consensus of a general historicism, a turn to theoretical tendencies marked by the affirmative, and the sedimentation of creative writing (at least in Britain), in which the creative has triumphed over the critical.

This explains why this book is structured by the pairing of crisis and criticism. Crisis calls for criticism, I will argue, and criticism is the mode to grasp the cultural mediations of crisis. Criticism is a necessary thinking to disrupt and undermine the acceptance that structures ideological forms. It is why the essays in this book run against the current of affirmation and the post-critical and why they aim to restate and reclaim the virtues of critique. In particular,

9   Mulhern 2000.
10   Althusser 2020; Montag 1994.
11   Brouillette 2017.

they are oriented by Marx's claim that 'the criticism of religion is the pre-requisite of all criticism'.[12] While the explicitly religious impulse remains more present than our self-congratulatory secularism would like to believe, especially in the literary humanities, here my concern is the criticism of religion in regard to the religious or theological elements of capitalism itself.

Walter Benjamin wrote a fragment on capitalism as religion, drawing-out the theological implications of capitalism and the value-form that Marx had indicated in *Capital* Volume I (1867).[13] Benjamin, also informed by the work of Weber, argued that capitalism was a cultic religion with no particular sacred day – instead it demands endless celebration by the acts of generating and consuming value. This religion, Benjamin concluded, was driven by the generation of a guilt without end, and it is Nietzsche's thinking which best gives expression to the secret religion of capitalism. While this appears as a criticism of Nietzsche, the difficulty does remain of traces of Nietzscheanism within Benjamin's work, here in the inflation of the religious. If we adopt a focus on religion as the primary metaphysical site of combat we risk giving capitalism as religion a metaphysical weight that merely reflects its own ideological self-image. It is not a matter of replacing Marxist ideology criticism with a Nietzschean critique (or metacritique),[14] but of maintaining the relations Marx insisted on between capitalism as an economic system and the ideological forms it generates.

What is central to my argument is the implication that there is an ideological form of capitalism that constitutes its everyday life. These daily acts of faith are disrupted by crisis, but not necessarily ended by crisis. It may even be that crisis, as has often been noted with believers, leads to a reinvigoration, even if in an apocalyptic mode, of faith. The ideological forms of capitalism that mimic the forms of religion remain in the structure of a religion that demands observance without dogma. This seeming lack of dogma, characteristic of certain forms of observance of capitalist norms, goes along with an overproduction of dogma, in the form of pro-capitalist ideological forms and in the forms of anti-communism as a cultural norm. The task of criticism is to address both this banality of observance as ideology and this cultural overproduction of ideology. Critique has to engage with this daily faith that capitalism proffers, while exposing the possibilities of transcending this faith.

---

12   Marx 1975, p. 243.
13   Benjamin 1996.
14   Losurdo 2019, pp. 431–58.

This is why the critique of Nietzsche is such a crucial operation. While Nietzsche styles himself as the most strident critic of religion, even as the anti-Christ,[15] his own thinking both explicates the core of capitalist thought and provides a re-enchantment of the capitalist universe. Max Weber, borrowing from Nietzsche, described capitalist modernity as an 'iron cage', but also held out the Nietzschean possibility of 'a great rebirth of old ideas and ideals'.[16] Certainly, it seems like Weber thought the actual fate of modernity one of 'mechanized petrifaction, embellished with a sort of convulsive self-importance'.[17] In response, Weber adopts a more chastened ethic of intellectual integrity for the scholar and an ethics of responsibility for the politician.[18] The Weberian response indicates the risks of the Nietzschean diagnosis: a blanket characterisation of modernity as inert, and then an oscillating response varying between claims for a total break and return to aristocratic ideals, or a self-sacrificing model of the small virtues of liberal conformity.

Nietzsche's own tone tended towards the more strident claims for a cultural revolution of the right, in the return to the slave-holding ideals of the Ancient world or of various ideal cultural heroes who incarnated a new defiance of modernity.[19] Nietzsche provides a metaphysics of violent conflict, summed-up in the will-to-power, but also proclaims the possibility of surpassing the limits of capitalist rationalisation, even if that is cast in the most toxic of forms. Nietzsche's aristocratic radicalism is often denied by contemporary adoptions of his work, but Nietzschean tenets remain, in ways that would have no doubt satisfied him, central to the intellectual field of contemporary life.

What is often retained is the Nietzsche of perspectivism, affirmation, chaotic materiality, the play of forces, the power of fictions, and the crisis of civilisation. In particular, Nietzsche, read by Gilles Deleuze,[20] is powerfully present in many of the movements of anti-critique and the post-critical that operate in the present. A recognition of the subterranean importance of Nietzsche to our theoretical present was also a revelation to me. My own thinking, especially via Georges Bataille, was heavily influenced by Nietzsche.[21] Bataille had offered some startling and I still think prescient criticisms of Nietzsche,[22] but the Nietzschean tones of Bataille's thinking remain strong. This is also true of

---

15   Nietzsche 2005.
16   Weber 1989, pp. 181–2.
17   Weber 1989, p. 182.
18   Weber 2020.
19   Dombowsky 2014.
20   Deleuze 1983.
21   Noys 2000.
22   Bataille 1985, pp. 32–44.

Jacques Derrida, another early influence on my work. While I may have always been sceptical of Nietzschean aristocratism and heroism, I had not fully settled accounts with all the ways in which Nietzsche informs our theoretical horizon.[23]

The problem of Nietzsche confronted here is of Nietzsche as a thinker of crisis. To put it simply, Nietzsche fuses the particular historical crises of capitalism, and revolutionary opposition to capitalism, with a crisis of civilisation itself. In *Ecce Homo* (1888) Nietzsche announces that 'one day my name will be connected with the memory of something tremendous, – a crisis such as the earth has never seen'.[24] Nietzsche's reading of crisis as a crisis of Western morality is specifically targeted against the anarchist and socialist traditions, which for Nietzsche partake in this crisis and can offer no resolution to it. Nietzsche had a famously tearful reaction to the rumoured excesses of the Paris Communards, when they were reported to have burned down the Louvre.[25] In *On the Genealogy of Morals* (1887), Nietzsche remarks that the anarchist and socialist 'inclination' for the commune is a 'tremendous counterattack' against the master race in the name of a 'primitive' social form.[26] For Nietzsche the commune was an assault on civilisation itself.

This treatment of socialism and anarchism as expressions of nihilism and crisis is also evident in Nietzsche's reading of European nihilism, traced especially in the notebooks collected as *The Will to Power*.[27] Crisis is given a metaphysical resonance, as a crisis of western civilisation and philosophy that must be overcome, and a political resonance, by being seen as the result of pity and morality. In the process, the metaphysical or theological forms of capitalist modernity are expressed but in a distorted fashion. The pitiless violence of capitalism is celebrated and exacerbated, while the role of capitalism as motor of crisis is displaced onto the victims of crisis or those who would contest the assumption that capitalism is the natural order of things.

Nietzsche's powerful criticisms of notions of unity and totality, his criticisms of *ressentiment*, and his affirmation of the consolatory powers of culture have had their influence on the left as well as right. This Nietzschean thinking of crisis continues to shape left-wing thinking, and my reflection here is on the

---

23   Losurdo 2019.
24   Nietzsche 2005, p. 143.
25   Losurdo 2019, p. 27; Toscano 2021, 666–9.
26   Nietzsche 2008a, p. 16. For a defence of the Paris commune as mode of thought and politics, see Ross 2016 and on the commune as a globally resonant form, see Ciccariello-Maher 2016.
27   Nietzsche 1968.

difficulty of shaking such an influence. To do so, I first aim to defuse the melding of the crisis of civilisation with capitalist crisis. What is seen as a crisis of civilisation should, in fact, be thought of as a crisis of capitalism. While not pursued explicitly through every essay, this task of separation between the senses of crisis emerges as a central one for criticism as practised here. This also involves the criticism of a widespread soft Nietzscheanism, evident in the various attempts to detoxify Nietzsche as a thinker available for use. While often originating in objection to the fascist and Nazi appropriations of Nietzsche – again Bataille would be a key example –[28] such detoxifications occlude Nietzsche's own politics and the damaging implications of his thought for any politics of liberation.

In the case of contemporary theory, the literary humanities, and literary culture, this detoxification has mainly been vectored through the French 'new Nietzsche', developed by Gilles Deleuze, Pierre Klossowski, Jacques Derrida, and Michel Foucault.[29] In this reading Nietzsche emerges as a thinker of difference and dispersion, which is played against Nietzsche's own re-inscription of hierarchies through establishing the 'pathos of distance'.[30] Nietzsche's adopted pose of aristocratic disdain is translated into a play of forces and a play of powers. We have a chaotic and materialist Nietzsche designated as a figure disrupting the Nietzsche of the overman and selection. This chaotic Nietzsche, however, retains a sense of the will-to-power as decisive, and while trying to undermine hierarchical difference struggles to define any decisive resistance to such forms. It also studiously tends to ignore Nietzsche's own ideology of aristocratic radicalism. Such detoxifications, by failing to work through the persistence of hierarchy and the risks of dispersion in Nietzsche's thinking, remain inadvertently toxic themselves.[31]

In particular, within the literary humanities and literary culture this softened Nietzscheanism appears most obviously in the currents of anti-critique and the post-critical, which is the focus of the first section of this collection and a recurrent concern. Rejecting Nietzsche's stridency of tone and Deleuze's own more rigorous reading, except as a background, such readings create a soft image of plural dispersion, which they suggest needs to be preserved. In the current context of ongoing ecological crisis and the damage done by contemporary capitalism it is not surprising that calls to care and preserve resonate. That said, while appealing, such post-critical gestures disable the possibilities

---

28   Bataille 1985, pp. 182–96. See also Bataille 2022, pp. 3–5.
29   Deleuze 1983; Allison (ed.) 1985.
30   Nietzsche 1973; Nietzsche 2008a, p. 12.
31   Sharpe 2021.

of ruthless criticism and, again, inadvertently or deliberately celebrate a world of plural matter that defies rational comprehension. They fuse the two options sketched by Weber, in which the rebirth of ideals is accompanied by a sense of ethical responsibility, but in doing so they do not evade the damaging effects of Nietzsche's thinking but inadvertently intensify it. The critical task of analysis – tracing causal effects, grasping the place of works in a totality, developing critical knowledge – is replaced by aesthetic contemplation and curation, treating works as singularities, and a quasi-religious (or explicitly religious) treatment of the world as object of belief.

In relationship to crisis, we have to secularise crisis and differentiate between a conception of crisis as a result of capitalism, to do with the continual attempt to extract and accumulate value at all costs, and a Nietzschean conception of metaphysical crisis as the crisis of civilisation. In one sense, it is understandable that some degree of confusion and lamination between these forms of crisis has taken place. The totalising effect of contemporary capitalism, its global dominance, and its penetration into life at all levels, mean that a crisis of capitalism is a crisis of civilisation, in the sense of a crisis of a global way of life. To take that as a given, however, or to give it the metaphysical resonances that Nietzsche does, and after him Heidegger, is to mystify global capitalism and to concede to it more power than it has. Capitalism is not commensurate with the totality of life and existence; instead a sense of totality requires we understand capitalism as an historical phenomenon that is riven with crisis and subsidiary to the totality of existence. If crisis demands criticism, as I have suggested, then this criticism should clarify our sense of crisis.

We have witnessed a recent critical reaction to Nietzsche and to the dominance of Nietzschean thinking.[32] These criticisms insist that Nietzsche's celebration of difference and the material has to be understood as central to an aristocratic radicalism that insists on multiplying difference and materialising it into new hierarchical forms. Such criticisms were already preceded by Lukács' *The Destruction of Reason* (1952),[33] which while certainly marred by compromises with Stalinism also indicated the way in which Nietzsche's thought serves the imperialist order of capitalism. The critical turn against Nietzsche remains, however, a minor current, and the dominant trend in the literary humanities is still to lay claim to soft Nietzschean positions. Such a general Nietzschean is, in a way, more pernicious in that it actively denies Nietzsche's aristocratic radicalism or claims to have neutralised it through a minor politics and minor theory.

---

32   Landa 2007; Bull 2011; Dombowsky 2014; Brennan 2014; Losurdo 2019.
33   Lukács 2021.

This seeming modesty, in contrast to the metaphysical reading of a thinker like Deleuze, risks leaving all the philosophical and political problems in place. It also further conceals such problems by blithely claiming to have escaped the demands of grand theory. It is not that such claims to modesty are not always genuine or genuinely felt, but that they function ideologically by reproducing Nietzschean tropes in a seemingly harmless form.

These criticisms are not some claim to purity on my part. My own position is ambiguous and no doubt significant traces of that ambiguity remain from my own intellectual formation through currents of French thought inspired by Nietzsche. Gramsci argued that our consciousness is the product of historical processes which leave us with 'an infinity of traces gathered together without the advantage of an inventory. First of all, it is necessary to compile such an inventory'.[34] This collection does not amount to such a complete inventory, but I do think it demonstrates the attempt to come to terms with the Nietzschean traces in contemporary thought, including my own. Perhaps such a proximity not only generates problems and weaknesses, but also at least the familiarity with the problem.

This is also a work of what I call, with tongue somewhat in cheek, English Theory, although like most suggestions laced with irony it carries its own disavowed truth.[35] My reference here is to Perry Anderson's *Arguments within English Marxism* (1980),[36] which refers to E.P. Thompson and a particular and particularly English debate and also, of course, to coinages like French theory or Continental Philosophy.[37] Of course, the transfer of these currents of thought into English (and into Britain) is often told as a tale of the fall. The original impulses, often heavily-dependent on French-language debates and the resources of that language, are traduced in an English reception that results in illegitimate syntheses and the collapsing of heterogenous thinkers into a singular theory (or post-structuralism). There is some truth to this image. I do not, however, only want to treat English Theory as a negative designation.

First of all, many of the works of synthesis, especially in the 1970s, were driven by political imperatives that saw the fusion of Althusser and Lacan as an essential political task, not least in the case of socialist-feminist interventions. Second, the reception of theory in England or Britain – these national designations remain a problem –[38] was also driven by a work of differentiation and

---

34   Gramsci 1957, p. 59.
35   Easthope 1991.
36   Anderson 1980.
37   Cusset 2008; Critchley 2001.
38   Nairn 1988.

analysis that remained less visible but no less essential. While the initial works of synthesis rapidly composed a canon, patient working-throughs were continuing. Finally, I would suggest the vice and virtue of English Theory was that its practitioners took these theoretical ideas seriously and tried to make them work in practice. Even if we consider this a legacy of a utilitarian and practical cast of mind, to resort to speculation about national philosophical character, the point here was a more or less honest attempt to live out the claims made by the original thinkers via a necessary transit into practice.

It is in this spirit, I hope, that this book can be read as a work of English Theory, rather than in any chauvinistic or nationalist sense. The unlikeliness of the formulation and the negative image of such appropriations of theory perhaps guard against this being seen as a positive claim. That said, it is also important to assess the space in which theoretical and critical articulations develop and, particularly in relation to Britain and England, important work has been done. Perry Anderson,[39] along with Tom Nairn, has been a crucial figure in tracing this intellectual history as well as for my project. There is no doubt that the sense of crisis and criticism that emerges through these essays is inflected by this national legacy and also the attempt to challenge and escape its limits.[40] This national legacy is something not only to be treated as a problem, but also as central to the possibility of such a project. Marx famously remarked 'men make their own history, but not of their own free will; not under circumstances they themselves have chosen but under the given and inherited circumstances with which they are directly confronted'.[41] Those conditions include the peculiarities and possibilities of national forms in the modern era, with its particular form of nationhood,[42] even and especially if we practice a mode of thought that is always internationalist and aiming to challenge those forms. Criticism, if it is to be ruthless, must also confront and overcome this tension.

This book is divided into four sections. The first, The Moment of Critique, consists of essays that address contemporary forms of the post-critical and try to reconstruct a critical thinking of crisis. This is a response to the Nietzschean tones I identify in contemporary theory, although these tones are often cast in the softer tones of care and saving. While recognising the attraction of such demands, especially in a time in which ecological and capitalist crisis intertwine, the post-critical also avoids the need for criticism to grasp and understand the totality and the social processes that drive crisis. The aim is to defend

---

39   Anderson 1992a.
40   Wright 1985.
41   Marx 2019, p. 480.
42   Anderson 2016.

and rehabilitate the notions of critique and materialism, to stress the necessity of ruthless criticism, and also to engage with the fate of criticism in contemporary Marxist thought. In this latter case the discussion turns on the contrasting apocalyptic tone and how we might grasp crisis as a secular form.

The second section, Crisis Culture, consists of critical studies, primarily focused on the novel form, of the cultural impact of crisis and cultural responses to crisis. Here I aim to justify the claims made by criticism in a critical practice that is attentive to the traces of crisis as registered and displaced by cultural forms. In each case the aim is to explore crisis as a dimension of cultural forms including, in the last essay of this section, philosophy. The essays work through the modalities in which crisis appears, drawing especially on the work of Lukács and his analysis of crisis and the possibilities of realism.[43] They offer direct engagements with Nietzschean versions of crisis as matters of civilisation and how we might respond in developing a critical and Marxist account.

The next section, Crisis and Communisation, focuses on the debates that have emerged in the 2010s concerning the radical left current of communisation theory. This theory is, in many ways, a return to classical formulations of Marxism, but also casts them into a radically new mode of analysis and a new language of critique. Communisation supposes the end of a dependence of capitalism on the identity of the worker, a period it identifies as programmatism, and a new time in which the proletariat can only appear as a defiantly negative phenomenon in a rift from the identity of the worker. In this way it aims to account for the crisis of previous forms of Marxist practice – social democratic, Leninist, and ultra-left – and suggest new modes of struggle and analysis. Originally formulated in the 1970s, it is certainly not surprising that it has proved influential in what appear to be the death throes of traditional left forms in response to global capitalist crisis. These essays present a critical balance-sheet in relation to the original theory, to the thinking of art and communisation, and to the issues surrounding military conflict and the militarisation of protest. While communisation theory only has an indirect and tenuous relation to Nietzschean thinking, vectored most strongly through certain elements in the thinking of Guy Debord and the Situationists, in a different mode communisation risks a flattening and inflation of crisis. The extremity of its formulations of crisis and its indifference to fully specifying the relationship of class consciousness to the crisis of programmatism leave a problematic legacy in negotiating the uneven modes of protest and struggle today.

---

43   Lukács 1963 and Lukács 2007. On Marx's call for realism as a mode of analysis, see Marx 1990, p. 102. For a contemporary discussion of realism and art, see Day 2011.

The final section, Critical Figures, consists of four essays considering what we could call companions in critique – critical thinkers indebted to Marxism who have tried to sustain critique in these unpropitious times. This is in no sense an exhaustive survey and may, I think apparently, appear highly conventional. The risk is run as, in various ways, these critical projects also indicate limits and problems of critique in the present moment. My aim is respectful appreciation, but not laudatory celebration. Also, I aim to constellate such work in broader critical reconstructions of left thought in the present moment. Fredric Jameson is obviously a significant figure in sustaining and revitalising Marxist reading and a significant figure for this book as well. Gregory Elliott and Francis Mulhern are less well-known, but belong to the tradition of critical Marxism associated with the *New Left Review* and deserve to have their projects better known. They have also engaged, in different ways, with some of the issues of national modes of thought and how we might develop a true internationalism that I have argued is vital. Finally, Mark Fisher emerged as a critical thinker within the span of this book and offers a fascinating point of reference for the renovation of the left project in the present moment. Fisher's project is also indicative of the tensions of left Nietzscheanism that remain resonant in the present moment. These figures are not meant to be representative – they obviously are not – but they do indicate a particular trajectory and, in the case of Elliott, Mulhern and Fisher, the attempt to theorise a cultural politics of Marxism out of the ambivalences of an English or British cultural formation.

In the conclusion I draw a broader balance sheet of the intellectual trends that inform our understanding of crisis and criticism. Using the work of Lukács as a guide, I argue that much of twentieth- and twenty-first-century thought has been informed by a subjectivism that disables its ability to grasp reality and crisis. Nietzsche is the crucial figure for this subjectivism and, in particular, for the way in which such subjectivism is projected onto the world. In Nietzsche we find a full-blown sense of the inflation of the subject to the point that it coincides with reality. This gives Nietzsche's understanding of crisis the sense that it is not only a crisis of civilisation but also a crisis of subjectivity that must be resolved by the subject. While abandoning the strident tones of Nietzsche, contemporary readings maintain many of the coordinates of his thinking. Therefore, my conclusion attempts to develop beyond the limits of our moment and of these essays to pose anew our thinking of crisis and criticism.

The book is selective and also selected out of a body of work I produced in this period. There are many other reference points and projects that could have been considered and that also proved vital to this book. Signs of those should be evident in the essays, footnotes, and acknowledgements. It would, perhaps, be best to read these essays as belonging to a wider invisible or barely visible collective that composed the various projects, activities, and developments of these years, including the regressions and failures that belong to this moment. This book is also a partial, truncated and interrupted summary of a time that resists easy summation. It is always difficult to avoid treating the urgencies of the present for long-term developments, although also easy to miss such developments by mistaking them for short-term urgencies. In a sense the selection and revising of these essays is some attempt to cast a critical eye over this project, never intended as such, and to assess the risks of analysing the tendencies of the present.

Therefore, the overall aim of this collection, in retrospect, is to maintain the necessity of critique and particularly critique as a reading of crisis. This is, of course, not any critique, but one inspired by and indebted to Marx and Marxism, which itself both valorises critique and aims to transcend its limits. Critique is a stage of thought and not its end. It requires a coordination with practice to realise the results of critique, and my intellectual project does not remain bound by the notion of critique as a matter of establishing limits. That is to say, Marx and Marxist critique is not Kantian critique, with its focus on limits, just as it is not Nietzschean critique, with its disabling of rational analysis. I hope, therefore, that the essays collected here offer some clarification of the dimensions of this form of critique and the endeavour to develop a positive project of transcending the limits both of critique and of capitalist society.

PART 1

The Moment of Critique

∴

The Distance of Critique

The problem of critique in the current moment appears to be one of distance. The claim of the post-critical consensus, which suggests that we need to abandon critique, is that critique is too distant.[1] Critique, especially in the forms of Marxism and psychoanalysis, assumes a position of distance over its object that equates to a position of mastery. Critique stands over and above its object, refuses to get too close, and issues judgements. And yet, critique is also accused of getting too close, of being mired in what it criticises and unable to escape from the gravitational pull of the object of critique. Too distant and too close, at the same time. The seeming paradox suggests the desperate need to be rid of critique; after all, as Jacques Derrida wrote in another context, 'coherence in contradiction expresses the force of a desire'.[2]

Here I want to restate the need for critique and to present a model that grasps the peculiar position of critique as 'within and against'.[3] I propose this model against the movements of the post-critical that propose a new model of distance that aims to get close and yet to remain distinct and distant.[4] This is the claimed virtue of the post-critical. While this is the preferred term of its exponents, here I use anti-critique, which I think restores the disavowed violence at work in this position. This anti-critique claims to be both intimate and exterior to the object it engages with. In contrast, focusing on the case of Marxism, I suggest that critique has its own necessary model of closeness and, eventual, distance. Contrary to the twin images of critique as a gesture of mastery combined with a fascinated gaze for the object of critique, a strange model of the hypnotiser hypnotised, I argue that critique has better worked through the problem of distance and proximity in its own terms as the experience of being within and against.

We can begin with a classic example of critique: the early work of Roland Barthes in *Mythologies* (1957), which combines an attention to language with a Marxist critique of ideology as a mechanism that transforms what is cultural into something natural. In the essay 'Soap-powders and Detergents', Barthes offers a witty critique of the language of advertising. He remarks that the claim

---

1   Felski 2015.
2   Derrida 1978, p. 279.
3   Tronti 2020.
4   For parallel criticisms of the post-critical see Kornbluh 2017 and Tally 2022, pp. 75–82.

made by advertisers that their product can 'clean in depth' is 'to assume that linen is deep, which no one had previously thought'.[5] This amusing act of sarcasm chides petit-bourgeois ideology with the production of false depth by using the surface effect of the linguistic sign. The sign, a surface effect par excellence, points to a depth that it creates before our eyes. Critique, therefore, is not seeking the hidden depths but rather claiming the surface as the point of traction by arguing that the secret of ideology is the production of depth, the production of a sense of naturalness, out of the mere surface effects of language. Barthes would oppose to this creation of depth an embrace of the theatricality and provisional form of the sign itself. Hence Barthes's delight in the world of wrestling, which presents itself as a semi-deliberate play with signs,[6] rather than the spurious claims to emotion and veracity that characterise historical film.[7] This already indicates that contemporary anti-critique may not have grasped the modes of distance at work in critique.

I open with this brief account of a classical gesture of critique, which Barthes would later disavow and modify,[8] to suggest that our usual images of surface and depth in critique might not be as simple as we think. As I have suggested, that common image is one in which critique is too distant and too close. Critique retains a distant stance of mastery while remaining reactively dependent on what it negates.[9] Bruno Latour, the exemplary figure of anti-critique, characterises critique as beginning in disbelief before the 'wheeling [in] of causal explanations coming out of the dark depth below'.[10] The position of distance is seen to correlate with mastery over the objects. The critic knows what is really going on beneath the mere appearance of things. At the same time such mastery disguises the dependence of the critic on the object of critique. This is evident in Jacques Rancière's *cri de Coeur*: 'If there is a circulation that should be stopped at this point, it's this circulation of stereotypes that critique stereotypes, giant stuffed animals that denounce our infantilization, media images that denounce the media, spectacular installations that denounce the spectacle, etc'.[11] Here the knee-jerk critical gesture merely repeats the terms of the problem it faces and proximity shades into complicity. The failure of critique is a failure of critical distance: too distant or too close.

---

5   Barthes 1973, p. 41.
6   Barthes 1973, pp. 15–26.
7   Barthes 1973, pp. 27–30.
8   Barthes 1973, pp. 9–10; Barthes 1977, p. 167.
9   Best and Marcus 2009.
10   Latour 2004, p. 229.
11   Rancière 2007, p. 266.

The post-critical alternative anti-critique offers is the suggestion that we get closer. We should give up the smug security and superiority of critical distance by getting our hands dirty in tracing the actual construction of things, or, better, in the affirmative practice of adding or reconfiguring, rather than subtracting and disfiguring. We should not assume a distance that grants a position of mastery. At the same time as we are called to get closer, we are also called to be more careful. What Latour calls the sledge hammer of critique has to be replaced with new tools, more suited to building than destroying (see also Chapter 2).[12] Our role is not so much to intervene as to compose, to develop, and to describe. I want to describe this mode as one of skimming the surface in such a way as to at once abolish distance and re-inscribe it. We can get close to anything, but never too close to any one thing. It is, finally, a model of analysis as an aesthetic mode.

This inscription of proximity and distance can be mapped across a spectrum of various forms of anti-critique. Here I will focus on the version of this spectrum of distance offered in contemporary literary studies.[13] At one end, there is the messiness of getting as near as possible to objects, which always recede from our grasp, of object-oriented criticism.[14] We then pass through the neutrality claimed by Heather Love,[15] with her descriptive reading, before we reach so-called distant reading, in which we count books rather than read them, as suggested by Franco Moretti.[16] This is a spectrum of increasing distance, but we should note that in each case the aim is to get closer by having the right kind of distance. All these instances of anti-critique mix distance and proximity in different degrees. There is no closing of the distance completely, but neither should we refuse to get close, at least to the surface. This double inscription of proximity and distance is designed to answer critique's inscription of mastery through distance and its closeness to its own objects of critique. While critique is both too distant and too close, anti-critique aims to be distant enough to be close enough; what Heather Love calls 'close but not deep'.[17]

My aim here is to dispute this collapsing or displacing of critical distance in contemporary thinking. I first want to challenge the originality of these forms of skimming the surface and to develop the irony, suggested by my opening, that surfaces have been a longer-term concern, and that various theoretical

12   Latour 2010, p. 475.
13   Foster 2017, pp. 115–24.
14   Harman 2012a.
15   Love 2010.
16   Moretti 2005.
17   Love 2010.

gestures had already engaged with anti-critique and the post-critical. In his polemic against Alain Badiou, François Laruelle notes that a taste for planes, or layers, or surfaces, 'is a "modern ideal", which can serve proliferation or the stratification of instances'.[18] This sense of the surface as modern ideal is crucial, I think, to positioning the post-critical within a longer narrative that it disavows. As Laruelle indicates, the surface can lead to both proliferation and stratification – hierarchy is not absent from attention to surfaces. Here I will be using the ultra-modernist 1970s work of Jean-François Lyotard as one prefigurative example of the early turn to surfaces. There is nothing like the modern, or modernist, to produce the ire of anti-critique, yet the emphasis on surface does not necessarily imply escape from the modern. Critique, I would say, is a rarer and more contested gesture than some of the new heroic accounts of anti-critique suggest – in which the post-critical is posed against some hegemony of critique that never really existed.

In turning to critique I will focus on the case of Marxism, for anti-critique the worst offender, along with psychoanalysis, of critical mastery and critical miring. Marxism is treated as a classic instance of what Ricœur called the 'hermeneutics of suspicion',[19] with Marx seen as dissolving the falsity of surface experiences to reveal the true reality of things. There is, of course, justice to this claim: in *Capital* Marx famously announces the necessity to descend to the 'hidden abode of production'.[20] In Ricœur's account Marx appears alongside Freud and Nietzsche, and it is telling that of these three masters of suspicion Marx and Freud are now seen as primary instances of critique while Nietzsche has been adopted as the patron saint of the anti-critique. Nietzsche's affirmative thinking, his embrace of chaotic materiality, his disputing of certain forms of depth, are all seen as exempting him from the sins of critique.

I want to explore Marxism as a site of debate about forms of distance rather than a settled instance of critique. The emphasis on immersion in relations of production, also a problem for anti-critique, generates a thinking that tries to gauge the possibilities of critique as emerging from immersion and requiring distance. Here I will focus on debates in Marxism that turn on the tension between immersion and distance required by a Marxist analysis. This suggests that rather than a smug mastery, Marxism itself is a site of struggle in working out these issues of critical distance. I then focus this problem through the issue of negativity. The anti-critique suspicion of the masters of suspicion is often

---

18   Laruelle 2013, p. 33.
19   Ricoeur 1977, p. 32.
20   Marx 1990, p. 279.

predicated on a suspicion of negativity and the negative. Whereas critique operates through a negativity that binds the object of critique to the subject, anti-critique regards this as getting too close. Instead, I will suggest, negativity is what binds us to think our own immersion in relations critically, but is also generative of a necessary distance. Critique does not imply the choice of distance, but rather sees distance and immersion as problems we already confront in our lives.

This problem of immersion and distance, driven by negativity, had already been noted within the discourse of critique. Louis Althusser, who is the figure of critique often identified by anti-critique as exemplary of the failings of Marxism, offers a reflection in *Reading Capital* (1968), with Étienne Balibar, anticipatory of the post-critical: Marx is trapped in 'the ambiguity of a *negation* which still clings to the universe of the concepts it rejects, without having succeeded in adequately formulating ... new and positive concepts'.[21] While Althusser locates this ambiguity in the young Marx, allowing him to transcend the problem with the mature Marx, we could say that anti-critique sees this problem as running through all of Marx. Marx is, to adapt Baudrillard's critical title, the mirror of capital.[22] Anti-critique claims the alternative of an affirmative or affirmationist thinking,[23] that formulates the new and positive against the ambiguity of negation.

In contrast, there is still something useful in this ambiguity of negation, which suggests an inscription of critical distance that does not necessarily imply mastery. Contrary to Althusser and to the anti-critique consensus, the ambiguity of negation is not something to be dissolved and displaced without a working through of the negation of negation. Of course, this can be regarded as a tarrying with the negative that never reaches a positive moment. The truth of anti-critique lies in this suggestion that Marxism, and cognate discourses, can be left tarrying with negativity and not articulate the negation of the negation and their own new discourse.

There is an irony in that this position of negativity is often identified as a position of weakness and modesty that tries to refuse the mastery it sees implied by traditional critique. It is another variant of anti-critique. By claiming the modesty of staying with negativity such a position then opens itself up to the criticism that it is not affirmative enough. The further irony is that this weakened position is also the result of anti-critique cutting off critique from

---

21   Althusser and Balibar 2009, p. 42 n. 18.
22   Baudrillard 1975.
23   Noys 2010, pp. ix–x.

any revolutionary position. If anti-critique denies critique the power necessary to overturn negativity and trace the determinations of new social forms,
then critique is left in a position of perpetual criticism. Therefore, contrary to
anti-critique, which encourages a dwelling in negativity and return to modest
virtues, the negativity of critique has to be a within and against that is also oriented to a negation of the negation.[24] The process of negativity is oriented by
this revolutionary claim, not in the sense that critique makes revolution, but
in the sense that it offers a revolutionary critique. This, I will suggest, is the
difficult task and reconstruction we have to make to rediscover revolutionary
critique.

1 Flaying Theory

One of the many ironies of anti-critique is that the attention to the surface,
which is articulated against theory, has eminently theoretical origins. Of
course, contemporary anti-critique takes as one of its main targets the moment
of theory, usually treated under the familiar and inaccurate cliché of the moment of linguistic imperialism. If, as we saw in Barthes, theory remains on the
surface, it remains on the wrong surface – the surface of language or the signifier, which is taken to determine the signified or even the referent. The result,
for anti-critique, is something idealist and not materialist, something coolly
abstract rather than hotly involved, and something too clean and not messy
enough.

I want to select one moment of theory that suggests the failure of anti-
critique to read history: the libidinal works of Jean-François Lyotard. Lyotard's
work was always far from any linguistic imperialism, being concerned to integrate the insights of phenomenology, especially the work of Merleau-Ponty on
the visual, and to explore a depth that complicates the surfaces of structuralism.[25] Lyotard's interest in the figural and in painting would drive a reluctance
to embrace any thinking of language as primary or central, arguably until his
later interest in Wittgenstein and language games.[26] What concerns me here
are the hyper-theoretical libidinal works, especially *Libidinal Economy* (1974),
which refuse the white terror of critique for the insurgent red cruelty of singularities.[27] This is a work posed specifically against critique in a way quite as

24   Engels 1976, pp. 164–82.
25   Bennington 1988, p. 57.
26   Lyotard and Thébaud 1985.
27   Lyotard 1993, p. 242.

violent, if not more so, than any proponent of anti-critique. My aim is not to celebrate Lyotard as a more successful example of anti-critique or as an unknown forerunner. Instead, Lyotard stands as one example, among others, of a disavowed history of anti-critique within theory, as we already saw with Althusser. Also, the problems which beset Lyotard's attempt to justify this stance also haunt contemporary forms of anti-critique.

Lyotard's *Libidinal Economy* begins with the bravura scene of the flaying and unfolding of the human body into a libidinal surface in which depth is only produced through the twisting of the surface into a Möbius band.[28] All that is left after this flaying of the body is the task of following the intensities as they pass across this band or film (as in the images passing on a strip of celluloid). There is no place remaining for any critique, because there is no depth or interiority on which it could stand to judge. If critique requires a minimal position of exteriority or distance, this is abolished in the ceaseless flux of libidinal intensities, leaving only one option: '*be inside and forget it*'.[29] In contrast to the position of critique as within and against, Lyotard's libidinal thinker dissolves themselves in the act of Nietzschean 'active forgetting'.[30] Of course, critique does exist, and so therefore has to be accounted for. In Lyotard's libidinal economy critique is the result of a libidinal de-intensification or cooling off – a studied distance that tries to canalise the libidinal into mere representation. In the libidinal schema critique embodies an intensity, but an intensity that forms a cold passion, disguised within an appearance of distance and mastery it can never actually achieve. It is, as Nietzsche would describe it, reactive.[31] In contrast to the active pulsations of libidinal intensity, critique is an intensity that de-intensifies itself, in a somewhat paradoxical fashion.

This kind of anti-critique is clearly set-out in Lyotard's 1974 introduction to Anton Ehrenzweig's *The Hidden Order of Art* (1967), tellingly titled 'Beyond Representation'. Lyotard's target, like many at the time and since, is psychoanalysis as a mechanism of critique and normalisation. For Lyotard psychoanalysis performs a de-libidinisation by turning the unconscious into a theatrical space, structured by the forms of the stage, spectators and actors, which allocates roles and contains and channels libidinal energy into static forms. It is this theatrical set-up (*dispositif*) that for Lyotard is central to the apparatus of representation and critique.

---

28   Lyotard 1993, pp. 1–3.
29   Lyotard 1993, p. 3.
30   Nietzsche 1983, p. 62.
31   Nietzsche 2008a, pp. 54–6.

Lyotard's alternative libidinal analysis is predicated on the affirmation of art, rather than its critique, and it seeks no hidden meaning. For libidinal analysis 'there is only surface'.[32] Psychoanalysis cannot function as a master discourse because it cannot impose a plane over and above art – they are both on the same surface. Instead of critique and its object we instead only have 'transformations of libidinal energy' that 'are all on the surface'.[33] This is why Lyotard is interested in Ehrenzweig's hidden order of art, because although this seems to incarnate the classical operation of a psychoanalytic hermeneutics in finding a hidden order, Lyotard reads it against the grain. There needs to be no decryption of some hidden order, because everything is already on the surface. The operation that interests Lyotard in Ehrenzweig is that of 'scanning',[34] which characterises the organisation of the drives. Far from the primary processes being merely disorganised and chaotic, Lyotard argues that this form of scanning suggests a proto-organisation that underlies and exceeds the cooling order of representation. The unconscious does not need ordering from outside, but orders itself in a way that ruptures representation.

Therefore, for Lyotard, we need to trace how 'the waves of the libidinal drives meet the rigid secondary structures'.[35] The space of libidinal analysis is the 'endless and anonymous film of primary drives'.[36] This is also the space of art, as 'all art is flat, as it were, pellicular, like a film'.[37] Crucial here, and this will be taken-up by anti-critique, is a commonality between art and the process by which we read art. This is a flattening, an archetypal flat ontology, and in this flattening theoretical discourse and art become one. The creativity of art can only be met by a creative criticism that refuses to be critical and becomes a co-creating. This may account for the contemporary popularity of the later work of Roland Barthes and the development of theory-fiction or autofiction – this is also a flattening or folding of theory within fiction. In all cases there is no critical distance. Of course, critique exists and so critique must create distance, which is, for Lyotard, merely 'one of the adventures that befalls the libidinal skin'.[38] In response, Lyotard suggests a descaling that places everything on the same level, while at the same time

32   Lyotard 1989, p. 158.
33   Lyotard 1989, p. 160.
34   Lyotard 1989, p. 160.
35   Lyotard 1989, p. 161.
36   Lyotard 1989, p. 159.
37   Lyotard 1989, p. 166.
38   Lyotard 1989, p. 167.

inscribing this level as a flux of intensities. To get closer, in this case, is to get closer to these intensities without the mediation of representation. In this way the gesture of critique is dissolved as just one adventure that cannot admit its own status as one adventure among other intensities without privilege.

The difficulty that constantly besets Lyotard is the extraction of the libidinal from the apparatus of representation. While libidinal economy is supposed to account for all representation as merely cooled-off intensities, this can be reversed to argue that libidinal economy is merely another representation.[39] From the relaxed position of anti-critique *Libidinal Economy* remains too locked in conflict with critique, taking it too seriously. The alternative Lyotard proposes of a libidinal monism risks repeating the gesture of critique by discovering yet another underlying force. Contemporary anti-critique has little time for the anguish that besets Lyotard, who would later reflect that 'the readers of this book – thank God there were very few – generally accepted the product as a rhetorical exercise and gave no consideration to the upheaval it required of my soul'.[40] The dispersion of contemporary anti-critique resists identification of any underlying force, and departs from the inscription of intensities. We might say it takes seriously Lyotard's injunction to 'be inside and forget it', precisely by forgetting this anguished engagement with critique.

It is for this reason that I do not want to generate a false genealogy by linking contemporary anti-critique to Lyotard's libidinal economy as if these were one and the same thing. What I want to stress is a parallel in the search for an affirmative, non-linguistic and material form that defies the distance of critique. There is also a parallel in the identification of critical discourse with creative discourse and the identification of the critical with a new mode of scanning that is both involved and carries a degree of separation. I also want to stress that the impasse Lyotard encounters in trying to detach himself from critique and enter a purely affirmative discourse does not disappear, even if contemporary anti-critique styles itself in a more relaxed mode. Lyotard's attempt to abolish completely critical distance onto one affirmative band or skin suggests the difficulty of a discourse that evacuates itself of any distance or tries to reinscribe distance in a non- or anti-critical fashion. Anti-critique still faces the difficulty of distinguishing itself from its object, even as it comes to identify itself more and more with that object.

---

39   Bennington 1988, p. 50.
40   Lyotard 1988, p. 13.

Lyotard relentlessly targeted psychoanalysis and Marxism as *the* forms of critique, hence one of his collections of articles from his libidinal period is called *Dérive à partir de Marx et Freud* (1973). This set a programme that many would follow. Virtually all instances of contemporary anti-critique take aim at either or both psychoanalysis and Marxism. This targeting serves a number of purposes. First, it homogenises the theoretical and critical field of the past under these banners. It is not true that Marxism and psychoanalysis have been hegemonic in the humanities, and certainly not in Britain or the United States. To claim that once we were all Marxists or all influenced by psychoanalysis is an exaggeration that serves the claim for resistance and novelty of contemporary anti-critique. It also – and this is my particular concern here – homogenises Marxism (and psychoanalysis) into stable bodies of knowledge that are exhausted by the usual clichés of critical mastery. The result is that anti-critique can claim novelty, obviously a core value in the contemporary context, and dismiss as beneath concern previous critical work. This serves the purpose of permitting benign or hostile neglect of how Marxism engaged critical distance as only ever a tentative and fleeting moment, due to our being primarily embedded in the contexts we criticise. Anti-critique borrows or steals this insight, but in ways that generate a far more free-floating discourse than critique ever was.

2   The View from Mount Olympus

Marxism is a discourse that has always engaged with critique and with the problem of critical distance. It is central to the classical arguments by Marx and Engels against projections of utopian futures or idyllic pasts,[41] as well as Marx's tracing of the dynamics of capital in terms of humans as bearers of particular social relation.[42] At the heart of Marxism as a critical practice is an insistence on historical embeddedness, which includes Marxism itself. In the 'Theses on Feuerbach' (1845), Marx famously displaced the concept of 'human essence' by declaring it 'in its reality' to be 'the ensemble of social relations'.[43] This does not dissolve human nature, but rather re-inscribes it as fundamentally embedded in natural and social relations.[44] We live in, and even as, an ensemble of social relations, but relations that are fractured and divided by conflict and ant-

---

41   Marx 2019, pp. 81–91.
42   Marx 1990, p. 92.
43   Marx 1975, p. 423.
44   Geras 2016.

agonism. The necessarily historically-situated nature of thought puts pressure on its critical function. We are cast within the moment we are critical of and, again, classically the proletariat forms the moment or clarification of negativity that inhabits this social form.[45] This will not simply emerge as a solution but also bequeath a series of problems for Marxism to negotiate as a critical discourse.

I want to focus this problem of critical distance through one case study: critical responses to the work of the English Marxist Perry Anderson. The reason for this choice is that Anderson has seemed to many of his fellow Marxists as the incarnation of critical distance as mastery. Gregory Elliott (see Chapter 11), remarking on Perry Anderson's editorial for the *New Left Review* titled 'Renewals' (2000), noted that Anderson's failure to evince much enthusiasm for the anti-globalisation movement left critics concluding that this 'rendered his habitually Olympian perspective positively intergalactic and his posture of reality instructor irksome'.[46] While Elliott is a sympathetic reader of Anderson, and author of the best account of Anderson's work,[47] even he seems to register frustration at the position of critic as reality instructor. Anderson's distance as an historian and commentator has seemed to many the incarnation of the superior critical position.

This criticism of Anderson's Olympian perspective has a long history. Before exploring that history, we should first clarify his status. Anderson, as a Marxist historian and editor of the *New Left Review*, is not a figure usually identified with theory, if we give that word its usual sense to refer to currents of structuralism, post-structuralism and later trends. On the contrary, Anderson has been a notable critic of theory,[48] preferring to articulate his work in terms of historical sociology. Despite this, Anderson's work has taken a position of critical distance that has led to cognate criticisms of his work as a form of high theory, in the sense of distant from real human relations.

In 1964, Peter Sedgwick wrote an essay, 'The Two New Lefts', which targeted the writers around the then nascent *New Left Review*, including Anderson. What interests me is the metaphors that Sedgwick deployed in his criticism. He argued that their historical work, at that point largely focused on Britain, evinced a 'lack nostalgia; when they survey the past, it is with a time-machine's traverse, plotting the orbit of elements in the historical ensemble, rather than

---

45   Marx 1975, p. 256.
46   Elliott 2008, p. 105.
47   Elliott 1998.
48   Anderson 1983.

registering sensuously the impact of men and events'.[49] The distance Sedgwick chastises is temporal ('time-machine's traverse') and spatial ('plotting the orbit of elements'). The fatal flaw of this critical distance is that it lacks the capacity to register the impact of humans and events in shaping history.

In an aside on intellectual history, we might note that the grounds of the later ferocious battles concerning Althusser's anti-humanism were already laid here. The problem was not simply a matter of a desiccating structuralism – as Derrida noted, the design of structures appears more easily when living energy is neutralised, as in 'the architecture of an uninhabited or deserted city, reduced to its skeleton by some catastrophe'.[50] Already the kind of historian's gaze these critics used was regarded as a form of practical anti-humanism, rendering history as empty of people and events, even before that charge was levelled again against Althusser, most venomously by E.P. Thompson.[51] This is perhaps why Perry Anderson would write a measured response to Thompson's charges, which primarily targeted Althusser, but also took in the style of Anderson's own earlier work.[52] I would even suggest that his practical anti-humanism might have been more disturbing than Althusser's theoretical anti-humanism, the latter being easier to dismiss as an excess of theory, while the former operated on the ground of history – the ground of Thompson and many others on the British left.

For Sedgwick, Anderson's Olympian distance had a class origin. In a memorable characterisation, he suggested that the second New Left 'is an openly self-articulated, self-powered outfit, an Olympian *autogestion* of roving postgraduates that descends at will from its own space onto the target-terrains of Angola, Persia, Cuba, Algeria, Britain ...'.[53] It is class-analysis, of a fairly brutal type, which is used to explain the critical mastery claimed by this form of Marxism. Critical distance is associated with class distance, and vice versa. This class gaze is rendered as a targeting and a matter of will, offering no real involvement in the world. Here, again, we see the articulation of the problem of critique as one of distance and mastery.

This would be a recurrent trope for those defending a more humanist historical Marxism derived from the lineage of Thompson. Peter Linebaugh, in his 1986 review of Perry Anderson's *In the Tracks of Historical Materialism*

---

49   Sedgwick 1964, p. 15.
50   Derrida 1978, p. 5.
51   Thompson 1978.
52   Anderson 1980.
53   Sedgwick 1964, p. 15.

(1983), uses a conceit of reading the book on a flight to literalise the usual metaphoric condemnation of the Olympian perspective. In this case Anderson's work belongs to the 'stratosphere', cruising above the abode of production and class struggle.[54] His style is 'Ultramontane', and so 'authoritarian and unresponsive to pressures from below'.[55] Not content with a critique of spatialised authority, Linebaugh also makes the temporal (and class) point as well: '[Anderson] lives in an interesting time-warp: partly Baroque, partly public-school Bohemian, partly 60s-style Trotskyism'.[56] Anderson is both far above and far behind, rendered as a nostalgic remnant refusing to get his hands messy with the business of the day. Again, we find a mixture of spatial and temporal figures of distance combined with a class or vaguely sociological claim.

My aim is not to settle the dispute between these perspectives, but to indicate an internal debate within Marxism concerning critical distance, and many other examples could have been used. In the debate I have just traced, this emerges between Anderson's traversal or tracking of positions, which seems to exit history, in opposition to those who stress the role of those who make history in their struggles. This recapitulates the tension Anderson himself probed between structure and subject in Marxism.[57] Certainly, this tension of analysis is not resolved by Marx or Marxism, but it is hard to see how it could simply be accused of assuming a mastery that dissolves this problem – except in its most scientifically reductionist and mechanical forms. It is an effect of being in close relation to the historical that generates the tension with which Marxism tries to work to gain critical traction on its material. This would be the reply of Anderson's scanning position, which is one committed to a position that can engage historical developments over long periods and also spatial developments in analysis of different national forms of capitalism.[58]

While Sedgwick and Linebaugh appear to have the virtue of class position and the masses on their side, we should be aware that the equation of closeness to a particular class position with insight is itself a complex debate within Marxism. Althusser can claim, for example, that the working-class reader has an immediate understanding of *Capital* denied to the philosophical reader.[59]

---

54   Linebaugh 1986, p. 143.
55   Linebaugh 1986, p. 143.
56   Linebaugh 1986, p. 143.
57   Anderson 1983, p. 33, p. 34.
58   Anderson 2009; Anderson 2012; Anderson 2019.
59   Althusser 1971, p. 72.

Here we seem to have the highest of high critique suddenly fusing or even collapsing into an identification of an immediate working-class knowledge. Certainly, the denial of working-class knowledge is itself constitutive for educational and social forms in capitalist society. The difficulty, beyond the level of accusations, is generating and mediating the relation of knowledge and critique as an act of distance and immanence. It can also be a rhetorical gesture, as it is not evident that Sedgwick and Linebaugh necessarily preserve a greater class truth as a result of their claim to immersion. In these scenes, we witness claim and counter-claim that can appear to be sterile, but in fact turn on vital issues of our position in capitalist society, the knowledge accrued by such positions, and how such knowledge is to be organised or fused into an understanding of the totality of that society.

It can be grist to anti-critique that Marxism seems to remain preoccupied with such problems, a sign that it has failed to achieve the right distance and the right closeness. It serves the image of anti-critique as a gay science – again the Nietzschean reference is deliberate –[60] which happily forgets such archaic debates, and even claims in its happiness to transcend the strident tones of Nietzsche. Models of distance are doubled by models of seriousness. Too distant and too serious, we might say. Instead, I am suggesting, such debates are a result of the recognition of immersion and negation required by the activity of critique, which is also a work of mutual and self-critique in trying to establish claims to knowledge. While it may appear as serious, which is not untrue, such a seriousness is a recognition of the stakes of knowledge. Therefore, to undermine the happy self-image of anti-critique we have to turn a critical and serious eye on the claims of anti-critique to a correct distance.

3   The Aesthetics of Relation

While anti-critique abolishes critical distance in the name of getting close to things, it also re-inscribes an autonomy and distance in its capacity to skim over many things. In the set-up of anti-critique, critique remains bound to the object of its critique, in a reactive and limited fashion. Again, the reference to Nietzsche's objection to reactive thought should be noted. The drive of critique to negate leaves it mired, as if in bird lime. In contrast anti-critique gets close

---

60   Nietzsche 2001.

to things, but never too close, and in doing so affirms its distance from things. To get close, to endorse, is also to escape any particular tie. This has been aptly characterised by Rosenberg as a 'theoretical primitivism', which involves 'the occlusion of the dynamics of social mediation'.[61] This kind of detachment is well-captured in Rancière's description of the nature of contemporary art: 'The Idea of the contemporary artist, on the contrary, is withdrawn, hovering in survey over the work of its realisation'.[62] The artist becomes a curator, an archivist, a collector,[63] and so too does the critic. In addition, the turn to aesthetics as a fundamental model is Nietzschean in inspiration, drawing on Nietzsche's contention that 'the existence of the world is only *justified* as an aesthetic phenomenon'.[64]

The reference to art is apposite because the role of the contemporary post-critic merges with that of the artist. Bromberg describes the convergence between contemporary forms of speculative realism and object-oriented philosophy; realist currents that have emerged within Continental thought, with art.[65] This convergence, as she notes, is not simply by chance, as aesthetics plays a crucial role in this thinking for the affirming of extra-human objects. It is aesthetics, in an impoverished form, that makes the bridge from ever-receding objects to humans. The relation of thinker or philosopher to their material is an aesthetic one, which inscribes both closeness and distance.[66] It is not surprising that such thinking appeals to artists, who are humans making (usually) objects. Both artist and, in this case, philosopher trace an aesthetic that affirms the non-human through affirming the multiplicity of objects that escape any control, including the control of capitalism.[67] They do so through an aesthetic appreciation of the possibilities of objects that are irreducible to capitalist capture.[68] In this way this affirmative discourse, which also draws on currents of anti-critique, displays a politics that affirms fluidity and escape through constant attachment and detachment.

There are two things to draw out here. The first is that a commonplace critique of anti-critique and speculative currents is that they treat their material in a reductively technical fashion. This, I argue, misses the point of the aes-

---

61   Rosenberg 2014.
62   Rancière 2010, p. 104.
63   Foster 2017, pp. 31–60.
64   Nietzsche 2008b, p. 8.
65   Bromberg 2013.
66   Fuller and Weizman 2021.
67   On the intimate legal dimension of the relation of objects to capitalism see Edwards 2020.
68   Berardi 2021.

thetic relation the post-critic makes with their material. The second is that this aesthetic relation is not simply that of the spectator, the classical position of Western aesthetics, but an aesthetics of the creator or curator. The post-critic is fused with the creative artist. The claim that anti-critique and speculative realism is technical or technological is a re-statement of what, with irony, we can call traditional critical theory: the danger of intellectual work mirroring the instrumental and positivist rationality of contemporary capitalism.[69]

Alexander R. Galloway makes the traditional criticism when he argues that 'mathification' is not only at the heart of some of these tendencies of speculative realism,[70] and we should stress some, but also at the heart of a contemporary capitalism of financial instruments and computerisation.[71] In a parallel critique of Franco Moretti's *Distant Reading*, Galloway argues that Moretti treats literature as a technical object. The result, he suggests, is that due to the arrival of the computer 'everything becomes computational'.[72] While not objecting to this per se – Galloway himself has worked extensively on computational structures – he argues that the result is a 'techno-mimicry'.[73] The need, instead, is to grasp critically the algorithms that make such research possible, rather than to accept them as given.[74] While there is some truth to this, the post-critic or speculative thinker can easily regard it as a typical sign of anti-scientific or anti-technological thinking dominant in the humanities. Galloway's critique, while useful, seems to miss the mark about the actual nature of anti-critique.

While not dismissing this re-statement of critique I want to re-iterate that the relation to objects is not so much technical as aesthetic. It is not so much a matter of instrumental rationality per se, but the aesthetic appreciation and use of material to form a counter-relation that will be warm and not cold. Post-critical thinking and certain currents of speculative realism, especially the work of Graham Harman,[75] work implicitly or explicitly by an aestheticisation of relation. It is the aesthetic that will constitute our relation to the world and objects and so any critical matter is, in fact, an aesthetic matter. In fact, anti-critique can evade critique on its own ground, by claiming to rework the

---

69   Horkheimer 2012.

70   Galloway 2019.

71   Galloway 2013a, p. 359.

72   Galloway 2013b.

73   Galloway 2013b.

74   Galloway 2004.

75   Harman 2012a; 2012b; 2016; 2020.

technical from the cliché of cold use into a relation of warm contact, which is the substance of Bruno Latour's work (see Chapter 2). In this swerve, the scientist becomes another creative figure allied with the artist, while the critic is condemned, as usual, to a purely negative form. All the negativity in the world, it sometimes seems, is to be found in the critic or projected on to the critic.

This aesthetic relation is, as I have suggested, not simply that of the spectator but that of the creator of art. In his critique of Western aesthetics Giorgio Agamben argues that the dominant aesthetic model, primarily instantiated by Kant, is an aesthetics of the spectator. It presumes a distance and a possibility of judgement upon a work, and it is not hard to make the same point in regards to the anti-critical distance anti-critique takes. Agamben's suggested alternative, derived from Nietzsche, is an aesthetics of the creator.[76] What interests me is how anti-critique bridges and synthesises these two positions. It is, at the same time, an aesthetics of the spectator and the creator, partly because the creator takes the role of the spectator in relation to the material they use. They scan over material as a spectator, but then get close to a particular object as a creator, or co-creator. This is why anti-critique offers a particular appeal to artists, because both theorists and artists insist on being constructive and creative to make something out of this capacity to skim over many things and then focus on particular selected things.

In the terms of literary criticism, the convergence I am tracing here on the aesthetic takes the form of an alliance between currents of anti-critique and the continuing and developing emergence of creative writing in the academy, especially in Britain. The history, and tensions, of the integration of creative writing in the US academy have been traced by Mark McGurl.[77] McGurl has pointed out the performative function of creative writing on the university campus, as the creative writer is hired as the means to personify and instantiate creativity. This marks a convergence with currents of anti-critique, which also affirmatively insist on their creativity. The accepted antonym of creative writing is critical writing, and the fact that this critical writing is in the process of abandoning critique indicates the possible convergence. Critics become creative at the same moment as the creative writer establishes a position in the academy. The creative writer treats literature and theory as potential material to be integrated into creative writing, as anti-critique treats objects as things to be skimmed over to produce a satisfying aesthetic reading.

---

76   Agamben 1999, p. 12.
77   McGurl 2009.

4　　Negative Relations

The real point of tension for anti-critique is the negativity on which critique depends for its critical distance. In contrast to the critical distance of negation, anti-critique prefers the affirmative distance of skimming the surface and zooming in to particular objects. The reason for this rejection is one consonant with a general theoretical trend that predates contemporary anti-critique. I have already mentioned Althusser's assertion that negativity belongs to the young Marx and that the mature Marx sets-out an affirmative and scientific procedure geared to generating new concepts. It should be no surprise that Deleuze, who defines philosophy as the invention of concepts, would appreciate Althusser's intervention and use it, in *Difference and Repetition* (1968), to further establish an affirmative Marx.[78] Negativity, to repeat, is mired in what it negates. The irony is that it does not achieve sufficient detachment.

A similar point, from a position more critical of Marxism, would be made by Jean Baudrillard. Marx's negativity is, according to Baudrillard, 'subtly haunted by the very form that it negates'.[79] Subtle hauntings are out, with a tendency to replace them with instances of brute material horror. This is evident in current theoretical interest in the writer H.P. Lovecraft, with his weird cosmology of alien horrors that once ruled the earth and will rule again. These monstrous alien creatures are not supernatural, they do not haunt, because, as Michel Houellebecq has indicated in regard to Lovecraft's Cthulhu, they are material:

> What is Great Cthulhu? An arrangement of electrons, like us. Lovecraft's terror is rigorously material.[80]

This excessive or weird materialism, or 'weird realism' as Graham Harman prefers,[81] probes a matter in excess of any determination: rigorously *positive* (even if cast as horrible) in its existence. While apparently an absolute negativity, we are again confronted with a matter that is regarded as resolutely positive. In contrast to a materialism concerned with the negativity of a relation to matter, especially in its making through labour, we have a post-critical emphasis on matter as affirmed against any capture.

78　Deleuze 1994, p. 186.
79　Baudrillard 1975, p. 52.
80　Houellebecq 1991, p. 32.
81　Harman 2012b.

This speaks not only to the rejection of negativity, but to the rejection of the negative in the name of the concrete or material. It is not only that the negative is too close, too tied to what it rejects, but this proximity is what forbids the finding or affirming of a materiality that escapes capture. What I want to suggest as an alternative is a return to critique and negativity without the clichés and assumptions that anti-critique has brought us. This involves being very close and very deep, in contrast to Love's 'close but not deep': in the sense of recognising our immersion in forms of capitalist value and state power. It does not assume an irreducible point of resistance, a matter beyond relation, or the aesthetic capacity both to take a distance and rely on a superior creative power.

In particular, as I have previously suggested,[82] this immersion is one way to grasp the particular function of capitalist value as a mechanism of abstraction. This is a materialism that does not simply reach for the concrete, but one which recognises that, as Marx put it, 'individuals are now ruled by *abstractions*'.[83] Marx also argues that: 'The abstraction, or idea, however, is nothing more than the theoretical expression of those material relations which are their lord and master'.[84] I would suggest that these 'real abstractions', the form of value, cuts across the alternatives of abstract / concrete, or material / ideal, in ways that anti-critique prefers not to consider.[85] They are real, materially embodied in relation of production and all the disciplinary modes of organisation applied to humans and nature to generate value, and abstract, in that these processes result in the global production of general equivalence and all the resulting theological and metaphysical effects known as the commodity-form. Against the real, anti-critique prefers a matter that does not fully enter into relations, against the abstract, post-critique prefers a concrete positivity that affirms things as they are.

To get very close would involve grasping these forms of abstraction through abstraction, in the very proximity and haunting that negativity implies. At the same time tracing negativity does not simply mire us in abstractions, but suggests the antagonisms and tensions that run through these forms. Werner Hamacher has suggested the risk run by conventional forms of Marxism is that they might reproduce the teleology of labour implied by capitalism: 'the true unveiling of its theo-economic secrets – of the sacrament of labour'.[86] But he also suggests that a Marxism re-thought as a mode of critique might also allow

82   Noys 2010, pp. 165–9.
83   Marx 1973, p. 164.
84   Marx 1973, p. 164.
85   Sohn-Rethel 1978; Toscano 2008a; 2008b.
86   Hamacher 2008, p. 179.

us to grasp the 'internal disjunction of labour and its autoteleology'.[87] I would like to stress this '*internal* disjunction' as the site of traction and intervention, which is given form by negativity. To be very close and very deep is not to enter into despair. This is the common accusation of anti-critique. Instead, while perhaps sceptical of the immediate joy proclaimed by anti-critique, this traction through negativity is, precisely, to pass through negation to affirm a revolutionary rupture.

Heather Love argues that post-critical reading that is close but not deep is more rigorously anti-humanist than the usual forms of anti-humanism associated with contemporary theory.[88] This is because they displace more radically, she contends, depth and a religious relation of meaning by departing from human concerns. Unlike, again, the anguish of various attempts to come to terms with humanism and escape it, Love suggests a kind of forgetting that would leave humanity behind. My argument, in contrast, is that attention to the forms of negativity and abstraction in relation disrupts the theological hermeneutic, without abandoning political questions and the question of the human. This is not an anti-humanism that leaves the human behind as one object among others, but a humanism that probes the relations to objects and the tensions and negativity at work in those relations. In place of an aesthetic contemplation of surfaces, or an aesthetic creativity of new forms, we need to attend to a critical distance that places us in contact with these relations of negativity, as distance, embedded within relation. This is not to smuggle back in a claim to critical superiority, but to understand how we are riven by these forms of relation and negativity. It is to suggest there is no safe haven from which we can skim and select.

The messy proximity I have traced should also include the relation between critique and anti-critique. These categories can be overly homogenising and result in a reduction that aims to counter a reduction. If the skimming of surface also includes the characterisation of critique, then complexity and messiness should also be restored to the forms of anti-critique. This means that we should not just dismiss the challenge of anti-critique or assume the ease of a reconstructive return to order. Another flattening of positions into abstract opposition is limiting. Some of the most interesting recent critical work has tried to integrate the fascination with matter evident in anti-critique with the concern with relation and negativity found in critique. Walter Johnson's reconstruction of the 'Cotton Kingdom' in the Mississippi Valley attends to the mater-

---

87   Hamacher 2008, p. 180.
88   Love 2010, p. 375.

iality of slavery: 'The Cotton Kingdom was built out of sun, water, and soil; animal energy, human labour, and mother wit; grain, flesh, and cotton; pain, hunger, and fatigue; blood, milk, semen, and shit'.[89] In this case the attention to materiality and networks is concerned with tracing the process of transformation of these forms of matter into abstractions. Matter is not simply cast as resistance, but as an ecology of relations that constitutes the relation of slavery to capitalist forms. Similarly, Timothy Mitchell's *Carbon Democracy* (2011) also pays attention to networks of carbon extraction, especially the transition from coal to oil, but also as a means to complicate and provoke reflection on possibilities of political intervention.[90] These works rightly distance themselves from some of the abstractions of critical discourse, but also attend to the emergence and constitution of real abstractions as forces and forms that act-upon and transform materiality.

We could also add that in terms of reading critique, recent work has started to probe some of the most reductionist and problematic forms of critique. Glyn Salton-Cox, for example, has explored the writing of the British Marxist Edward Upward, who is often taken as one of the most reductionist and Stalinist writers of the British Left. While not diminishing the problems of Upward's critical discourse and his own experiments in writing socialist-realist novels, Slaton-Cox sensitively registers the complexities within socialist realism and within Upward's own 'leftist self-fashioning'.[91] We could add the recent reissues of work by Christopher Caudwell,[92] usually treated as the most reductive instance of Marxist literary criticism. Caudwell's work, while problematic, is also insightful into the fundamental dimension of bourgeois ideology as posing a subject without relations. For Caudwell freedom lies in entering into social relations rather than trying to escape from them, which is a useful corrective to singular attempts to break with relation.[93] Again, the point is not to deny the reductive forms of critique or problems of a negativity treated as a melancholy incapacity. These are and were present in critique. The point is to read and re-read critique and currents within anti-critique that can be developed into a path through negativity to a rupture and a new critical conception of a mode of freedom. Critique that it is true to its aim is also self-critical, not simply in the mode of eternal doubt and hesitation but as a means to transcend the limits of critique.

---

89   Johnson 2013, p. 9.
90   Mitchell 2011.
91   Slaton-Cox 2013.
92   Caudwell 2017; 2018.
93   Hallward 2001.

The lack of a safe haven for critique requires thinking through in all these dimensions. In particular, it re-inscribes the notion of critical distance to refuse the consolation of a safe affirmative distance from which we can sally forth. Instead, the distance we have emerges out of the rupturing effects of negativity *within* forms of relation and abstraction. The tendency to abandon or distance ourselves from this thinking literary criticism or literary theory is a particular matter of concern. This is because questions of form and fiction, the traditional domain of literary studies, are crucial to grasping the seemingly paradoxical conjunction real abstraction. This is a pressing need at exactly the moment when the real damage that real abstractions have inflicted, and continue to inflict, are self-evident to all. A cursory reading of any daily newspaper, of virtually any political persuasion, should be sufficient. The consolatory resting in contemplation or creation of the material, vital, or concrete is an evasion of this need at the moment of the abandonment of many to a material destitution through the voiding of value.

Matter against Materialism

Bruno Latour, according to Andrew Barry, has been 'extraordinarily influential across the social sciences in Britain'.[1] Latour's 'actor-network theory' has,[2] however, only become influential in literary and cultural studies comparatively recently.[3] The construction of Latourian literary studies is something of a synthetic phenomenon. It had been prepared by the currents of new historicism, cultural materialism, and thing theory, all of which attended to objects as sites of critical attention.[4] Also, it has been reinforced by, and coincided with, the turn to object-oriented philosophy,[5] the new materialisms,[6] and Latour's own turn to metaphysical and philosophical questions.[7] What I would characterise as a general historicism, coupled with an attention to the complexity of social and material relations, is the default mode of the contemporary humanities. The arrival of Latour in this context is, surprisingly, somewhat belated. My concern here is to dispute this arrival of Latour or, to be more precise, this synthetic Latourianism, in literary studies. My point of attack concerns Latour's rehabilitation of matter, primarily in the form of objects, posed against materialism – which is to say posed against broadly Marxist currents that insist on the role of the economic, on the ensemble of social and historical relations, as crucial to the analysis of literature.

Bruno Latour has never hidden his hostility to Marxist materialism. For Latour Marxist determinism by the economic is a signature form of reductionism and critical mastery. In its place Latour insists on 'irreduction'[8] – the treatment of matter and objects as matters of concern that resist stabilisation.[9] Latour turns Marxism against itself. He argues that reification – the congealing of social relations in material things – is not simply an act of capitalism, but also an act of Marxism. Marxism reifies the economy as fundamental cause and condition, and Latour's response is to suggest the necessity to de-reify the

1 Barry 2011, p. 36.
2 Latour 2005.
3 Love 2010, Felski 2011a.
4 Vesser (ed.) 1989; Dollimore and Sinfield 1985; Brown 2001.
5 Harman 2009; 2012a.
6 Bennett 2010.
7 Latour 2013.
8 Latour 1988.
9 Latour 2004.

economy into another network, another ensemble of relations and objects. In this way objects are extracted from their determination by capital to – in an inversion of Marx's commodity table, which stands on its head[10] – stand, or dance, on their own feet.

In terms of literary studies this attention to matter takes a number of forms: concern with the materiality of books as objects, including the materiality of printed page,[11] book covers, and the physical nature of reading; concern with the appearance of objects within texts, such as in 'it-narratives', which are literary works focused on the passage of a particular object, such as a coin;[12] and interest in the descriptive surface of texts, rather than probing beneath to reveal some deeper meaning.[13] While explicit reference to Latour is fairly sparse, and should not be exaggerated, it is possible to argue that there is a wider structure of feeling, which is precisely concerned with the feeling of objects (in both senses): a haptic attention to the material surfaces of objects and a sense or defence of the rights or status of objects as sites of feeling. We can already note the emerging tendency to donate to objects a set of qualities that were usually associated with traditional models of literary subjectivity and character: depth of feeling, complexity, fluidity, and a sense of the living.

There is no doubt something salutary and even necessary in the turn to objects as a curbing of hubris, especially at the time of the Anthropocene and ongoing financial crisis. This turn has been less successful, I contend, in giving deeper attention to the relation of these objects to human practice, and also how these objects carry imprinted on them forms of practice.[14] The result of separating matter from materialism is to sunder an understanding of the relations between humans and objects, especially as commodities, and leave us with a mystified view of both humans and objects. There is also a risk of underestimating how fiction, that uncanny form that destabilises truth, can unlock these forms of relation. To make this argument I return to Marx to probe his account of materialism and commodities again. Against the reading of Marx as economic determinist, itself a reductionist reading, we can find in Marx an exploration of the forms of what Sohn-Rethel, after Marx, called 'real abstraction'.[15] The paradoxical category of real abstraction cuts across the terms of the current debate, belonging neither to the material nor the non-material.

---

10   Marx 1990, p. 163.
11   Lupton 2008.
12   Lupton 2011.
13   Love 2010.
14   Edwards 2020.
15   Sohn-Rethel 1978, p. 20.

The weaponising of matter against materialism is not a turn to the concrete, as claimed, but rather the turn to a 'warm abstraction' posed against the 'cold abstractions' of capitalism.[16]

To explore the resonance of real abstraction I turn to Gordon Lish's experimental novel *Peru* (1986). This is a defiantly abstract novel, but one that will therefore help us access the real abstractions that structure our existence without making an appeal to the concrete that claims to bypass the abstract. Against the delights of warm abstractions, Lish's novel pursuit of a particular form of cold abstraction is more revealing of the possible path to the concrete through the abstract. The nature of fiction helps us to resist the supposed charm of the concrete and the supposedly unmediated object, especially in the case of a fiction that undeniably engages the abstract with experience. Literary theory, I claim, cannot be updated by a turn to the material and concrete, but instead it must traverse the path of abstraction.[17]

1   Object and Commodities

In his *Philosophy of Marx* (1994) Étienne Balibar notes that in the case of Marx 'we are dealing with a strange "materialism without matter"'.[18] Balibar is referring to Marx's theses on Feuerbach, where Marx argues that 'the chief defect of all hitherto existing materialism [...] is that the thing, reality, sensuousness is conceived only in the form of the *object or of contemplation*, but not as *sensuous human activity, practice*'.[19] This is crucial to the displacement of a certain image of Marx in which materialism is considered as a reductive or contemplative notion, in which the world is reduced to the material as static stuff. Instead, Marx's argument suggests that materialism is not only about objects, but a concern with practice and relations. Certainly, Marx's materialism begins from the priority of matter and never departs from that, but it also tries to grasp the relations formed between humans and objects and especially as those objects take the form of commodities.

We could suggest that Balibar exaggerates the position by suggesting a materialism without matter, when we might be better off considering how Marx's materialism develops a new relation to the understanding of matter. This is especially true of Marx's later discussion of the fetishism of commodities in

---

16   Toscano 2008a, p. 58.
17   Lustig 2019.
18   Balibar 2007, p. 23.
19   Marx 1975, p. 421.

Capital.[20] The form of the commodity, as we shall see, is precisely the trans-formation of the object through a social practice, a practice Marx traces and delimits. Here the point of resistance does not so much lie in the matter that is the resistant inertia residing in the object, but in a critical attention to the transformation of the object 'into a thing which transcends sensuousness', as Marx states, or, as Michael Heinrich corrects the translation, 'into a sensuous extrasensory thing' (*sinnlich übersinnliches Ding*).[21]

For Latour such activities of de-mystification and the attention to relations at the expense of the resistance of the object are problematic. They are the root of the gesture of critique, which for Latour is an anti-fetishism that pro-jects naivety onto the other and claims a superior knowledge of true causes.[22] Symptomatically, Latour does not mention Marx, although the target is obvi-ous. This would be the Marx who explains commodity-fetishism as a social practice based in the 'hidden abode of production',[23] which is invisible to its practitioners while visible to Marx. Such an explanation, for Latour, is an exem-plary act of reduction that cannot account for the complexity and density of objects and networks.

If Latour favours the object over the commodity, then we could say an inverse problem emerges on Derrida's account of Marx's discussion of spectres. In this case, Derrida's account of Marx's battles with spectres and ghosts also suggests that, finally, Marx exorcises the ghostly to establish an ontology of presence at the expense of a hauntology.[24] For Latour Marx cannot deal with the complexity of the object, while for Derrida Marx cannot deal with the com-plexity of the spectral. Latour argues that the focus on the fetish obscures the materiality of the object, which is finally reduced to the 'hieroglyph' that can only be read by the Marxist critic.[25] For Derrida the problem lies with dis-pensing with the fetish to reveal the true use-value of the commodity, which obscures the irreducibly spectral nature of the object.[26] In both cases, Marx's level of the commodity as fetish and real abstraction is denied. The symmetry of the criticisms, one focused on the object and the other on the spectral, sug-gests that what is missed lies in the relation of the object to the fetish, or of the object to the commodity, which is, precisely, the 'value-form'.[27]

---

20   Marx 1990, pp. 163–77.
21   Marx 1990, p. 163; Heinrich 2012, p. 72.
22   Latour 2004, pp. 237–8.
23   Marx 1990, p. 279.
24   Derrida 1994, p. 170.
25   Marx 1990, p. 167.
26   Derrida 1994, pp. 159–60.
27   Marx 1990, p. 160.

Hylton White has already drawn attention to Latour's wilfully reductive reading of Marx's account of fetishism. In an ironic inversion White notes that Marx produces a much more complex account of the human relation with objects in the production of commodities than does Latour.[28] Marx is not making a claim about an epistemological failure of people to understand their own projections, but how a social practice generates the transcendence of the thing into the commodity. Slavoj Žižek, invoking Sohn-Rethel's analysis of 'real abstractions', has insisted that commodity fetishism is an objective illusion that operates precisely *because* the subject is unconscious of it.[29] What these accounts suggest is that the transformation of the object into the commodity is not an act of will or mind, but a result of a social practice determined by abstract labour – the transformation of labour into an equivalence which is then embedded into objects. This then suggests that the act of the critic, in this case Marx, is also not another wilful imposition, but a critical reconstruction that reveals what had left all blind. Certainly, there is an undeniable claim to critical superiority here, but quite as much as in Latour's or Derrida's claims to insights into objects or the spectral. Marx's point is that his critical reconstruction can be followed and reconstructed by all to explain our subjection to real abstraction.

While these correctives are useful in refuting Latour and the many other dismissals of Marx that rest on a similar characterisation, something more can be said about commodity fetishism. Marx's account of the commodity as a 'sensuous super-sensuous thing' (*sinnlich-übersinnlich*),[30] with its occult or mystical character, also allows us to probe the fetishisation of matter as what resists materialism. The two-fold nature of the commodity form, which combines use-value and exchange-value, the material and the abstract, suggests that the accusations that Marx tries to separate these things misfire. In fact, Latour's emphasis on matter and Derrida's insistence on the spectral risk missing this historically-specific transformation of the object into the commodity form wrought by capital. They risk missing the combination or fusing of the material and the spectral.

Werner Hamacher has traced the congealing of abstract labour in the commodity as a transcendental action of capital as a '*formaterialism*'.[31] The form of value attaches itself to the material object, through a social practice, to generate the commodity which is an object that then behaves like a subject.

28   White 2013, pp. 667–8.
29   Žižek 1989, pp. 16–21.
30   Marx 1990, p. 163.
31   Hamacher 2008, p. 178.

While Marx attributes the revelation of occult qualities to the analysis of the commodity-form, which appears as natural in everyday life, we can add that the commodity also takes on a spectral or occult form in everyday life. If, often, nature does not appear wholly natural, but rather uncanny or weird, so the everyday life of the commodity is naturalised for us, but this is also a second nature that leads to the weird state of objects behaving badly or madly. The deranged nature of the commodity-form, with its 'metaphysical subtleties and theological niceties',[32] is true to capitalist reality as a weird second reality.[33]

Marx is not, pace Latour, merely anthropocentric, arguing that all the powers of objects are projected human powers. Latour's criticism, like so many criticisms of Marx, attributes to Marx the position he is criticising. It is capitalism that is anthropocentric, in creating a world that treats objects as only of interest insofar as they embody value, that is, human labour. The result of this anthropocentrism is that the commodity world is an anthropomorphic world, 'a bewitched, distorted and upside-down world',[34] in which we are dominated by things with quasi-divine powers.[35] While Latour can target an anthropocentrism that reduces objects to inert things, he cannot grasp how this is a result of capitalist social relations. Latour also cannot grasp how these relations imbue objects with occult and magical powers, mistaking these endowed powers for the truth of objects. The result is a fetishisation of the object, but an object rendered as fetish through the aesthetic mode. It may therefore be through fiction, as a mode of the aesthetic, that we can put the object back on its feet and understand how our upside-down world is the result of the real abstraction of value.

2   Form and Deformation

The question is how fiction might come to terms with what Marx calls 'commodity-language': that attempt to transcribe the world into the transcendental form of value, into an abstract system of equivalence.[36] Hamacher argues that this coming to terms involves not simply a transcription of this language, of the promise of the commodity-language to provide equivalence, but also of the

---

32   Marx 1990, p. 163.
33   Lukács 1971a, p. 64.
34   Marx 1992, p. 969.
35   Heinrich 2012, p. 184.
36   Marx 1990, p. 144.

exhaustion of this promise.[37] To do so, I will argue, requires attention to form, as this is the central element of the character of the commodity. In terms of literary fiction and literary theory, form has obviously been a central category, although notably displaced by the generalised historicism that characterises literary studies at the present moment.[38] To attend to form is not simply to replicate the formaterialism of capitalism, but to attend to the deformation of form in contact with the equalising force of the commodity.

Gordon Lish is perhaps best-known as the severe editor of Raymond Carver's short stories and as a teacher of creative writing. His teaching and writing are heavily inspired by contemporary theory, and his own writing is defiantly experimental. While Lish might be regarded as an outlier to contemporary fiction, a representative of the fading avant-garde or postmodernism, I want to treat him as a crucial figure due to his emphasis on literary form. In particular, his novel *Peru* (1986) offers a singular articulation of literary form, abstraction, and questions of violence. It concerns Gordon, a fifty-year-old father, who witnesses a violent prison uprising on late-night television, which he later finds out takes place in Peru, before he is due to take his son to summer camp. Taking his son to camp he strikes his head on the trunk lid of a taxi and, badly-hurt, he recalls how, as a child, he killed a playmate in a neighbour's sand pit (though we cannot tell whether or not the memory is real).

The novel operates through a repetitive style, which aims at consistency or what Lish calls 'consecution',[39] or 'the language of Peru'.[40] This is a recursive procedure in which each sentence works on the words of the previous sentence to produce an emergent sense.[41] The result is a patterning of repetition and return that also aims to swerve from the expected sense, something like a Lucretian or Epicurean materialism. The swerve, however, is not simply the introduction of contingency or chance into the system, but the result of registering material pressure. This deeply abstract practice of working on language as a set of units or objects is also concerned with inscribing instances of traumatic violence and the violence of the forms of abstraction.

Reflecting on his killing of his childhood playmate Steven Adinoff in Andy Lieblich's sandbox, the narrator recalls his desire to be like Andy Lieblich. This desire is expressed in the desire to have hair that smells like Lieblich's and then expands out into identifications with others through objects; he wants

37   Hamacher 2008.
38   For a critical rehabilitation of form see Levine 2015.
39   Winters 2013.
40   Lish 2013, p. 187.
41   Lutz 2009.

to be his teacher Miss Donnelly's hankie, lilac, or bodice. The narrator concludes: 'I tell you, when you live next door to someone richer, there is no
end to what will enter your thoughts'.[42] The repetitive thoughts of the narrator are shaped by this lack of equivalence created by wealth as it operates within the equivalence formed by language and the abstraction of value.
Here, there is a dialectic of equivalence and lack of equivalence, form and
deformation, between the equalising force of the commodity-form and the
force of differentiation of value in that form. It is this pressure that *Peru*
probes.

The enumerative logic of the narration equalises objects, people, and activities, including murder: 'Killing Steven Adinoff – there is no sense in not saying
so, there is no reason for me not to say so – killing Steven Adinoff was one of the
best of these things'.[43] Killing is one of the best of these things, part of the chain
of equivalence, but as 'one of the best', also stands out in the chain, although
still grouped with the objects and feelings that are the narrator's thoughts.
Killing becomes an object that removes the person treated as a series of qualities or objects, Steven Adinoff. This logic of reification constantly attends to the
differentiation of value; the abstract chain is not purely abstract. Andy Lieblich has 'rich skin', which 'looked much cleaner than mine did'.[44] Again, we
have a sense of value, 'rich', which deliberately equivocates between a quality
of the skin and a social quality, wealth, which has led to the quality of the skin.
It is tempting to read Lish's novel as, in part, a commentary on or repetition
of Barthes's *Mythologies*, with its reflection on how consumer objects accrue
metaphysical and social value by the transformation of historical values into
seemingly natural facts.[45]

While Lish's repetitions attest to the force of language, and the deformation
of sense under the drive of language, they also constantly return to differences
in status. The narrator eats leftover meat loaf, while Andy Lieblich has meat
patties, the narrator's parents rent their house, lack a car, and to save water he
showers with his father. The fetish of the commodity is given form in a feeling:
'But I can't think of anything else of theirs which did not give you the feeling of
being a creaminess, of it being smoothed over and a creaminess'.[46] The promise
of the commodity-language is registered in these series of exceptions, a kind of
shine on the commodity that takes a material form, or more precisely sensual-

---

42   Lish 2013, p. 13.
43   Lish 2013, p. 23.
44   Lish 2013, p. 30.
45   Barthes 1973.
46   Lish 2013, p. 104.

super-sensual form, of this feeling of creaminess. Again, we recollect Barthes's discussion of the foaminess of soap as a kind of spiritual incarnation of material luxury.[47]

Far from capitalist abstraction being anti-material, it works over the material, even producing the feeling of the material. Lish's probing of language as a medium, which is his primary concern, is also revealing of this generation of the material and of affect through and by abstraction. There is not an opposition of matter to the forms of abstraction, but their intertwining. This is not the fault of Marx, as in Latour's reductive reading, but something Marx probes in his attention to how the effect of value creates the 'creaminess' of the commodity-form, that desirable excess in repetition. In Lish's narrative, which is centrally concerned with trauma – the violence on the prison roof seen on television, the killing of Steven Adinoff, and the narrator's injury – this trauma is also placed within the abstraction of language. The preface to the reissue of the novel insists on the truth of *Peru*, while also recalling how Lish's misspelling of his father's name as Philip, rather than Phillip, is as much a crime as the murder of Steven Adinoff. This perhaps bathetic inflation suggests the force of abstraction belonging to language, which is tapped but not exhausted by commodity-language.

While Latour-inspired literary critics often choose to analyse work that concerns objects, I might easily be charged with choosing a defiantly abstract work to prove my case. David Winters, in his excellent discussion of *Peru*, remarks 'such a book is a black box, an object at odds with the world around it'.[48] The issue of the object is not posed internally to the narrative, but at the level of the work itself. This is a peculiar kind of object – a work of fiction, a work of language, which does not cohere into the creamy materiality so much desired today. This novel does attest, however, to the repetitive force of abstraction at work everywhere and left unnoticed in works which take for granted creaminess of the object or, perhaps more often, try to produce it for us. The sometime nausea and difficulty we experience in reading, or trying to read, *Peru* is a sign of the intrusion of abstraction into our awareness; we experience not the fleshy materiality of matter as such, as Sartre's narrator does in *Nausea* (1938) when he contemplates the roots of a tree,[49] but the forming and deforming force of the language of abstraction that produces the object as material for us.

---

47   Barthes 1973, p. 36.
48   Winters 2013.
49   Sartre 2000, p. 186.

3   Non-materialism

Bruno Latour claims constantly to do justice to matter as a complex and connected 'matter of concern'.[50] It is this attention to materiality that, he claims,
distances him from a materialism that subsumes matter under a singular determination. Is it true, however, that Latour's primary concern is with matter? Henning Schmidgen argues, via a reading of Latour's early philosophical
and religious work, that Latour is not so interested in material assemblages
as he is in how things are passed on via 'inscribed surfaces and registration
devices'.[51] While literary studies has turned to Latour for his concern with matter and objects, it may be that Latour was much more concerned with texts
than objects. This ironic textualisation threatens revenge on a literary studies
that tries to displace or dispose of the literary or fictional in the name of matter,
which is subject to a literary or fictional representation.

   More interesting for my argument is Schmidgen's key point: 'In Latour the
things of science retain a lightness and transcendence, which eventually cannot be referred back to material, economical and/or social configurations'.[52]
Latour, according to Schmidgen, is not simply religious as a matter of personal preference, but a certain drive or desire for transcendence operates in
the core of his materialism. Objects are not so much stable and inert things,
but become thresholds between worlds, or even thresholds that open onto
worlds.[53] This is a spiritualisation of matter, which concerns itself with inscrip-
tions and objects insofar as they refuse to stay merely material. This is not only a
matter of Latour's misapprehension of the sensuous-supersensuousness of the
commodity-form, as I have suggested. There is a stronger agenda in his desire
to turn to matter as a form of transcendence, in a kind of mystical materialism.
The hubris of human mastery is displaced by the supposed humility before the
divine powers of matter. This is not only true of Latour, but also of other itera-
tions of the new materialism or concern with matter against materialism. Jane
Bennett's pan-animist vitalism is a 'creed' for the appreciation for the sacred-
ness of things,[54] while William Connolly's stress on becoming and flux aims to
restore belief in the world.[55] In all cases, the potential for the analysis of matter

---

50   Latour 2004.
51   Schmidgen 2013, p. 15; Schmidgen 2015.
52   Schmidgen 2013, p. 8.
53   Schmidgen 2013, p. 22.
54   Bennett 2010, p. 122.
55   Connolly 2011, p. 61.

and materiality is, in the end, abandoned for a mystical contemplation of the material as such, which ironically becomes indistinguishable from the textual or the sign.

This religious or theological notion of matter suggests that we not treat the historical and material turn of literary theory, and theory more broadly, at face value. The novelty claims made by the new materialisms rest on the enchantment and animation of matter that not only takes over the powers of the humanist subject, but also of the divine. Contrary to the image of secular advance, we can see these supposedly new claims as a return to the initial theological or religious imperative in literary studies. It has been regularly noted by critics that the emergence of literary studies as a subject was often justified by giving that discipline the moral and cohesive power formerly ascribed to religion.[56] If, formerly, this cohesion was to be found in the moral and ethical truths encoded in fiction, which were to be transmitted by the accredited scholar-cum-priest, today the claims for cohesion are to be found in an agreement that matter and objects escape all determination. In this way a defiantly non-determinist materialism, resistant to all forms of reduction, tends to find in matter a transcendence that frees it from the inert and weighty. Felski, following Latour, insists that context is not a box and that texts themselves are actors which escape rigid determination to enter into all sorts of relations.[57] The identification of text and object is complete, in which both become that resistant matter and incarnate that 'creaminess' *Peru* suggested, a shine or glow that passes out of the control of capitalism and into a heavenly realm of promiscuous objects.

This is not to deny the attentiveness religious thought can bring to matter. Contrary to a simple-minded accusation of having eyes only for heaven, religious discourses attend to the immanence of the world as the creation of God.[58] We only have to think here of the poetry of Gerard Manley Hopkins or David Jones, with its attempts to fuse language and matter into sacred sign.[59] The difficulty I am indicating, however, is how this oscillation between immanence and transcendence risks missing the 'sensuous super-sensuous' nature of the commodity. To presume to escape this effect by an embrace of the transcendence of matter does not dispute the commodity-form but remains as a celebration of its power. At the more local level, it also enforces a doxa of transcendence

---

56   Eagleton 1996, pp. 21–3.
57   Felski 2011a, p. 584.
58   Urpeth 2014; Noys 2023.
59   Noys 2023.

in the name of a freedom from determination.[60] Connections are everywhere, but there is never any exhausted connection, licensing a discourse of flight and unworldliness as the final determination of the literary.

4   The Misery of Criticism

Rita Felski summarises critique as 'a ubiquitous academic ethos of detachment, negativity, and doubt'.[61] In this she is the direct heir of Nietzsche, who remarks on the 'eternally hungry, the weak and joyless "critic", the Alexandrian man, who is basically a wretched librarian and proof reader blinded by book dust and printer's errors'.[62] There is no doubt that part of the appeal of the turn to objects lies in claims to abandon this negative attitude and the embrace of a more practical and positive orientation. There is, however, some difficulty in this story of a turn to the happy world of objects. The first is the overstatement of the dominance of the ethos of critique. Certainly, in the field of theory, one might characterise the recent past as easily in terms of a defiant affirmation-ism – insisting on a Nietzschean laughter, embrace and affirmation of what is, in all its becoming.[63] Claims to Nietzschean joyousness and rejection of the misery associated with critique, and by implication the left, are everywhere.[64] More specifically, in the field of literary theory, many of the characterisations of critique rest on a persistent invocation of clichéd versions of psychoanalysis and Marxism to justify the novelty of their own position (see Chapter 1). The second difficulty is, at what cost is this happiness bought? Here, as we have shown, the turn to the material is, in fact, a turn to the lightness of matter as transcendent, an escape into a promiscuous world of connections and inter-actions. It is a movement away from actual objects and into a spiritual realm detached from reality. The *sprezzatura* of the turn to objects feels, at times, all-too studied and more of a faith than a reality, an escapism that denies reality.

To dispute this claim to novelty is to risk being seen as irredeemably ret-rograde, as a defensive and miserable critic clinging to claims of power over matter that have been rescinded.[65] That we need to rethink critique is certainly

---

60   Berardi 2021.
61   Felski 2011a, p. 575; Felski 2011b.
62   Nietzsche 2008b, p. 100.
63   Noys 2010, p. ix.
64   Land 2013, pp. 623–8.
65   See Tally 2022, p. 108, on the persistent tendency to characterise critique as elitist and arrogant.

true, that we should abandon it for the charms of a new happy post-critical state, not. What is forgotten in the forgetting of critique is not simply an affective sensibility,[66] but a thinking that tried to take the measure of the forces and forms of abstraction. The post-critic treats the choice to be post-critical as an aesthetic matter, to choose pleasure over pain, and so reduces the question of critique to a matter of aesthetics and style. Such an aestheticisation of reading beyond the critical could already be found in Sontag's 1960s work,[67] which was part of a broader Nietzschean heritage. In fact, the novelty of the post-critical is overstated.

It is perhaps surprising that the turn away from abstraction and towards matter should take place at a point where the violent effects of abstraction have become obvious and real, notably in global financial crisis, the further development of digital technologies, and, linked to both, an awareness of the power of financial instruments, from Collateralised Debt Obligations (CDOs) to High-Frequency Trading (HFT), effects in which abstraction is bound to the material.[68] In the face of effects of dematerialisation it may not be surprising, however, that we find a turn to matter. The increasing powers of abstraction may drive the turn to matter and away from abstraction. But, and this is crucial, this return to matter is not a return to matter as a simple point of stability but it is a return to matter as fluid, contingent and transcendent which exerts its charms. Here matter can play the role of a point beyond capture in its very capacity to elude inert materialisation. To reiterate, the risk of such an appeal is that, while consoling, it evades the embedded nature of objects, in particular socially-produced forms of abstraction.

What we have pursued here is Balibar's suggestion of Marx's 'materialism without matter', to emphasise the relations at the centre of Marx's vision, but also the relation of materialism to matter as what has priority for materialism. In that sense, Balibar concedes too much to critics of materialism and leaves the door open for the abandonment of matter, which is dissolved into relations, or for the return of matter as ever-receding mystical object. The power of Marx's vision was to coordinate matter and relations within an historical materialism that traced the evolution of the relations between matter and objects. In the context of contemporary capitalism this involves attention to those relations of real abstraction that have to be explained by a series of relations that transform objects and humans into commodities.

---

66   Felski 2011b, p. 215.
67   Sontag 2009, pp. 3–14.
68   Toscano 2013.

In terms of literary studies, this also involves an attention to the material forms that structure the experience of the literary commodity. For example, recent attention to literary objects as embedded within forms of institutional practice that shape literary production and consumption,[69] offers a path to grasp and traverse abstraction without invoking theological forms of transcendence. The choice, then, is not between objects, literary or otherwise, as mere passive victims of processes of abstraction, and objects as always possible sites of transcendence escaping final determination. Instead, the literary object can be considered as a site which engages with the forms of abstraction that shape and constitute it. This engagement does not simply result in some essential innocence, some re-inscribed religious, moral, or ethical value as such, but rather, due to the embedded nature of the literary object and its attempt to write or fictionalise this position, the literary object can deform or test current forms of abstraction. Here we can find a defence of the literary object which allows us to take seriously the test of abstraction which we all face.

---

69   McGurl 2009, p. xii; Brouillette 2014, p. 52.

CHAPTER 3

Apocalypse and Crisis

In a time of crisis apocalyptic desires and fantasies become pressing and real. Norman Cohn's *In Pursuit of the Millennium* (1957) offered a secret history of the periodic emergence of a revolutionary eschatology in the Middle Ages in response to a collapsing social order, immiseration, disease, and war. Responding to crisis these dreamers dared to imagine an apocalypse that would turn the world upside down, and create a new heaven on earth in which princes would bow to peasants. Of course, the apocalypse that became real was often the apocalypse of repression: the wake of the Peasants' War in Germany (1524–6) led to the deaths of over a hundred thousand peasants and the eventual execution of its leader Thomas Müntzer who, under torture, proclaimed *'Omnia sunt communia'* (All things are to be held in common).[1] Cohn, an anti-communist liberal, regarded these millenarians as dangerous forerunners of the totalitarian movements of the twentieth century and, in the 1970 edition, extended this to condemn the revolutionary aims of the movements of the 1960s.[2] Of course, the Situationists would deliberately re-purpose Cohn, reclaiming these rebels from 'the condescension of posterity', to use E.P. Thompson's famous phrase, as heralds of a radical communist future.[3] Apocalyptic desires are ambiguous: at once consolatory fantasies, deferred hopes, and, potentially, spurs to radical re-orderings.

We are living in a time of crisis and potential apocalypse, with the overlapping of the financial crisis, ecological crisis, and the crisis of movements of resistance. The apocalyptic imagination feeds on this to produce dreams or nightmares of a world cleansed of humanity, from the film *2012* (2009) to the History Channel's television series *Life After People* (2009–10). These fundamentally reactionary fantasies can only imagine the redemption of our fallen world on the condition that humanity ceases to exist, or is reduced to the right number of the saved. With the Coronavirus pandemic that began in 2019 we have seen a further revival of apocalyptic thinking.[4] What concerns me here is thinking more closely the relation between radical and revolutionary thought and an apocalyptic tone in the context of crisis. The usual model of such a tone

---

1 Müntzer 2010.
2 Cohn 1970, p. 286.
3 Not Bored! 1999; see also Blisset 2004.
4 Berardi 2021, pp. 97–102.

was proposed by Kant, when he argued that it was the result of the illegitimate extension of reason beyond its limits towards a transcendent 'exalted vision' (*schwärmerische Vision*).[5] Failing to recognise the limits of reason, for Kant the apocalyptic dreamer was a fanatic (*Schwärmer*) trying to impose an abstract vision on reality.[6] I am more interested in another version of this apocalyptic tone, one which is generated by a claimed immanence of thought to reality rather than its transcendence.

In this case apocalypse is not generated by some external superior transcendent vision but by the immanent tendencies of the present. This is a tone which remains within, if often heretically, the ambit of Marxism. Marx, writing with Engels in *The Communist Manifesto* (1848), argued that class struggle would each time end 'either in a revolutionary reconstitution of society at large, or in the common ruin of the contending classes'.[7] While history was a history of class struggles, the model was that the immanent tendencies of capitalism would make possible their own transcendence into a new social order, or collapse into barbarism. The difficulty or tension in this model lies in how these tendencies advance and how far the contradictions of the present have to sharpen before they can be transcended. If plunging into crisis is a necessary feature of capitalism then how do we trace a way out of that crisis that intensifies the crisis for capitalism and not for its victims?

In the context of the global capitalist crisis of 2008–9 we can think of those who argued the need to radicalise and deepen the tendencies that led to the crisis or that the crisis was an opportunity that would lead inevitably to radicalisation if followed through. This included Franco 'Bifo' Berardi's contention that the crisis was actually the demise of capitalism under the pressure 'of the potency of productive forces (cognitive labour in the global network)';[8] the claim by Angela Mitropolous and Melinda Cooper that the crisis is generated by 'usury from below ... that extended beyond the limits which were tolerable to capital';[9] and Antonio Negri's argument that 'no New Deal is possible', and so we must go on to more radical demands.[10] These thinkers, associated with the currents of Autonomia and post-Autonomia, stressed the radically subjective elements of crisis. They saw crisis as the result of insurgent agency and so as leading to the possibilities of apocalyptic transformation. This is an ana-

---

5   Derrida 1984, p. 7.
6   Toscano 2017.
7   Marx 2019, p. 62.
8   Berardi 2009.
9   Mitropolous and Cooper 2009, p. 107.
10   Negri 2009.

lysis with Nietzschean tones, in the sense that the world-breaking capacities of subjectivity, now ascribed to the proletariat (or its updated variants, in the multitude or cognitariat), maintain an emphasis on will overcoming reality. While these thinkers keep the sense of crisis as capitalist crisis, these solutions court a subjectivism that aims to accelerate the powers of the will to dictate the birth of a new world.

Of course, all these thinkers are trying to call for a new inventiveness in the face of crisis and resisting, rightly I think, the usual calls for sacrifice and austerity – calls which usually fall on the victims of the crisis rather than those who caused it. That said, they also imply that by a kind of radical or quasi-Marxist cunning of reason the very worst will produce the good, or at least the moment of choice between the revolutionary reconstitution of society at large and the common ruin of contending classes. What they also offer is a remarkably teleological model of the development of the revolutionary forces emerging from capitalist society. In the 1859 Preface Marx wrote that 'the material productive forces of society come in conflict, with the existing relations of production ... [and] [f]rom forms of development of the productive forces these relations turn into their fetters. Then begins an era of social revolution'.[11] These post-Autonomist thinkers transform the productive forces into the powers of the multitude or the cognitariat and this carries the implication that the crisis will deliver its own radical solution. They lack a dialectic between material productive forces and relations of production, as those material productive forces are treated as subjective capacities embodied in the multitude or its equivalents.

This voluntarism runs contrary to the suggestion of the 1859 Preface, that 'mankind always sets itself only such tasks as it can solve; since, looking at the matter more closely, it will always show that the task itself arises only when the material conditions for its solution already exist or at least in the process of formation'.[12] While Marx reads the tasks of revolution as related to its material conditions, treated as objective forms, in these apocalyptic thinkers of crisis the material conditions are displaced by being treated as only ever instantiations of the power of subjectivity.[13] In this way the complex relations between subjective activity and objective conditions, as well as the mediation of this relation, are leapt over through a direct translation of those conditions into radical subjective activity. I want to problematise this apocalyptic tone by

---

11   Marx 2000, p. 425.
12   Marx 2000, p. 426.
13   Tronti 2019.

returning to the Marxist concept of the tendency, and by suggesting the need to complicate the model that claims that the tendencies of the present will deliver the apocalyptic realisation of communism as the realisation of subjective powers.

1   The Method of the Tendency

The concept of the tendency makes a key appearance in Volume III of *Capital*.[14] Here I do not want to consider the lengthy and vituperative debate on Marx's speculation, but rather to attend to the way in which Marx's remarks on the tendency became re-worked into a method of analysis. Crucial here is Lukács' *History and Class Consciousness* (1923) and his argument, in the central essay on 'Reification and the Consciousness of the Proletariat', that the tendency is the key tool in allowing us to grasp the historical process by dissolving the reified appearance of capital: 'This image of a frozen reality that nevertheless is caught up in an unremitting, ghostly movement at once becomes meaningful when this reality is dissolved into the process of which man is the driving force'.[15] This dissolution of reified appearance means, as Lukács notes, 'that the *developing tendencies of history constitute a higher reality than the empirical "facts"*'.[16] These facts are to be dissolved, but also reconstituted in the tendency as a tendency of the development of history.

The tendency or tendencies therefore have a particularly tricky form – a dialectical form in fact – in which 'the objective forms of the objects are themselves transformed into a process, a flux'.[17] This flux is no Bergsonian 'duration' (*durée réelle*), which is merely 'vacuous' according to Lukács, but a tracing of the 'unbroken production and reproduction of ... [social] relations'.[18] Of course the tension is that such a dissolution of the (reified) facts can easily be regarded as mere speculation detached from reality, which is often the way in which the dialectic has been taken by bourgeois thought, and even by certain forms of Marxism. Lukács recognises that this is a 'theory of reality which allots a higher place to the prevailing trends of the total development than to the facts of the empirical world'.[19] It is the very immediacy of facts which is the sign of

---

14   Marx 1992, pp. 317–38.
15   Lukács 1971b, p. 181.
16   Lukács 1971b, p. 181.
17   Lukács 1971b, p. 180.
18   Lukács 1971b, p. 180.
19   Lukács 1971b, p. 183.

their reification, and instead the tendency returns reality to its mediation, to the complex totality that can only be truly registered, and so given empirical confirmation, from the standpoint of the proletariat.

The ambiguities of the tendency are resolved in the knowledge of the totality, which takes place from the position of the proletariat, but which is not simply a point of view or standpoint. Instead, the capacities of the proletariat to see the totality are what must then lead to empirical confirmation. Considering Karl Popper's well-known criticism of Marxism as always self-confirming,[20] we could argue that the method of the tendency is actually closer to the model he proposed for science of bold conjectures that can be tested by possible refutation.[21] It remains distinct from Popper, however, because it retains the notion of a rational knowledge of the totality and not a model of the advancing frontiers of knowledge, conjectures, which confront an always present and ineliminable unknowable reality. Reality is potentially knowable, not a point beyond which we cannot advance.

Of course, my brief overview of the contemporary apocalyptic tone, in Autonomist and Post-Autonomist currents, would suggest that Lukács is not at all the key reference point. The retention by Lukács of the notion of totality, reinforced by his later work which corrects his earlier tendency to dismiss the dialectics of nature, results in an objectivism that puts him at odds with the subjectivism of contemporary uses of the tendency. To be more precise, Lukács aims to mediate between subjectivity and objectivity by understanding historical reality as structured by conflict.[22] In fact, within Italian Marxist thought of this type, including its original formulations by Operaismo, it has been the early Lukács, inclined to subjectivist formulations, who has been the dominant reference.[23]

The theoretical references for contemporary thinkers of the apocalyptic tone are rooted in the thinkers that emerged in the breakdown of the Fordist compact in the 1970s and the switch to financialisation to deal with dropping corporate profits, which would also be the origin for our current experience of crisis. The examples of contemporary post-Autonomist thought that I have cited, which embody the apocalyptic tone, all take off from the fusion of the work of Antonio Negri with that of Deleuze and Guattari. In particular they draw on Negri and Deleuze and Guattari's re-imagining of the concept of the tendency in the early 1970s. I am not suggesting a simple isomorphism between

---

20   Popper 2002.
21   Popper 2002; Lakatos and Musgrave (ed.) 2008.
22   Dainotto 2020, p. 29.
23   Tronti 2019, p. 328.

capitalist base and theoretical superstructure; after all, this re-tooling of the tendency was precisely an attempt to articulate a theoretical means to grasp the precise effects of the economic base. I am, however, suggesting that we do not simply regard theory as a hermetically-sealed realm that has no relation to economic, political, and social forms. In fact, as will become clear, this is a moment of theoretical reaction and response to the crisis of Fordism.

In the case of Negri, his canonical statement of the method of the tendency is given in his 1971 work 'Crisis of the Planner-State'. At this point Negri remains within remarkably classical and dialectical terms, arguing that 'the tendency gives us a determinate forecast, specified by the material dialectic that develops the factors comprising it'.[24] In a way remarkably similar to Lukács, Negri correlated the tendency with the viewpoint of the workers, and he also stressed that 'the procedure of the tendency is far from being rigid or deterministic. Instead, it represents an adventure of reason as it comes to encounter the complexities of reality, an adventure of reason that is prepared to accept risks: in fact, the truth of the tendency lies in its verification'.[25] As in Lukács, the tendency is here deliberately pitched between the necessity of departing from the facts, it is an adventure of reason, but also of returning to a newly re-ordered world through the mechanism of revolutionary verification.

Negri's practising of this method in the 1970s was predicated on accepting and radicalising the crisis of the Fordist social compact to license a thinking of the imminent, and immanent, apocalypse of capitalist relations. If capitalism started to rupture the structure of the factory and guaranteed employment then one should not regret this and go backwards to some lost world of social democracy, but push the tendency further into exodus, sabotage, and destruction of the fetters of the remnants of Fordism. The implication of his work, reflecting on the crisis of Fordism and its planner-state, was that communism had already arrived and would simply need to be realised. Negri was obviously prepared to accept risks, and the uncharitable could say that his own reading of the tendency fell victim to the failure of verification, with the defeat of the movement of Autonomy and Negri's imprisonment. This failure did not, however, lead to a further nuancing of the method of the trajectory in his work. Rather, especially in *Empire* (2000), co-written with Michael Hardt, Negri would exchange the encounter with the complexities of reality for an adventure of reason in which the tendency was flattened further into the pure immanence and positivity of communism.[26]

---

24   Negri 2005, p. 27.
25   Negri 2005, p. 27.
26   Badiou 2012, p. 10.

2 Accelerate the Tendency

The second element of the fusion, which would partly license Negri's later anti-dialectical positivisation of the tendency, is derived from the work of Deleuze and Guattari. In their 1972 work *Anti-Oedipus*, they gave a different spin to the notion of the tendency as the means of liberation and rupture. In a by now well-known argument they indicated two fundamental tendencies of capitalism: a primary axiomatic of deterritorialisation or decoding (something like Karl Polanyi's 'disembedding'),[27] and a secondary, but also essential, axiomatic of reterritorialisation, in which capitalism recoded and reabsorbed the desires it unleashed. They posed the question:

> But which is the revolutionary path? Is there one? – To withdraw from the world market, as Samir Amin advises Third World Countries to do, in a curious revival of the fascist 'economic solution'? Or might it be to go in the opposite direction? To go further still, that is, in the movement of the market, of decoding and deterritorialization? For perhaps the flows are not yet deterritorialized enough, not decoded enough, from the viewpoint of a theory and practice of a highly schizophrenic character. Not to withdraw from the process, but to go further, to 'accelerate the process', as Nietzsche put it: in this matter, the truth is that we haven't seen anything yet.[28]

The tendency now becomes the immanent radicalisation of capital's own dynamic of deterritorialisation, a theoretical manoeuvre I have called accelerationism.[29] It is obviously, as this quotation indicates, heavily indebted to Nietzsche and a Nietzschean posing of crisis as a crisis of civilisation to be resolved by a new kind of subject (or by an experience beyond the limits of subjectivity).[30]

Deleuze and Guattari were not the only practitioners of this form of the method of the tendency in the early-to-mid-1970s. In the wake of the failures of the movements of May '68 a number of French thinkers, particularly Jean-François Lyotard and Jean Baudrillard, also argued for a nihilist embrace of the disenchanting forces of capitalism as the means for achieving a strange kind of liberation through absolute immersion in the flows and fluxes of a libidinal

---

27   Polanyi 1980.
28   Deleuze and Guattari 1983, pp. 239–40.
29   Noys 2010, pp. 4–9; Noys 2014.
30   Klossowski 2007, pp. 99–122.

capitalism. Lyotard couched accelerationism in its most extreme form in his 1974 work *Libidinal Economy*: 'the English unemployed did not have to become workers to survive, they – hang on tight and spit on me – *enjoyed* the hysterical, masochistic, whatever exhaustion it was of *hanging on* in the mines, in the foundries, in the factories, in hell, they enjoyed it, enjoyed the mad destruction of their organic body which was indeed imposed upon them, they enjoyed the decomposition of their personal identity, the identity that the peasant tradition had constructed for them, enjoyed the dissolutions of their families and villages, and enjoyed the new monstrous *anonymity* of the suburbs and the pubs in morning and evening'.[31] This statement develops Marx's contention that capitalism offers a liberation and progress over feudal conditions, but decides to treat this without its dialectical complement of the experience of exploitation as negativity. Truly we may not have seen anything like this before, and it is no surprise that this would prove a remarkably unpopular theoretical moment.

Of course, Deleuze and Guattari did put the brakes on before conclusions like Lyotard's could be reached. They still held faith in an anti-capitalist project of liberation, but one that certainly still courted confusion with a simple faith in capitalism to deliver the goods. Negri, on the other hand, fuses his work with that of Deleuze and Guattari by mapping this accelerationism together with the desire of workers to flee the Fordist compact. Rather than the valorisation of capitalism *per se*, as Deleuze and Guattari's model might seem to intimate, we have the valorisation of deterritorialisation, later often refigured in terms of exodus,[32] as a proletarian strategy of resistance and rupture. In *Empire* (2000), Hardt and Negri are critical of Deleuze and Guattari's model of 'continuous movement and absolute flows', regarding it as 'insubstantial and impotent'.[33] The difficulty is, however, that their solution to this problem is to substantialise the tendency, but this substance is only the projection of human powers. This is achieved by the ontologisation of the tendency in the immanent and positive power of the multitude. It appears, then, that the dispute is not so much that Deleuze and Guattari valorise flux or movement, but that they cannot ground that flux and movement in an absolute immanent power of collective potential communism. Once again, the positive and accelerating tendency is that flux that can override and dissolve reified reality located in the subject.

---

31   Lyotard 1993, p. 214.
32   Hardt and Negri 2000, pp. 210–14.
33   Hardt and Negri 2000, p. 28.

3   Deviations of the Tendency

In a strange case of unlikely bedfellows, Alain Badiou, in his 1982 work *Theory of the Subject*, also makes recourse to the method of the tendency: 'To the logic of the trajectory, which the structural dialectic comes up against and which announces the new only in the retroactive operation of its *mise-en-scène*, we oppose the logic of tendencies, of currents, of vanguards, wherein that which is barely at its birth, though placed and subjected, links up with the most terrible force of the future'.[34] Badiou's presentation of a contrast between the logic of tendencies and a quasi-structuralist logic of the trajectory is cast in surprisingly Lukácsian terms – considering that they would usually be regarded as antithetical figures. Badiou's comment that in the logic of the trajectory 'time is extinguished by space', could easily be mistaken for a quotation from Lukács.[35]

More relevantly to this discussion, Badiou also identifies a second possible deviation of the method or logic of tendencies: this is committed by 'the dynamicists' who 'posit ... the multiplicity of variable intensities' and 'who believe in the insoluble tendency'.[36] These thinkers, and Badiou obviously has in mind Deleuze and Guattari, emphasise the priority of the flowing tendency over any objective moment. In Badiou's diagnostic: 'the asymptotic perspective of flight makes of the empiricist a wandering materialist, a vagabond philosopher of natural substances. Ignorance of the mirror turns the empiricist into the mirror of the world'.[37] Badiou's contention is that in their haste to depart from the static or reified nature of capital's logic of economic and political places, the dynamicists, ironically, end up *reflecting* capital's logic of accumulation.[38]

The importance of Badiou's analysis of the tendency is that he suggests the necessity for a careful practice of this method. What is particularly interesting is that Badiou does not simply suggest we condemn the errors of these deviations, but that the method of the tendency can only proceed by zig-zagging between these errors, which in this way correct each other. Those who emphasise a static logic of the trajectory and the necessity of patient analysis of the world as it is prevent us from rushing into revisions of our method that would leave it detached from reality. At the same time, the dynamicists provide a necessary sense that we must take risks with the method and cannot simply

34   Badiou 2009a, p. 109.
35   Badiou 2009a, p. 108.
36   Badiou 2009a, p. 209.
37   Badiou 2009a, p. 209.
38   Baudrillard 1987, p. 25.

follow the contours of reality. Badiou's suggestion aims at balancing between those sorts of pessimistic analyses which suggest an all-encompassing capitalism that always allocates people to their ideological place (as we find in certain moments in Althusser, Adorno, and contemporary value-form theorists like Moishe Postone),[39] and those optimistic analyses that always stress that resistance comes first, and foresee the imminent arrival of a new era of flux and freedom (precisely Negri, Deleuze and Guattari, and even certain moments in Jacques Rancière).

This balancing is, however, problematic. Badiou plays off the tendencies to subjectivism of the dynamicists against the objectivism of the structuralists; for the latter, we can assume here Badiou has in mind certain tendencies in the early Althusser, although the later Althusser of the encounter would turn to another 'wandering materialist'.[40] The difficulty is that this zig-zagging never seems to stabilise as Badiou's own theorisation of the subject, as with his later thinking of the event,[41] remains based in the moment of rupture identified with the subject. There is no real capacity for mediating between subjectivity and objectivity, to bring the zig-zagging to a halt in the form of knowledge. This is exactly what Lukács aimed at. So, while Badiou can provide useful criticisms, his own solutions remain within the subjectivising form of the tendency.

Considering Badiou's criticism of Deleuze and Guattari, and his suggestion that we practice a method of the tendency that does not embrace the perspective of flight, it comes as no surprise that Badiou should later vehemently reject Negri's own variant of accelerationism: 'As is well known, for Negri, the Spinozist, there is only one historic substance, so that the capitalist empire is also the scene of an unprecedented communist deployment. This surely has the advantage of authorising the belief that the worse it gets, the better it gets; or of getting you to (mis)take those demonstrations – fruitlessly convened to meet wherever the powerful re-unite – for the 'creation' and the 'multiform invention' of new petit-bourgeois proletarians'.[42]

Badiou notes what we earlier gestured towards: the tendency is taken by Negri as the immediate fusion of reason and reality in one Spinozist historic substance (or a version of that substance that remains Deleuzian and Nietzschean in inflection). What is lost is any nuancing of the tendency, any real sense of the tendency as riven by contradictions, tensions, and reversals. There is no mediation of subjectivity and objectivity here, but a projection of sub-

---

39   Postone 1993.
40   Althusser 2006.
41   Badiou 2005.
42   Badiou 2006, p. 45.

jectivity into a form of substance that becomes something like what Nietzsche called the will-to-power, a chaotic flux of forces.[43] The implication of such a reading of the tendency is that crisis is not to be reined in by the rationality of socialist or communist planning, but exacerbated by new forms of flight and flow – truly we have not seen anything yet.

Perhaps the best indication of the fatality of Negri's mirroring of capital is his constant stress that the revolutionary movements of the 1960s and 1970s were successful. Negri argued that the recuperation of the revolutionary impulses of the 1970s was not a sign of defeat, but of actual communist success lurking beneath the rotted carapace of capital. One more effort and the fetters of capital would be shaken free, releasing the communist content within. This perpetual chant can crescendo at the onset of any crisis. Paolo Virno, in contrast, and rightly in my view, argued that the defeat of the revolutions of the 1960s and 1970s led to a 'communism of capital'; rather than a hyper-capitalism leading to communism, instead capitalism recuperated and redeployed communist elements (abolition of wage labour, extinction of the state and valorisation of the individual's uniqueness) for its own purposes.[44] Negri, in contrast, magically parlays defeat into victory.

4   Decelerating Tendencies

The criticism that Negri's theorisation of the multitude is a mirror of capital is not particularly original. My concern is not simply to point out the possible confusion of a supposedly communist apocalypse with an actually capitalist apocalypse. Instead, another, more important, irony is at work in this apocalyptic accelerationism. Fredric Jameson has insisted on the unevenness of capitalist accumulation and its increasing turn to speculation as a sign of deceleration or inertia in the forms of accumulation.[45] Deleuze and Guattari had argued that Marx's contention that 'the *real barrier* of capitalist production is *capital itself*' did not so much indicate that capitalism was doomed by its own limits of accumulation, but rather that this barrier should be smashed by the radicalisation of capitalism's deterritorialising tendencies.[46] In contrast, as Robert Brenner had argued and as Jameson developed, we can see a slowing down in the forces and forms of accumulation and a turn to speculative

43   Nietzsche 1968.
44   Virno 2005, pp. 110–11.
45   Jameson 2009a.
46   Marx 1992, p. 358.

financialisation that leads from real estate to digital real estate. Rather than a following of the tendency, the tendency is obscured by an overly rote vision of capitalist accumulation.

This form of accelerationism, as cultural and theoretical moment, is predicated on economic deceleration – there is a disjuncture, or even inversion, between the superstructure and the base. The mirror of 1970s accelerationism is, as in Marx's famous metaphor of ideology as *camera obscura*, in fact an 'upside-down' image of 'historical life-processes'.[47] Although claiming to track the tendencies, the analyses of these accelerationist readings took appearance for reality, or to put it in more precise Marxist terms, could only grasp the real abstractions of the capitalist form of value at face value.[48] While these real abstractions truly are real, they shape and determine the forms of value, they lack the dynamism that accelerationists detected, and which such forms had, of necessity, to project. This is what makes Deleuze and Guattari's analysis of capital as an axiomatic machine or virus of deterritorialisation at once so resonant a characterisation and so problematic.[49]

Jameson's own writing illustrates this tension in a more dialectical manner. His writing on postmodernism initially maps superstructure and base, but takes an image of later or third stage capitalism as driven by the inhuman immensity of cybernetic and nuclear forces of production (and destruction).[50] Here we have a postmodern sublime given emblematic form in the confusing attempt to navigate the Bonaventure hotel in Los Angeles. It is also given form in cyberpunk fiction and the various cultural fictions that try to inhabit the exuberant moment of initial capitalist triumphalism, the 1980s, before that second moment of capitalist triumphalism after the collapse of the remnants of actually-existing socialism during the 1990s. Jameson's work at this time would be inspired by the accelerationist theoretical forms of Deleuze and Guattari and Baudrillard, but try to map them much more closely to economic reality. During that later period Jameson would also presciently start to grasp the turn to financial speculation and the symptomatic role this played for mapping both the economic and cultural forms of late capitalism. While he made a cautious shift, beginning to note the cultural signs of impasse, the perennial apocalyptic attraction of this form of accelerationism, which has persisted up to and through the current financial crisis, is a cultural and theoretical bubble which has yet to burst.

---

47   Marx and Engels 2011, p. 14.
48   Toscano 2008a; 2008b.
49   Noys 2015a.
50   Jameson 1991.

Of course, part of the irony is that any such slowing down or inertia can lead to further calls for acceleration or the desire to identity the real moments of acceleration within the inertial forms of contemporary capitalism.[51] Here, often, the apocalyptic re-enters with the selection of particular innovations as truly innovative and as the basis for a new post-capitalist social order. In this vein, continuing the dynamics of cyberpunk culture, we can note the contemporary fascination with developments in genetics, neuro-science, and research in artificial intelligence. Fantasies of re-sleeving consciousness, or, as Lyotard speculated,[52] of escaping a dying or doomed earth in a radically modified or downloaded post-human form, persistently haunt the zeitgeist.

To adapt T.S. Eliot's 'The Hollow Men', the apocalyptic tone can only imagine the end of the world in the form of a bang, and never a whimper.[53] While I am not suggesting the complacency of simply denying out of hand any possibility of apocalypse, which seems most likely at the moment to come in an ecological form, the apocalyptic tone I have been tracing is one which actually welcomes apocalypse as the decisive moment, the moment of the 'lifting of the veil' (the Greek meaning of the word 'apocalypse'). More particularly I am suggesting that the cycle of this tone, especially its particular accelerationism, is closely imbricated with the shift to a neo-liberal financial and political regime and its crisis. Of course, it was an attempt to grasp and resist that order, whatever we think of what I regard as its failings. The difficulty I am pointing to is that it mistook the tendency of that order, taking a real appearance for reality and missing the structural and economic limits of that order.

5   Bursting the Theoretical Bubble

The method of the tendency is, precisely, a method that does not offer guarantees, except in the starting point of totality and in the form of future verification or confirmation. The apocalyptic tone of accelerationism is, quite unusually, predicated on a firm and traditional belief that reality was on our side and that reason and reality were fused. This fusion, however, is a subjectivist one, which translates all the powers of capital into the will of subjectivity. The integration of reason with a subjectivised reality was unusual because, more commonly, radical thought in the last century saw a detachment between reason and reality; not such a surprising conclusion in light of the events of the age of extremes.

---

51   Fisher 2018.
52   Lyotard 2003, pp. 83–101.
53   Eliot 1974, p. 92.

Perhaps, in the wake of the events of the 1960s, as Marcuse suggested,[54] the hope that reason and reality could be re-aligned was once again on the agenda.

The error of this apocalyptic tone is to presume the fusion too quickly and in a subjective form – that the tendency will deliver on its own, or, in Badiou's words, that there is one historic substance, which, in fact, is a subject masquerading as substance. It would be Nietzschean elements that would permit this inflation and fusion of the subject with reality treated as crisis.[55] It could be contrasted, as a symmetrical error, with those forms of negative dialectics which seem to presume no possible integration of reason with reality.[56] These negative forms also took on Nietzschean notes, but this time of despair at the capacities of the masses and of a tendency that inflated the subject as judge of a fallen reality. So, we have an oscillation or zig-zagging, but not between subjective experience and reality, but rather within and between forms of subjective experience. In the case of the thinking of the tendency, the particular form of Communist accelerationism we are examining, capitalism is accepted as crisis, but also taken at its word by treating capitalism's promise of endless accelerating productivity as a given actuality.[57] Whether the positive affirmation of this mode of accelerationism or the negative mode of despair, in both cases subjective forms trump social reality.

I am not, as seems to be the case in some currents of ecological thought, arguing for a return to the detachment of reason and reality. In this case pessimism licenses retreat, with reason reduced to ever diminishing pockets or niches of resistance – often art, the body, or a certain elect. These chastened forms of retreat remain in the ambit of subjectivism and Nietzschean tones of despair. Instead, as should be evident, I am arguing that we return to a more nuanced realism about the contemporary conjuncture, and a closer analysis of its possibilities and limits. In his closing address to the *Historical Materialism* conference in London, 2009, Fredric Jameson argued that the aim of critical intellectuals should be to present or represent the contradictions of the time, even to sharpen them. We could add that we need the thought of totality and the tracing of the tendency as a tracing of objective development. In this way, we are not reduced to merely reflecting reality but to a necessary and radical process of re-ordering and, even, cultural struggle. We must attend to the problem of the mediation of crisis in the relation between subjective experience and the objective forms of crisis.

---

54   Marcuse 1972.
55   Deleuze and Guattari 1983, p. 21.
56   Adorno 1973.
57   Noys 2014.

With the bursting of the financial bubble and resulting economic crisis we could argue that a gap, perhaps only temporary, has opened up globally in our perception of the real abstractions of capitalism. If not exactly the fabled moment of the Emperor's New Clothes, at least capitalism's jingoism, and the thinness or weakness of its claims to constitute an order of development, freedom, and liberation, ring hollow. Of course, into that gap capital has responded as it knows best: by redoubling abstractions, in creating what Alain Badiou has called the spectacle of the crisis-film, in which the financial crisis becomes another apocalyptic film to elicit our awe and terror.[58] It has not, as Mirowski argued, let a good crisis go to waste.[59] Perhaps, however, at this moment of the opening of the gap we could also burst the theoretical bubble of this form of accelerationism. We could renew our theoretical analysis by practising a method of the tendency that more closely aligns base and superstructure in our analysis, that permits a closer grasp of the failures, tensions, and contradictions of this order, and that may condition the possibility of a true fusion of reason and reality in practice.

---

58   Badiou 2010, pp. 91–100; Kinkle and Toscano 2011.
59   Mirowski 2014.

PART 2

Crisis Culture

∴

CHAPTER 4

The Aesthetics of Crisis

> You know it's an invisible hand, the market is always right, it's a life-form that has being in its own right. You know, in a sort of Gestalt sort of way ( ) it has form and meaning.[1]

∴

In a 2011 interview, reported in the *Latin American Herald Tribune*, the Peruvian novelist and Nobel Prize laureate Mario Vargas Llosa claimed that 'great traumas', such as the current financial crisis, were 'very stimulating' for literature, predicting the beginning of a 'good period' for literary creativity. He added, presciently, that the crisis was 'just beginning', and that 'we've never seen anything like it'.[2] On this reading, the slaughtering of capital values is not going to extend to literary value and, in this dialectic, bad times make for good literature, and presumably very bad times make for very good literature. It is easy enough to mock. Certainly, in retrospect, the moment of financial crisis did not lead to any great novel of crisis, at least so far.

In this situation of absence, what I want to trace here are critical possibilities for thinking the contemporary novel occasioned by the crisis, and to reconsider the question posed by Fredric Jameson: 'how to express the economic – or, even better, the peculiar realities and dynamics of money as such – in and through literary narrative'.[3] In particular, we could add, how to express the realities and dynamics of money turned toxic in literary narrative? My wager here is that the crisis of money, collapsing in malignant value-loss, may refigure aesthetic value, as well as the aesthetic forms used to represent that loss, impacting on the paradigm of the contemporary novel. The crisis may also force into appearance what is usually troped as the sublime unmappability of capitalism.[4]

---

1 Market trader qtd. in Knorr Cetina and Breugger 2000, p. 151.
2 Anon. 2011.
3 Jameson 2000, p. 13.
4 Jameson 1995.

In terms of tracing these problems we can use Joshua Clover's distinction, borrowed from Braudel, of capitalism in autumn, in the cycle of financialisation, and capitalism in winter, in the period of crisis.[5] What I will trace and analyse here are what we could call the signs of winter embedded within the literature of autumn, and particular the relation of contemporary narrative forms to the mediations of finance. Any predictive discourse is, by definition, vulnerable, but I want to suggest something of a kind of experiment in tracing possibilities and trend lines that may, or may not, become actualised. Such experiments no doubt operate in terms of a certain wish-fulfilment, as we might say the dream of the great American novel becomes the dream of the great financial crisis novel (and that this will probably be American is left hanging, implicit in that much of the literature of autumn I turn to is American). That said, we might suggest that the global financial crisis offers something of a test-bed not only for the perennial question of the future of the novel, but also for how we might theorise and grasp the mediations of the novel by finance that take a particular and striking form in the emergence of crisis.

1   Realism out of Balance

To begin this task, I first want to return to a moment of the theorisation of crisis and literature that emerged out of the fierce debates concerning aesthetics and politics conducted amongst German-language Marxists, and in particular to Georg Lukács' 1938 essay 'Realism in the Balance'. This is not just to rehash past debates, but to focus on one element of Lukács' argument: his reflection on the relation between aesthetic experience and capitalist crisis. He remarks, 'in periods when capitalism functions in a so-called normal manner, and its various processes appear autonomous, people living within capitalist society think and experience it as unitary, whereas in periods of crisis, when the autonomous elements are drawn together into unity, they experience it as disintegration'.[6] The schema is the remarkably simple one of the dialectical reversal of appearance and essence. It conforms to Marx and Engels' well-known metaphor of ideology: 'in all ideology men and their circumstances appear upside-down as in a *camera obscura*, this phenomenon arises just as much from their historical life-process as the inversion of objects on the retina does from their physical life-process'.[7]

---

5 Clover 2011, p. 34.
6 Lukács 2007, p. 32.
7 Marx and Engels 2011, p. 14; Kofman 2014.

And yet Lukács' schema is more complex than it might first appear, and the seeming clarity of his reversal of appearance and essence, and its polemical intent to condemn expressionism and valorise realism, intimate that this schema, although powerful, might require a more complex mediation. Capitalism, in its moment of smooth functioning, appears as a unity predicated on the differentiation and the autonomy of its sub-systems, notably finance, while capitalism in crisis produces a contraction, which manifests the unity of the system but appears as disintegration. These processes are reflected in consciousness in a form 'always back to front',[8] hence differentiation appears as unity and unity as differentiation or disintegration. This implies aesthetic correlates: so-called normal capitalism is experienced as unity, but requires a critical realism that can grasp both this appearance and the essence of differentiation that results. In the moment of crisis we have the aesthetic of expressionist or modernist disintegration, which reflects the *appearance* of capitalism in crisis, but which cannot grasp the true *unity* produced by the collapsing effects of crisis. Contrary to the usual claims, it is modernism which is merely reflective, 'abstract and one-dimensional',[9] not realism, and Lukács acerbically remarks that, '[a]fter all, a puddle can never be more than dirty water, even though it may contain rainbow tints'.[10]

Hence, expressionism or modernism is a false aesthetic, a valorisation of capitalist appearance of disintegration that can never track its essential unity – manifest in crisis. For Lukács the requirement is still the pursuit of critical realism that can grasp the Janus-faced dialectic of unity/disintegration that only reverses itself in experience. It is crucial to give a narrative form to capitalism, rather than to mimic the surface appearance of capitalism as non-narrative, or as a narrative form of disintegration. Brecht sarcastically summarised: 'writers just have to keep to the Old Masters, produce a rich life of the spirit, hold back the pace of events by a slow narrative, bring the individual back to the centre stage, and so on'.[11] Despite this lambasting of the ahistorical return to bourgeois realism, Brecht himself concedes to the Lukácsian objection of the failure of naturalism and anarchistic montage to truly grasp the forms of capitalist culture in crisis, agreeing that 'they merely reflect the symptoms of the surface of things and not the deeper causal complexes of society'.[12] So, despite a seeming disagreement we can see a measure of aesthetic agreement.

---

8   Lukács 2007, p. 32.
9   Lukács 2007, p. 37.
10   Lukács 2007, p. 43.
11   Brecht 2007, p. 69.
12   Brecht 2007, p. 72.

In the situation of capitalist crisis capitalism is mediated aesthetically in the form of disintegration but requires a *mediation* of its unity. The question then turns on the form of this unity-in-crisis: for Lukács, critical realism is still the key to any cognitive mapping of totality (to use Jameson's phrase),[13] while for Brecht although expressionism fails we require a more inventive use of montage and the techniques of modernism coordinated to read or narrate capitalism as unity-in-crisis.

This discourse implies a dual model: first, of the kind of existing literary and narrative forms that mediate capitalism at the level of appearances, in the passage from realism to modernism. Secondly, of the kind of literature and narrative that is necessary to consciously or truly mediate capitalism, and particularly capitalism in crisis, which is where Lukács and Brecht depart from each other. This tension, between descriptive and prescriptive moments is, of course, key to any Marxist cultural analysis which aims to pass from critique to practice. It is not enough to merely demonstrate the limits of existing literary or narrative forms; what is required is to indicate within those forms the new possibilities of successful critical mediations that could take the measure of capitalism. Therefore, we have a movement from a descriptive analysis of what kinds of literary mediations are taking place, and their limits, to a prescriptive analysis of what kinds of literary mediations are necessary. In this case I want to pursue this dual practice through the analysis of the literature of autumn, against the horizon of the winter of capitalist crisis that began to emerge in 2008. In doing so, of course, this means shifting the debate to very different critical coordinates to that of Lukács and Brecht: no longer realism and modernism but, for all the problems that attach to these categories, realism and the contemporary.[14]

2   Signs of Winter in Autumn

Of course, at the present moment the idea that the experience of capitalist crisis would be mediated by an aesthetics of disintegration, especially in a classically expressionist or modernist form, seems unlikely, if not impossible. Certainly, there are hold-out domains of neo-modernism (notably in British neo-modernist poetry), and Joshua Clover has recommended poetry, in its neo-modernist forms, as the best aesthetic to capture the spatialisation and financialisation of contemporary capitalism – 'the signal literary form of the

---

13   Jameson 1991.
14   Osborne 2013.

period'.[15] That said, these movements do not constitute a cultural dominant, and Clover's is a prescriptive rather than a descriptive claim. So, modernism appears, in the present context, to be something of a vanishing mediator. Also, of course, any return to modernism itself would now be mediated through the contemporary as aesthetic mode. To use the familiar distinctions proposed by Raymond Williams we might say modernism remains residual, the contemporary, in all its diversity, dominant,[16] and Clover's suggestion in regards to poetry is the hope for a new emergent configuration.

Therefore, we don't seem to simply face the choice between realism and modernism but between realism and the elastic category of the contemporary. Of course, we also have the attempt by Jameson to establish the category of the postmodern or postmodernism as the dominant aesthetic mode of the present.[17] We also have a looser use of postmodernism to classify strands of cultural experimentation beginning in the 1960s and stretching at least until the 1990s.[18] The picture is messy, but in literary terms we could argue that high postmodernism, of the kind found in Donald Barthelme, John Barth, and others, appears to have waned from critical attention and creative practice, and re-statements of realism, of the kind made by Jonathan Franzen, indicate the fragility of postmodernism as a category. In fact, we could argue that the tendency in American fiction of so-called blank fiction – thinking particularly of the work of Brett Easton Ellis or Denis Cooper, but which could be extended to Don DeLillo as well – is not so much postmodern as a new form of realism attuned to the informational overload and the period of financialised bubble economics. The postmodern experimentation of Latin American and postcolonial fiction also seems to narrate and register the particular fragmentations or fractures of the world-system of capitalism.[19] If the conflict between realism and modernism registered a dichotomy (although a complex one), one polemically inhabited by modernists themselves as in Virginia Woolf's critique of Arnold Bennett, the case of realism and postmodernism appears far more mobile and permeable. We might therefore, as I have done, speak of the contemporary to capture this sense of permeable currents between realism, modernism, and what was called the postmodern, as well as the impact of genre fiction in our current moment (thinking of the genre of fantasy fiction, in particular).

15   Clover 2011, p. 39.
16   Williams 1977, pp. 121–7.
17   Jameson 1991.
18   Anderson 1998.
19   WReC 2015.

Despite this changing context, I would suggest that Lukács' dialectical reversal does register something of the tensions between aesthetic forms and what Brecht calls the causal complexes of capitalism, and not least capitalism in crisis. Taking up this argument, we can adapt Lukács' claim that capitalism in unity registers as differentiated and capitalism in crisis registers as disintegration to argue that the proliferation and relative stability of fictional experimentation through the 1990s and early 2000s rested on a differentiation generated out of the relative stability of capital in the heartlands, although one obviously shaken by a circulating cycle of crises (Japan and the Far East, Argentina, etc.) that did not fully register. The experience of unity in capitalism was figured in the pursuit of various forms of differentiated experience, facilitated by a normally functioning capitalism, in which capitalism itself largely figured as stabilised domain or backdrop. The narratives of difference sprang from an assumption of a stable narrative of capitalist unity, which they mediated more or less critically.

Therefore, we could risk another characterisation of this phase of the contemporary novel in terms of a narrative form that operates through relatively autonomous sub-systems of differentiated and plural narratives, hence its appearance as non-narrative and contrary to Lukács' image of a critical realism. We could also reflect on the popularity of certain forms of theory in the 1990s that stressed difference and mutation, although often coagulated around differential identities, and which often took inspiration from a loosely handled use of Deleuze and Guattari's modelling of deterritorialisation and 'smoothing'.[20] This contemporary theoretical instantiation of difference also mediated the experience of capitalism as a differential unity in its own narratives.

Even the more explicitly political forms of contemporary fiction in the capitalist heartlands found themselves often unconsciously structured by this differentiation. Taking the work of Thomas Pynchon during this period, we find a mode of differential and fractured narrative, one which is also attuned to the unity of capitalism qua corporate and governmental conspiracy. This cognitive mapping, however, remained focused on various moments of the historical emergence of the forces of power: *Vineland* (1990) (the 1960s), *Mason & Dixon* (1997) (the 1700s), *Against the Day* (2006) (the 1890s), *Inherent Vice* (2009) (the 1960s again), *Bleeding Edge* (2013) (the early 2000s). Obviously, these historical digressions served an ontology of the present, but they seemed to find themselves stalled in a nostalgia for the moment of emergence and

---

20   Cusset 2008.

failed to fully link the remapping of the past as the ghosting of the present order, even as they get closer to that order. Joshua Clover takes a more sympathetic position, suggesting that Pynchon's *Against the Day* provides 'a parallax on the contemporary position of capital'.[21] And yet Clover goes on to note that despite the explicit resonances of Pynchon's project with a contemporary capitalism in financial drift and incipient crisis, his attempt at overview indexes the problem of time and space in capitalism without fully grasping it. In fact, we can note that it was precisely the differential form of capitalism pre-crisis that served to generate a narrative of its own unmappability.

What remains elusive in Pynchon – although as Clover notes, this is reflected in the sprawling non-narrative form of his fiction –[22] was the precise analysis of the contours of a differentiated capitalism in this phase of financialised bubble expansion, which was predicated on drift and inertia. One could draw a link here between the non-narrative sprawl of Thomas Pynchon's works and the theoretical non-narrative sprawl of Fredric Jameson's writing in this period. In both cases the mapping of a differentiated capitalist unity, read through an experience of political defeat, operates to try and grasp the limits of the narrative of a successful capitalism. While the novelist and the theorist are both attuned to a sense of the deceleration and drift encrypted within capitalist dynamism, they both tend to turn to an alternative or counter-factual or utopian dynamism in the past to break the capitalist horizon.[23]

In the 2000s the war on terror of course added an edge of the real to the series of fictions that engaged with American hegemony, from Don DeLillo's *Falling Man* (2007) to Ian McEwan's *Saturday* (2005), amongst many others; although this edge was related not so much to finance and capital as to questions of politics and power – was removed, in other words, from the power of appearance incarnated in the power of the real abstractions of financial capital.[24] Here the dynamic of differentiation was experienced as fragmentation, but only at the level of the polity and not at the level of the economic. The element of the spectacle of violence distracted or displaced the spectacle as capitalist category of abstraction.[25] In these cases disintegration took the form of the disruptive effects of trauma, often metonymically treated in the form

---

21   Clover 2011, p. 39.
22   Clover 2011, p. 43.
23   Jameson 2000; Pynchon 2007.
24   Toscano 2008a; Toscano 2008b.
25   Retort 2005.

of bodily violence, which incarnated what Alain Badiou would call the ideology of 'democratic materialism', in narratives of 'bodies and languages' that
could register no alternative truth to that of material suffering and excess.[26]
Don DeLillo's *The Body Artist* (2001) would be a resonant reflection on this need
for bodily experience and the experiences of grief and haunting that trouble
that immediacy.

It may be, I would suggest, a more minor work, such as Frederick Barthelme's
Waveland (2009), with its reflection on the devastation of Hurricane Katrina, that captures more of the moment of autumn, than the grander attempt
to address war and terror. This novel continues the persistent thematics of
Barthelme's work – the disintegrating marriage relation triangulated through
new partners, the attempt to forge new groupings out of that failing relationship, and an attention to the intersection of middle-class and lower middle-
class, or working-class, life. One irony is that Barthelme, unlike his better-
known brother, is not identified with postmodernism but often with 'dirty realism', although he regards his own work as a project between high (post)mod-
ernism and a certain type of realism, preferring the title 'minimalist'.[27] We
might see this as a signature negotiation of the contemporary as a mode.

In *Waveland* it is the setting of these thematics and Barthelme's usual tropes
(playing with model train sets, for example) against the backdrop of the aftermath of Hurricane Katrina and what Benedict Seymour has called, in the
context of New Orleans, non-reproduction,[28] that renders the effect of disintegration in the appearance of differentiation. Barthelme's central character narrates: 'On the Mississippi coast recovery was ridiculously slow, almost
non-existent. There wasn't much to recover since there wasn't much there any-
more, just flattened houses and empty lots piled with rubbish and wreckage'.[29]
Although the novel itself concerns a kind of tentative reconstruction or reproduction of personal relationships between the central characters, a kind of
uneasy peace, it figures also the pressures of non-reproduction and crisis which
do not simply stem from nature but from the failure of capitalist reproduction
– signalled in the work's attention to property and value (its central character
being an architect).

Another work directly attentive to an autumnal capitalism is Joshua Ferris's
Then We Came to the End (2007). Although the choice to write in the first-
person plural, to convey the group dynamics of the office, is perhaps overde-

---

26   Badiou 2009b, p. 12.
27   Barthelme 2009a.
28   Seymour 2006.
29   Barthelme 2009b, p. 9.

termined by a desire to experiment, what is more interesting is the attention to the threat and actuality of redundancy – 'walking the Spanish down the hall' (a phrase derived from a Tom Waits song and referring to a pirate punishment of being forced to walk on tip toes). Again, the novel turns on a kind of realism, vectored through the narrative device, and also recalls the drifting and iner-tial dynamics that underpinned the bubble of financialisation. In this case the slow attrition through redundancy erodes any dynamic of narrative, forcing the recognition of absence and instability operant within the dynamics of differ-entiation. These two works register effects of disintegration that reach towards an aesthetic knowledge of a decelerative and disintegrating capital, rather than remaining locked into the differential sub-systems that permitted the prolif-eration of the novel *qua* local and regional form coupled dialectically to the horizon of global capitalism. They prefigure the collapse of this distance in the collapse of the sub-systems into an imploded unity as a result of the financial crisis.

3   Dematerialisation under Pressure

We can trace this implosion of neoliberal capitalism aesthetically through the work of the science-fiction novelist William Gibson. Gibson is the author of the novel of prefigurative neoliberalism–1984's *Neuromancer*, with its Night City as 'a deranged experiment in social Darwinism, designed by a bored researcher who kept one thumb permanently on the fast-forward button'.[30] Joshua Clover has noted that Gibson's vision, so influential on contemporary culture, incarn-ates the 'thrill and threat of dematerialization' at the heart of financialisation.[31] Clover contends that the fate of the film version, delayed because of the fin-ancial crisis that resulted from the dematerialisation of wealth, is itself, in its absence, a sign of the aesthetics of crisis:

> It may be that Hollywood's inability to bring *Neuromancer* to the screen is itself the truth of the situation, more true than any version of the film could be. The story's displacement of crisis and transformation into science-fictional allegory is too visible: not enough blind spot for our moment's hysterical looking-via-looking away. But more pungently, it's endlessly telling that the film should founder in this exact moment: when

---

30   Gibson 1986, p. 14.
31   Clover 2010, p. 9.

the very developments it required – that is, the dematerializing and vir-
tualizing of the physical movie set, of the scene of real labour – have
blown up the economy and worse, pushing us toward another transformation, a far greater crisis. This is dialectical history in its most refined
form.[32]

The refinement has one more twist; Gibson's himself has written a crisis novel
– *Zero History* (2010) – although a crisis novel that, despite its contemporary
setting, remains highly derivative of his own previous science fiction, not least
Neuromancer itself.[33]

Continuing his informal trilogy of novels set in the contemporary moment,
after *Pattern Recognition* (2003) and *Spook Country* (2007), *Zero History*'s characters also echo those of the science fiction 'Sprawl trilogy', which consisted
of *Neuromancer* (1984), *Count Zero* (1986), *Mona Lisa Overdrive* (1988). This
is the case with *Zero History*'s Milgram, who has 'zero history' as a result
of ten years of drug abuse, and so mirrors Slick Henry's punishment with
the 'induced Korsakov's' in *Mona Lisa Overdrive* that left him with flashbacks
to a state in which consecutive memory only lasts for five minutes. If Slick
Henry's punishment allegorises the neoliberal sensorium as one of perpetual
flux with no capacity to constitute historical memory, it is Milgram's absence
from contemporary consumer culture that so finely attunes him to its trend
lines. This also links him to Colin Laney from the Bridge trilogy – *Virtual
Light* (1993), *Idoru* (1996), and *All Tomorrow's Parties* (1999) – whose attention deficit disorder, as a result of childhood pharmaceutical trials, allows him
to detect nodal points in culture. These are all figures of what Lauren Berlant characterises as the 'intuitionist', which are repeated across Gibson's fiction.[34]

Milgram is partnered with Hollis Henry, a kind of de-augmented Molly Millions. They both, in different ways, incarnate the obsessive, and repetitive, focus
of Gibson's recent fiction, being semioticians of capitalist commodification as
'assemblages of desire' (the Deleuzian language he uses in *Idoru* (1994)). These
node spotters, and the fictional magazine Hollis works for in *Spook Country* is
called *Node*, obviously and deliberately figure the role of the author and that of
the reader. The central irony, however, is that the prefigurative capture of the
ideological energy of emergent neoliberalism in *Neuromancer* and the Sprawl

---

32   Clover 2010, p. 9.
33   Gibson 2010.
34   Berlant 2008.

Trilogy has been replaced by a trend chasing in Gibson's own fiction, which as it approaches the present falls behind into a flattened lifestyle commodity-fetishism that lay implicit in the unobtainable commodities of his science fiction works. This is what Fredric Jameson, in a more laudatory fashion, refers to as 'a kind of hyped-up name-dropping'.[35]

In the case of *Zero History* the same Gibsonian stylistic tics, broadly Chandleresque clipped-narration, a focus on technical objects and commodities, a flat, writing-degree-zero style,[36] and a difficulty with characterisation, service a thriller plot driven initially by the pursuit of the designer of the secret anti-fashion brand Gabriel Hounds.[37] This narrative MacGuffin conceals the true aim of the commissioner of the quest, the amusingly named Hubertus Bigend, a slightly sinister Belgian advertising executive: to recover a mathematician who has found a predictive method to track in advance the order flow of markets by seventeen minutes. We could note the obvious allegorisation of Gibson-the-novelist: be ahead of the market by a metaphoric seventeen minutes to give the requisite predictive edge to his fiction. So far so familiarly postmodern, and also quite predictable considering the MacGuffin within a MacGuffin plotting that has characterised much of Gibson's writing. In fact, what is remarkable about the novel is not the fact that the characters are often driven back into these plots and pursuits by losses incurred by the global financial crisis, which at least marks an intrusion of money into the contemporary novel, but that the novel retains such faith in markets. Crisis very much is opportunity and creative destruction, as corporate espionage goes on as usual. The order flow is unceasing, as the flow of real abstractions continues.

The very materialisation of Gibson's novels into the present marks their seeming detachment from the decelerative dynamics of that present, and they recede into a striking Schumpeterian faith in innovation and renovation (again, this is a position also present in currents of post-Autonomist theory (see Chapter 3)). The irony of course is that the fiction itself becomes more and more inertial, less and less inventive, as Gibson tails rather than predicts the very trend lines he tracks. The result is an appropriately vacuous fiction, which constantly verges or lunges into the ludicrous. Perhaps unfortunately for Gibson we can track his work as the passing from autumn into winter in terms not of a good time for literature but of the extinction of the thrill of dematerialisa-

---

35   Jameson 2003, p. 108.
36   Barthes 1970.
37   Gibson 2008.

tion. Of course, Gibson's fiction has always been haunted by matter as junk – *Gomi*, to use the Japanese term he prefers – as the flipside to jacking-in to cyberspace and chemical and prosthetic enhancement. But the drag of junk is no longer a resource or the remains of an accelerated dynamics, but the crunch of credit grinding into the ground and non-reproduction that junks his fiction. Gibson has produced the fiction of crisis as the fiction of the obsolescence of his own work.

This drag is more literally allegorised in *Spook Country* (2007), ostensibly Gibson's novel of the war on terror, but also haunted by presentiments of the crisis to come, and involving the same central cast as *Zero History*. Here money literally turns toxic. First, with the reflections on 'the International currency of bad shit',[38] as one of the chapter titles has it. This refers to the use of the US hundred-dollar bill as the preferred currency of organised crime, and also the tendency to counterfeit these bills. Secondly, it refers to the central plot of the novel: the aim to contaminate with radiation a shipping container full of money stolen from a shipment intended for the reconstruction of Iraq. This literal turning of literal money toxic of course gains resonance, but also signals its limitations, against the toxicity of virtual money evidenced in the financial crisis.

Gibson's *Zero History* is a failed confrontation with the contraction of the sprawl of fiction under the impact of financial crisis. Gibson's first three science-fiction novels were known as the 'sprawl trilogy' after their imagining of a continuous urban space: The East Coast United States 'Boston-Atlanta Metropolitan axis' (BAMA). Joshua Clover argues that 'the postmodern novel's narrative instability and its frequent substitution of sprawl for story' reflects the fact 'that an organizing trope of Autumnal literature is *the conversion of the temporal to the spatial*'.[39] What we might say of winter fiction is that this spatialisation is confronted by the unity of capitalism in crisis that collapses the fictional space of the contemporary novel. While Clover attends to poetry as the non-narrative form able to grasp this spatialisation, or at least mediate it, and here we might recall the debates concerning montage, I am not suggesting the novel as a counter-privileged site. Rather, what concerns me is the possible spacing of the novel in regards to this relatively sudden unification of capitalism that presents itself not as differentiation (sprawl) but *disintegration*.

---

38   Gibson 2008, p. 131.
39   Clover 2011, p. 43.

4   Collapsing Value

As I noted, speculation concerning the future of the novel is an oversubscribed area littered with false predictions. Here what I want to suggest, drawing on the signs of winter in the literature of autumn, is a perhaps obvious point. The global financial crisis, however it shakes out, impinges directly on the space of fiction through what appears as a certain effect of contraction. The material, social and psychic condition of differentiation, predicated on the normal functioning of capital, is wrecked by the differentiated sub-system of finance that ruptures the edifice and reveals its true unity. In doing so much that is taken for granted in the literature of autumn, notably the financial and material conditions that allow the characters of these novels to live as they do, to become characters in novels, has been put into question. No doubt, as evidence already indicates, the rich have benefited from the crisis and the poor have suffered, but the taken-for-granted nature of the wealth necessary to live a life in fiction has contracted. The inner life always requires the necessary financial requirements to be lived.

Even if token indexing, as seen in Gibson's motivation of characters through relative losses incurred in the financial crisis (although none of the characters are simply reduced to destitution), or in the subtler probing of the dependence on disappearing labour, as in Joshua Ferris's analysis of the psychopathologies of middle-class precarity, money itself becomes present as a character or persona (which was so self-evident in eighteenth- and nineteenth-century British fiction). At the same time the participation of the state in non-reproduction, often through non-intervention as tracked in Barthelme's novel, undercuts its supporting role (to use an appropriate metaphor) in the condition of differential and sprawling fiction. This contraction cuts both ways: it not only cuts into the expansiveness of sprawling fiction, which played on the differentiation of a normal capitalism, but also into the psychic intensiveness or local density of realist, minimalist or experimental fiction, which again depended on the horizon of capitalism to create or play on the specificity of differentiation. Jameson's analysis of postmodernism proved a quite accurate prediction of the terms in which the contemporary novel would explore this differentiated condition: spatial sprawl (long-form fictions, notably borrowing from the fantasy genre), psychic disintegration (the neuro-novel,[40] the various novels of psychopathology, and certain forms of auto-fiction), and history treated as memory bank (as in the return of the neo-historical novel).

---

40   Roth 2009.

Of course, even if such a space has contracted, there is no simple necessity that fiction need register this. In the line of Marx's method of the tendency,[41] one can imagine various counter-tendencies and the retention or continuing exploration of existent forms. The very shaping of the response to the crisis at the level of the political, in terms of austerity measures, the ideology of keep calm and carry on operating in Britain (drawn from British wartime experience),[42] and the vicious exacerbation of neo-liberalism as *pharmakon*, all imply the necessity to maintain the status quo. It is certainly possible that the same would apply to fiction. Conservative retreat to safe forms is as probable as further leaps of experimentation, although these retreats are themselves inflected by crisis. Even continuity throws such older forms into relief as the horizon of capitalism has contracted into the unity of the crisis form. The denuding of monetary value dates these forms of fiction for their very distanciation from the economic and their acceptance of the differential as the condition for their functioning.

5   World Reduction

In his 1975 essay 'World Reduction in Le Guin: The Emergence of Utopian Narrative', Jameson traces the process whereby the attenuation of the world in science fiction generates utopian possibility. He argues that this is 'a principle of systematic exclusion, a kind of surgical excision of empirical reality, something like a process of ontological attenuation in which the sheer teeming multiplicity of what exists, of what we call reality, is deliberately thinned and weeded out through an operation of radical abstraction and simplification which I will henceforth term *world reduction*'.[43] In the case of Le Guin's novel, appropriately enough for the metaphorics we have been using, this effect is firstly achieved through the use of winter – radical cold as an isolating mechanism. In particular, however, Jameson singles out Le Guin's reduction of the function of sexuality as the opening of a space of utopian reimagining.

For Jameson this process of world reduction offered some purchase on the *excess* of capitalism, the possibility of 'weeding out the immense waste-and-junk landscape' to give us a breathing space from the 'overwhelming presence of late capitalism'.[44] What I am suggesting is that the financial crisis produces

---

41   Balibar 2007, p. 120.
42   Hatherley 2016.
43   Jameson 2006, p. 271.
44   Jameson 2006, p. 278, p. 279.

an effect of world reduction in reality, and one not directly attuned to utopian possibility (obviously). The reduction here falls on the function of money, hollowed out through debt, devaluation, banking crisis, and the failed speculative moment of financial instruments. Although these instruments have a baroque complexity, itself appropriate to the age of the revalorisation of the baroque aesthetic and philosophy in the contemporary moment,[45] at the moment they stand reduced into their real-world effects. The rest offered here is a sudden withdrawal of the capitalist horizon as horizon of reproduction – of an experience of abandonment in which the presence of capitalism withdraws, leaving us exposed to the void of value and our own surplus status. The Marxist utopia of a 'world without money' is realised in the form of a world of toxic money in which we remain monetary subjects, and capitalism has become 'negative-utopian'.[46] Gibson's irradiated currency of bad shit becomes the lived experience of money and debt turned toxic.[47]

In terms of fiction what we find, as we have traced, is the reduction of the space of alternatives. We should note that when this space did exist it was not much taken up with the imagination of alternatives, but rather with tracking the differentiations of contemporary capitalism.[48] Now the conceptual persona of money appears empty or malignant, and the tracking of this disintegration impinges on the forms of narrative. Instead of the dynamics of money *qua* dynamism requiring forming into narrative, with the usually linked questions of the sublime, excess, and a cognitive mapping that can never be fully completed, we have money *qua* deceleration and the necessity to put into narrative a reduced and meagre world that is all too graspable and lacking in sublimity. The turn to the apocalyptic is predictable in such a situation, thinking especially of Cormac McCarthy's *The Road* (2006) as prescient work, but this form of narrative only reads capitalism in crisis in terms of its appearance as disintegration and cannot read the unity that is the result of crisis. We can also see the turn to fantasy not simply as a desire to escape a destitute present but also, in the mode of the quest and the sprawling form of fantasy, a negotiation of the landscapes of crisis capitalism.[49]

Perhaps what is required is a novel, or novels, of world reduction, which do not re-start the process of making value or re-finding value in the novel, but which rather work on the attenuation and ruination of the condition of our

45   Calabrese 1992 and Deleuze 1993.
46   Kurz 2011.
47   McClanahan 2016.
48   Fisher 2010.
49   Noys 2023.

forms of narrative.[50] Instead of dreams of the speculative rebirth of value out of the compacted moment of crisis, we might have the realist exploration of the forms of contraction that we live as the manipulated alienation of the present. In this way, the return or renovation of critical realism remains vital to thinking the dialectics of crisis and mediating that experience of crisis as a secular one.[51] While the apocalyptic and fantastic register the global scale and level of crisis as catastrophe, they also risk maintaining us in this manipulated alienation of crisis,[52] which is transformed into a way of life. Such narratives can reflect the distortions of our crisis capitalism,[53] but we also need the current diversity of the contemporary novel to make good on its potential to explore and develop multiple forms. The differentiated aesthetic moment of a 'normal' capitalism must be placed into a new relation with the contracted experience of crisis capitalism to help us recognise our experience of disintegration as a social effect. In this way we might start to see beyond the horizon of crisis and capitalism.

---

50   Lustig 2019, pp. 270–1.
51   See Kornbluh 2019 for such a defence of critical realism.
52   Lukács 1970, p. 13.
53   Lukács 1963, p. 52.

CHAPTER 5

Scale, Commodity, Totality

The deaths of the avant-garde and of the epic have both been widely reported. In the first case, the avant-garde is seen as dead due to the exhaustion of the social forms and energies that sustained it in the first half of the twentieth century, especially in the West.[1] Similarly, the epic, with its aim to narrate the founding of a people, is also seen as lacking a referent or basis for this articulation, with the erosion of solidarity and the disenchantment of the world in the age of capital.[2] Despite the confidence of these teleologies of exhaustion, which can, in some cases, be ascribed to what Jean-François Lyotard called the 'period of slackening'[3] which celebrated the end of the dual ambition of the avant-garde and the epic, these verdicts have not gone unchallenged. In relation to the avant-garde, to choose two examples, Alain Badiou has suggested the possibility of reactivating the 'subtractive' avant-garde,[4] attentive to the problem of constituting a new critical relation to the totality of capitalism in the present moment. John Roberts, with a different emphasis, has argued for a 'suspensive avant-garde', which negotiates with the memory of the revolutionary moment, and maintains the 'suspension' of art from immediate use as a promise of freedom.[5] In regard to the epic, Franco Moretti has insisted on the possibility of a modern epic, although one correlated with high modernism: Joyce's *Ulysses* (1922) and Eliot's *The Waste Land* (1922) or, with some scepticism, Gabriel Garcia Marquez's magic realism.[6] In more avant-garde terms, there is also the 'pocket epic' of post-war avant-garde poetry,[7] in Britain particularly, which has maintained both the epic and avant-garde ambition.

Of course, the terms 'subtractive', 'suspensive', and 'pocket epic', indicate some scaling-down of the grand ambitions of the avant-garde and the epic. This suggests the truth of the death of the avant-garde and death of the epic theses, even as it gives the lie to them. In the chastened mood of the present,

---

1 Bürger 1984.
2 Lukács 1971a.
3 Lyotard 1984, p. 71.
4 Badiou 2007.
5 Roberts 2010, pp. 723–27; Roberts 2015.
6 Moretti 1996.
7 Alderman 2000.

after the avant-garde century of what Badiou calls 'the passion of the real',[8] we live in a moment transfixed by the limits of our powers to grasp, let alone change, the system; from the epic adventures of the early avant-garde, to a situation of sobriety and working through the minor.[9] At issue is the overdetermining problem of the triumph of capitalism as a global system, even if that triumph looks rather threadbare in the context of financial crisis and climate change. The powers of the capitalist market to recuperate and subsume avant-garde experimentation have been extensively discussed,[10] not least by the avant-gardes themselves.[11] Also, the form and complexity of the capitalist totality, as Fredric Jameson asserted,[12] poses problems that challenge all artworks engaged in mapping the totality, but especially those with the ambition associated with the avant-garde and the epic, let alone the conjunction of the two.

Here I want to assess that conjunction, of the avant-garde and the epic, as a site for engaging with these problems of mapping, representation and intervention. In *Brecht and Method* (1998), Fredric Jameson notes that, playing on Ezra Pound's definition of the epic as a poem that includes history, the epic better refers to the inclusion of the economic in the literary work: the question of 'how to express the economic – or, even better, the peculiar realities and dynamics of money as such – in and through literary narrative'.[13] This challenge engages both the avant-garde and the epic in their claims to totality. The totality of capitalism, even if this totality is contradictory, competes with the avant-garde claim to fuse art and life and the epic claim to tell the story of the tribe. There is a tension between totality, as the totality of life and existence, and the totality of capitalism, as what aims to subsume life and existence under the totality of value. We might note here a tension between Lukács' discussion of totality, which uses the sense of a totality of life and existence as the basis for the critique of capital,[14] and the tendency of Jameson to suggest that capitalism as totality becomes increasingly dominant.[15]

I retrace this problem, of putting the economic into literary narrative, through the historic avant-garde, particularly the figure of Brecht. This problem

---

8   Badiou 2007.
9   Wark 2015.
10   Frank 1997.
11   Situationist International 1989.
12   Jameson 1991, p. 51.
13   Jameson 2000, p. 13.
14   Lukács 1971b.
15   Jameson 1995.

is then engaged through a discussion of the capitalist epic, before considering, in the contemporary moment, the debate between poetry, as non-narrative
form, and the novel, as narrative form, as forms for grasping capitalist totality. In both cases, competition over the capacity to map 'the perpetual transformation of money into capital' places stresses and strains on form, including
on the notion of narrative.[16] We can also find the tension between mapping
capitalist totality and the totality of life and existence, as these texts try to
reveal that totality within and against the capitalist commodification of reality.

To focus this discussion, I will primarily be considering instances of what has
become known as commodity-chain analysis: the attempt to represent capitalist relations through tracing the fate of a particular signature commodity.[17]
This field, along with the commodities it traces, has been proliferating rapidly. To choose only a few examples, we have the commodity-chain analysis
of the pound-shop novelty item,[18] of gold,[19] of the flip-flop,[20] and even meta-
analyses of the cartographic impulse to map capital and the commodity.[21] Not
only has this been a proliferating mode of analysis but, as Alberto Toscano
and Jeff Kinkle have exhaustively detailed,[22] it has also become a mode of
artistic practice, from film to literature to contemporary art. The attraction of
following the commodity is that it promises to unlock the commodity fetish,
by re-tracing the emergence of the final product through its global transformations. In this way, as we can see with the choice of lowly commodities, we have
works which move between the local or the scaled-down, and the global field
of commodity production. As Fredric Jameson puts it, in a discussion of Eisen-
stein's film work, it is matter of following 'the chain of hidden links that leads
us from the surface of everyday life and experience to the very sources of production itself'.[23] While such works claim to unlock the problem of scale, I want
to suggest the tensions of this project: between realism and the avant-garde,
between local narratives and the epic scale of capital. It is within this tension
that any attempt to work out the inheritance of the avant-garde and the epic
finds itself.

---

16   Jameson 2000, p. 13.
17   Toscano and Kinkle 2015, pp. 190–5.
18   Hulme 2015.
19   Barragan 2014.
20   Knowles 2015.
21   Toscano and Kinkle 2015.
22   Toscano and Kinkle 2015.
23   Jameson 2009b, p. 113.

1   The Petroleum Complex

The figure of the historic avant-garde who engaged most explicitly with the epic was Bertolt Brecht. It was Brecht who proposed an epic theatre capable of breaking with the constraints of dramatic theatre. In a text from 1929, written as a series of theses, Brecht provided a telegraphic definition:

> Epic. It must report. It must not believe that one can identify oneself with our world by empathy, nor must it want this. The subject-matter is immense; our choice of the dramatic means must take account of the fact.[24]

The problem of scale is obvious: 'the subject-matter is immense'. Brecht would provide a series of definitions and even a table of contrasts between epic theatre and dramatic theatre, from which we can stress the educative aspect of epic theatre, which breaks with passivity, involvement, and growth, for a theatre of activity, reasoned reflection, and jumps and fractures. While Brecht's epic does track a story, it also tracks the fractures of this narrative as it tries to grasp, in Marxist fashion, how 'social being determines thought'.[25] It also tracks the problem of the scale of this story, as it tries to grasp the excess of economic processes through the jumps and fractures that compose the processes of production and consumption.

Amongst the examples Brecht uses to demonstrate the necessity of epic theatre, one resonates in particular with the contemporary moment:

> the extraction and refinement of petroleum spirit represents a new complex of subjects, and when one studies these carefully one becomes struck by quite new forms of human relationship. A particular mode of behaviour can be observed in the individual and in the mass, and it is clearly peculiar to the petroleum complex. But it wasn't the new mode of behaviour that created this particular way of refining petrol. The petroleum complex came first, and the new relationships are secondary.[26]

Brecht's invocation of the petroleum complex is one that signals a new artistic need: 'Petroleum resists the five-act form; today's catastrophes do not progress in a straight line but in cyclical crises'.[27]

---

24   Brecht 1978, p. 25.
25   Brecht 1978, p. 37.
26   Brecht 1978, p. 29.
27   Brecht 1978, p. 30.

Brecht worked on Leo Lania's 1928 play *Konjunktur* (*Oil Boom*), which dealt with the oil industry and international competition over oil extraction. Lania was part of Erwin Piscator's collective group and Piscator directed the play, which concluded with the 'petroleum song', 'Die Muschel von Margate', a play on the emblem of Royal Dutch Shell, for which Kurt Weil wrote the music.[28] The play was not particularly successful, focusing on a contrast between the efforts of the Russians and the capitalists, which, as the solidification of Stalinism became evident, was rendered problematic. It was, perhaps, these difficulties that prompted Brecht's remark about the difficulty of putting petroleum in the five-act form.

It is obvious why this remains a resonant problem. In our moment the grasping of the petroleum complex has become even more pressing with the arguments around peak oil and anthropogenic climate change. A large amount of material has emerged, in multiple forms, trying to capture the various dimensions of this complex. To select only some of this material, we have Timothy Mitchell's *Carbon Democracy* (2011), which explores how oil extraction, which requires a relatively small labour force, has shaped the erosion of democratic politics;[29] Reza Negarestani's *Cyclonopedia: Complicity with Anonymous Materials* (2008), offers a speculative theory-fiction in which oil is treated as a sentient and malignant entity;[30] Andreas Malm's *Fossil Capital* (2016) is a powerful articulation of the persistence of coal within the fossil economy as a form of stock, accumulated value, against the flow of alternate energy sources, whilst also acknowledging the petro-complex;[31] and Peter Mettler's documentary *Petropolis: Aerial Perspectives on the Alberta Tar Sands* (2009), shows images of what we could call the 'petroleum sublime': a landscape marred by the processes of tar oil extraction, yet presented in a gliding horizontal mapping view that renders it oddly fascinating. Wenzel, discussing Ben Okri's fiction as petromagic-realism, remarks on how it explores 'its vision in a recognisably devastated, if also recognisably fantastic, landscape'.[32] These texts all trace the disturbing fascinations of this landscape.

Mettler's *Petropolis* suggests another difficulty in grasping the scale of something like the petroleum complex. The excess of scale produces a sublime effect that threatens to stultify critical thought: 'In the depiction of cycles of energy extraction, circulation and waste, cause and effect implode into a

28   Schebera 1995, p. 103.
29   Mitchell 2011.
30   Negarestani 2008.
31   Malm 2016.
32   Wenzel 2006, p. 457.

kind of entropic destiny, which we can nonetheless artistically enjoy (while we simultaneously arrive at some kind of mindfulness of our total and terminal dependency)'.[33] Brecht's epic theatre was designed to address this kind of problem, through the production of knowledge and reflection, in which the spectator would say: 'I'd have never thought it – That's not the way – That's extraordinary, hardly believable – It's got to stop – The sufferings of this man appal me, because they are unnecessary – That's great art: nothing obvious in it – I laugh when they weep, I weep when they laugh'.[34] Yet Brecht was also canny enough to be sceptical about this production of knowledge: 'There is not much knowledge that leads to power, but plenty of knowledge to which only power can lead'.[35]

For Brecht the determination of social being by the cyclical crises of capitalism demands a new form that can provide this knowledge. It must not be linear in form, a 'five-act form', but operate 'in montage', 'curves', and 'jumps'.[36] This speaks to the difficult position of narrative and the narration of capital in Brecht. The dispute between Brecht and Lukács over realism and the avant-garde has tended to leave Brecht as the representative of the avant-garde and disruption, against the claims of Lukács for bourgeois realism as the path to a new proletarian realism, posed against naturalism and modernism.[37] Brecht's position was, however, more complicated. Brecht did not simply accept the expressionist avant-garde, but subjected it to criticism that placed him closer to Lukács than might first be apparent. For Brecht, 'anarchistic montage' did not grasp the forms of capitalist culture in crisis, rather such forms 'merely reflect the symptoms of the surface of things and not the deeper causal complexes of society'.[38] Lukács would also argue that Brecht's later work, after his avant-garde fascinations and his attempts to produce direct political art, would approach a more successful critical realism.[39]

Brecht certainly rejected the 'simple reproduction of reality' in his famous remark when he noted that 'A photograph of the Krupps works or GCE yields almost nothing about these institutions'.[40] He went on to make a point that prefigures Jameson's argument concerning totality: 'Reality is no longer exper-

---

33   Toscano and Kinkle 2015, p. 206.
34   Brecht 1978, p. 71.
35   Brecht 1978, p. 72.
36   Brecht 1978, p. 37.
37   Lukács 2007.
38   Brecht 2007, p. 72.
39   Lukács 1963, p. 87.
40   Brecht in Leslie 2015, p. 25.

ienceable in its totality'.[41] Yet, Brecht's project was not simply antagonistic to realism, instead it would lay claim to a better perception of reality more closely linked to the complexities of capitalist society. This is evident in the fact Brecht adopted realism as a banner for his work, on a certain understanding inspired by Lukács, but also differing from him: 'Realist means: laying bare society's causal network / showing up the dominant viewpoint as the viewpoint of the dominators / writing from the standpoint of the class which has prepared the broadest solutions for the most pressing problems afflicting human society / emphasizing the dynamics of development / concrete and so as to encourage abstraction'.[42] Brecht's position aimed to activate realism in a mode that was not beholden strictly to bourgeois realism, but rather one that remained in concert with the new radical proletarian energies resulting from the Russian Revolution.

The complexity of Brecht's position was further reduced when the dispute between Brecht and Lukács' dispute over realism was overlaid by the neo-avant-garde reactivations of Brecht. In particular, 'Screen theory', the articulation of Althusser and Lacan in the analysis of film pioneered by the British journal *Screen* in the 1970s, took Brecht as the model for anti-realism. In Colin MacCabe's 1974 article, 'Realism and the Cinema: Notes on some Brechtian theses', MacCabe solidified the opposition between the 'classic realist text', his example being Eliot's *Middlemarch* (1871), and the Brechtian avant-garde.[43] While polemical, this interpretation, perhaps influenced by Roland Barthes's tendency to binaries, reduced the difficulty Brecht had tried to engage with to a simplified alternative: ideological realism versus avant-garde anti-realism.

Certainly, Brecht belonged to the avant-garde, in the sense he regarded the social conditions of his time as having exhausted conventional forms and that they required new forms capable of grasping these conditions: 'Capitalism operates in this way by taking given needs on a massive scale, exorcizing them, organizing them and mechanizing them so as to revolutionize everything. Great areas of ideology are destroyed when capitalism concentrates on external action, dissolves everything into processes, abandons the hero as the vehicle for everything and mankind as the measure, and thereby smashes the introspective psychology of the bourgeois novel'.[44] Brecht welcomed the smashing of bourgeois psychology, going so far, along with elements of the Soviet avant-

---

41   Brecht in Leslie 2015, p. 25.
42   Brecht 1978, p. 109.
43   MacCabe 1974.
44   Brecht 1978, p. 50.

gardes, as regarding behaviourism as a science that could have possible communist uses. While behaviourism was based on the needs of industry, these limits were only proper to its function under capitalism and: 'Here again the road leads over capitalism's dead body; but here again the road is a good one'.[45]

The tension of Brecht's position, between realism and the avant-garde, is one, as I have suggested, that is often flattened to reinforce the image of the avant-garde – not so much the historic avant-garde, but the later rediscovery of Brecht and cognate theoretical work in the 1960s and 1970s. Of course, this is not to underestimate the complexity of that moment as well – which often wrestled with the same, or reactivated, tensions that beset the historic avant-garde. It is notable amongst contemporary theorisations of art, especially the otherwise antithetical work of Alain Badiou and Jacques Rancière, that it is the 1960s and 1970s avant-garde, especially the Situationist International, that is singled out as the worst example of didactic pedagogic political art.[46] Instead, I am suggesting that the tensions of realism and the avant-garde, to use two loose, baggy categories, persist and might be re-focused around the problem of something like the petroleum complex: the mapping and analysis of the commodity as key to totality.

2   The Subject of Totality

David Cunningham has argued that we reconceive the problem of epic, linked particularly to the novel form, in relation to the totality of capitalist relations.[47] Dialoguing with Lukács' argument in *Theory of the Novel* (1916) that the epic is now impossible, and that in the disenchanted world of capitalism it is the novel that captures the prose of the world, Cunningham suggests a twist. Instead of the novel being the epic of the rising bourgeois class, expressing its confidence and anxieties, but limited as such to this class, we instead have to recognise that: 'As regards the novel as a modern epic form – which still *thinks* in terms of totality – it must then be capital, on this reading, which constitutes its most properly "epic" subject'.[48] Instead of the novel recording the experience of an ascendant class fraction, we can recalibrate the novel as epic when its deals with the totality – with capitalism as 'automatic subject'.[49] What is absent here

---

45   Brecht 1978, p. 50.
46   Badiou 2007, p. 153; Rancière 2009, pp. 6–7.
47   Cunningham 2010.
48   Cunningham 2010, p. 18.
49   Marx 1990, p. 133.

is the possibility of a proletarian epic, of the type sketched by Badiou in relation to a communist poetics that wrote the epic of the struggle in the Spanish
civil war.[50] The collapse of historic socialism leaves the proletarian epic off the
agenda, a project which, in different ways, drove Lukács and Brecht. The totality
which was not capitalist totality has apparently disappeared and, with capital
triumphant, we are left only able to write the epic of capital.

The modern epic is impossible, as it cannot fully grasp capitalism as totality,
but it is possible if it acts out this impossible mapping. In trying to grasp the
abstract totality of capital, and failing, this failure opens to a negative function
that retains the critical function of the novel.[51] The success of the novel, as the
epic of capitalism, would lie in the way a work 'renders visible the essential limits on any artistic or cultural "representation" of "totality"'.[52] The question then,
is what kind of work would fit the bill, considering most novels remain within
the ambit of bourgeois subjectivity as the totality. Chris Kraus has acidly noted
that:

> Contemporary fiction takes this one step further: only upper-middle class
> domestic life is worth considering. My Grandmother's Cancer, My Di-
> vorce, My Subjectivity. And they could be right.[53]

In contrast, Cunningham's example of a novel is Roberto Saviano's work of
reportage *Gomorrah* (2006), focused on organised crime, the Neapolitan Cam-
orra, and capitalism.[54] While this might be stretching the definition of the
novel, we should note that Saviano's work opens with an exemplary scene
of following-the-commodity: the opening of a container full of dead Chinese
migrants.[55] While this story was likely to be apocryphal, since publication incid-
ents like the discovery of the bodies of thirty-nine Vietnamese people in a lorry
in Essex in 2019 eerily confirm in retrospect the truth of the violent disposal of
labour under contemporary capitalism. So, a novel that is not exactly a novel,
and then Cunningham turns to television, particularly the Baltimore police
procedural *The Wire* (2002–8). *The Wire* has, already, become something of a
cliché for discussion around the mapping of capital.[56] What is striking is that it

---

50   Badiou 2014, pp. 93–108.
51   Blanton 2015.
52   Cunningham 2010, p. 20.
53   Kraus 2011, p. 157.
54   Cunningham 2010, pp. 19–20.
55   Toscano and Kinkle 2015, pp. 198–9.
56   Toscano and Kinkle 2015, 137–56; Kraniauskas 2009.

remains difficult to identify a contemporary novel that fits the bill of the capit-alist epic, an issue to which we will return, and the turn to television instead.

This is reinforced by Cunningham's complementary analysis of the televi-sion series *Deadwood* (2004–6) as a 'capitalist epic'.[57] *Deadwood*, an historical drama of the wild west, is, according to Cunningham a '*"pre-history" of this cap-italist present*'.[58] In writing an origin story of capitalism, the process of what Marx called 'original accumulation', *Deadwood* constitutes 'a kind of historical epic of *capital itself*'.[59] The particular power of this epic lies in its narration of the incomprehension of the characters at the solidification of an abstract eco-nomy of exchange. In this way the work narrates own its limits: the difficulty of grasping 'fundamentally impersonal and systemic forces'.[60] *Deadwood*, while probing the limits of the generic form of the Western, remains a popular work, although one cancelled by HBO before its completion.

The Western, profoundly influenced by the fiction of Sir Walter Scott, has often reflected on radical historical change: from barbarism to civilisation, from anarchy to order. Lukács would take up Scott as exemplar of the historical novel precisely because of Scott's attention to sudden change.[61] Lukács would also use Scott's historical novel as the transitional form into bourgeois realism, as Balzac, for example, began his 'Human Comedy' sequence with an historical novel, *Les Chouans* (1829), deeply influenced by Scott. Two things can be noted: first, the return to the form of the historical novel to map the capitalist epic. The totality can be grasped only in its germination. Second, the realist form of this mapping, which also extends to *The Wire*, where experimentation lies in the extension of a sustained realist form to television, rather than any avant-garde gesture. Here the failure of the epic form seems to threaten the very possibility of a capitalist epic.

Franco Moretti, in his discussion of the modern epic, also notes the prob-lems and tensions that persist in these works. The modern epic is modern, we might say, because it engages with the failure to create the epic from within the epic form. Moretti's examples are not avant-garde, but the great works of modernism. In a brief discussion of T.S. Eliot's *The Waste Land* (1922) Moretti suggests that this modern epic is *the* epic of capitalism. Contrary to the sprawl-ing and totalising works he has previously discussed, it is the very compression of *The Waste Land* which, for Moretti, makes it the best form to grasp capital:

---

57 Cunningham 2013.
58 Cunningham 2013, p. 9.
59 Cunningham 2013, p. 9.
60 Cunningham 2013, p. 19.
61 Lukács 1962.

Between materials and plan, in short, a discrepancy subsists: a tension. But this is not a limit of *collage* and of *The Waste Land*: rather it is the specific form of their effectiveness. It is the allegory of a heterogeneous – but forcibly unified – reality. The most abstract form of 'totality' imaginable in the capitalist world-system. And, perhaps, the most truthful.[62]

The violent compression of the fragmentary form of *The Waste Land*, fragments 'shored against my ruins',[63] is, for Moretti, the best allegory, the most truthful, of the capitalist world-system. Implicitly referencing the argument of Lukács, that capitalism is a unified reality that presents itself as heterogeneous,[64] Moretti suggests Eliot, despite his reactionary politics, grasps something of this abstract totality.

Moretti's point may be more interesting than it is true, at least as regards *The Waste Land*. He raises the question of whether the representation of capital should merely reflect its sprawling appearance or be true to its compact essence, at least if we agree with the terms of Lukács' description of capital. This is further complicated by Lukács' assertion that in its normal functioning capitalism appears as a differentiated system of multiple forms, but is experienced as a unity, while in crisis it reveals its essence as a compact and determined system, and is experienced as disintegration.[65] In this case, the representation of capital turns not only on a mimesis of appearance or essence, but also, in the time of crisis, on the emergence of that essence in a forcibly unified reality. Therefore, we could say that Moretti suggests that a true epic of the capitalist world-system should be compact in form to capture the truth of capitalism's own shoring of fragments against its ruin.

This is why poetry, not the novel, may be the site of the capitalist epic. It is Joshua Clover who has insisted that poetry is the medium that can best answer the demands of writing capitalism, and especially capitalism in crisis. The expansive dynamic of capital, its 'spiral form',[66] requires a non-narrative mode, like poetry, to grasp the spatialisation of temporal relations.[67] For Clover, in a detailed discussion of Kevin Davies's poetry, it is the dissolution or displacement of narrative in that work which allows a scaling that can move 'from

---

62   Moretti 1996, p. 229.
63   Eliot 1974, p. 79.
64   Lukács 2007, p. 32.
65   Lukács 2007, p. 32.
66   Clover 2011, p. 36.
67   Clover 2011, p. 49.

word to world-system and back again'.[68] Clover's own poetic practice, particularly his *Red Epic* (2015), aims to embody these non-narrative possibilities of scaling. Borrowing from Dante's epic poem *The Divine Comedy* (1320), the grasping of totality by the Situationist International, the avant-garde poetics of Gertrude Stein and Frank O'Hara, and currents of communisation theory, this work is preoccupied, in ironic fashion, with 'the itch to make an account of it all'.[69]

Clover's poem 'Year of Analysis for a Day of Synthesis',[70] is exemplary of this strategy. The poem likens the 'adventure of value' to Francesca da Rimini 'circling immaterial' in Dante's *Inferno* as punishment for infidelity.[71] The 'unspooling' spiral of capital 'heaves up on Benicia's beaches / ten thousand cars',[72] abandoned due to the financial crisis, 'and they all hunch / in the weak sun too tired / to launch into the circuits'.[73] The circling expansion of capital, its Yeatsian gyre, is not only centrifugal but also centripetal, and so can be captured in its moment of spiralling collapse. In the freezing of the commodity chain the commodity is starkly rendered as useless, as weak, as object, as yet unable to launch again on the adventure of value. This is also, of course, the key object of the petro-complex, with the car now 'too tired' to enter into that complex, stalling it. In fact, one of the side effects of the financial crisis was a temporary drop in carbon emissions.[74] The poem concludes with a repeated question of who will make various figures of the financial crisis 'whole'.[75]

Clover's work constantly registers the object-world of capitalism as one dominated by abstraction: 'dude that's not emptiness it's abstraction / asserting itself on the home front now / who will love in your hollowed carapace'.[76] At the same time, this abstraction is always forming and deforming people and objects. Also, Clover's work resists a capitalist sublime that would celebrate or contemplate in awe the productive or destructive powers of capitalism. While tracing the spirals of value, the poem also focuses on the problem of resistance and struggle: 'Once fire is the form of the spectacle the problem / becomes

---

68   Clover 2011, p. 48.
69   Clover 2015, p. 58.
70   Clover 2015, pp. 5–9.
71   Clover 2015, p. 6.
72   Clover 2015, p. 7.
73   Clover 2015, p. 8.
74   Malm 2016, p. 12.
75   Clover 2015, p. 9.
76   Clover 2015, p. 39.

how to set fire to fire'.[77] In this case the problem of protest, the use of fire in the form of the Molotov cocktail, appropriately, is itself problematised as spectacle. Clover's is a self-conscious consideration of crisis and resistance as complex spirals still intimately linked to spirals of value even as those spirals stall. This problem is left unresolved, and this is one of the signs of the epic's tension, which falls here not so much on the mapping of capitalism as a totality, but on the mapping of capitalism as a totality that intrinsically involves forms of struggle. What remains difficult to view is the totality of which capitalism it itself a part. Certainly, this totality of life is evident in Clover's poetry, in its Debordian moments of friendship and struggle, but this remains difficult to coordinate with the failing spirals of value.

3 Only Connect

While Clover makes a defence of poetry as the mode of avant-garde epic, both in theory and practice, his discussion of the possibilities of poetry as the non-narrative art of capital also includes a discussion of the novel. Specifically, Clover discusses the sprawling work of Thomas Pynchon, in particular *Against the Day* (2006), as a work that tries to grapple with the problem of writing an epic of the emergence and sedimentation of capitalism. This work is, Clover notes, doomed to failure, and operates alongside a number of Pynchon's fictional inquiries into the rationalisation of territory: notably, *Gravity's Rainbow* (1973) and *Mason & Dixon* (1997).[78] We might say that, like *Deadwood*, Pynchon is focused on the scene of original accumulation as scene of original sin, although reversed from the meaning Marx ascribes to this notion in *Capital*. If original accumulation was original sin in political economy was the 'just so' story of our condemnation to labour, for Pynchon the fall is from stateless and capital-less freedom into the grid of control.[79] Here the totality of life and existence can only appear as this point of vanishing origin, or in recurrent moments of an outside that is in the process of disappearing.

As we have seen (see Chapter 4), Pynchon's novels of the recent past, like *Vineland* (1990), *Inherent Vice* (2009) and *Bleeding Edge* (2013), also still seem to tell stories of the fall: from the possibilities of the counter-culture and from the moment of cyber-utopianism. Johanna Isaacson,[80] in her analysis of *Vineland*,

---

77   Clover 2015, p. 3.
78   Clover 2011, p. 40.
79   Noys 2015a, p. 187.
80   Isaacson 2014.

has noted how this work also assesses the fate of counter-cultural moments in and against the global dominance of capital and the state. Therefore, Pynchon may not be as nostalgic as he might first appear, and these works carry a double address, a parallax, as Clover puts it,[81] which de-naturalises capitalist dominance through a reactivation of past struggles and hints at another totality. If Pynchon is the major example of the avant-garde novelist, and the avant-garde epic of capital, there are other, less obvious, attempts to engage with the problem of the cartography of the present. We previously discussed William Gibson's near-future 'Blue Ant' trilogy – *Pattern Recognition* (2003), *Spook Country* (2007), and *Zero History* (2010) – that plays with the trendlines of state power, the commodity, and technology, to map the emerging moment (see Chapter 4). *Spook Country* makes use of the signature device of commodity-chain analysis, the shipping container, which forms the empty centre of the plot.[82]

In an avant-garde key, the novels of Pierre Guyotat, notably *Éden, Éden, Éden* (1970), also make use of the epic, especially the use 'of a radically impartial tone'.[83] Guyotat's linguistic experimentation, with his text engaging sexuality and violence, inhabits, as Diarmuid Hester has argued, the neutrality and levelling of the epic form.[84] This indicates a particular link between the epic and capitalism, which itself levels and abstracts the world through the grid of monetary value. The flattened form of the epic, which exercises an abstract equivalence, radicalised in Guyotat's work, speaks also to the abstract totality of capitalism. Guyotat's work, evoking the peripheral experience of Algeria as site of colonial violence, also connects with those mappings of capital from the position of its colonialist implantation. We could consider here Jennifer Wenzel's analysis of 'petro-magic realism' in Nigerian literature, in which Nigerian novelists, especially Amos Tutuola and Ben Okri, struggle with 'negotiating the pressure of petroleum on literary representation'.[85] Another example would be Palestinian modernism, as identified by Bashir Abu-Manneh, with its reflections on the emergence of the 1970s oil society.[86] Michael Niblett has also made the argument that peripheral literatures, particularly magical realism, have grasped the violent ecological revolutions of capitalist world-making.[87]

---

81   Clover 2011, p. 39.
82   Toscano and Kinkle 2015, p. 200.
83   Hester 2015, p. 38.
84   Hester 2015.
85   Wenzel 2006, p. 456.
86   Abu-Manneh 2015, pp. 63–4. For a different critical reading, see Lustig 2019, pp. 207–22 and Malm 2017a.
87   Niblett 2012.

Guyotat's fiction is less immediately explicit about these effects, but his work does offer a powerful, flatter image of the wasteland of commodities, which circulate in an equivalence of objects and bodies.[88]

What is striking is that relatively little contemporary literary fiction appears focused on the present moment of crisis in the heartlands of capital. Don DeLillo's *Cosmopolis* (2003) took a small step-back to 2000 for its one day in the life of a master of the universe – billionaire asset manager Eric Packer. Packer's world, often confined to his luxury limousine in the novel, is certainly the contemporary bourgeois *Dingwelt*.[89] Also, Packer's reflections capture the financial vitalism characteristic of contemporary capitalism. Studying the streams of data from the financial markets, Packer muses that: 'It was shallow thinking to maintain that numbers and charts were the cold compression of unruly human energies, every sort of yearning and midnight sweat reduced to lucid units in the financial markets. In fact data was soulful and glowing, a dynamic aspect of the life process'.[90] This vitalism of data is certainly diagnostic of the mutated form of commodity fetishism, in the age of financialisation, while also indicating how capitalism's vampirism on life is now seen as consonant with life. Yet, this figuration of subsumption, beyond the psychic collapse of Packer, offers little sense of contradiction or struggle within that subsumption, with anti-capitalist protest rendered as fundamentally consonant with the desires of capital.

Ben Lerner's *10:04* (2014) presents a nice summary scene of the epiphany of the commodity chain. In the period before the arrival of Hurricane Irene in 2011, the narrator and his girlfriend prepare to do some emergency shopping:

> I want to say I felt stoned, did say so to Alex, who laughed and said, 'Me too', but what I meant was that the approaching storm was estranging the routine of shopping just enough to make me viscerally aware of both the miracle and insanity of the mundane economy. Finally I found something on the list, something vital: instant coffee. I held the red plastic container, one of the last three on the shelf, held it like the marvel it was: the seeds inside the purple fruits of coffee plants had been harvested on Andean slopes and roasted and ground and soaked and then dehydrated at a factory in Medellin and vacuum-sealed and flown to JFK and then driven upstate in bulk to Pearl River for repackaging and then transported back

---

88   Badiou 2014, pp. 194–205.
89   Adorno 1992, p. 177.
90   DeLillo 2003, p. 24.

by truck to the store where I now stood reading the label. It was as if the social relations that produced the object in my hand began to glow within it as they were threatened, stirred inside their packaging, lending it a certain aura – the majesty and murderous stupidity of that organization of time and space and fuel and labour becoming visible in the commodity itself now that planes were grounded and the highways were starting to close.[91]

The length of the quote is, in part, indicative of the meditative stance induced by the contemplation of the commodity chain. Lerner's narrator traces the transition from the mundane economy to the estranging effects of an emergency situation, the result of climate change,[92] which reveals the glow and aura of the social relations that inhere in the commodity.

What is interesting to note is that this is something of a reversal of terms familiar from Marxist analysis. The glow or aura of the commodity, the later obviously recalling and adapting Walter Benjamin, is not a deceptive fetishistic illusion, the 'shine on the nose' (*Glanz auf der Nase*), that obsesses Freud's fetishist.[93] Instead, the glow or aura is the revelation of social relations, of 'the majesty and murderous stupidity of that organization of time and space and fuel and labour becoming visible in the commodity itself'. This scene of revelation by estrangement is paired with another that occurs later in the novel. The narrator is invited to an exhibition by a friend of totalled art, art rendered empty of value due to damage that is held by insurance companies. His experience is one of shock, similar to the encounter with the instant coffee: 'I felt a fullness indistinguishable from being emptied as I held a work from which the exchange value had been extracted, an object that was otherwise unchanged'.[94] These two moments of epiphany, in the Joycean sense, are taken to render the mundane world in a utopian frame.

This links to the novel's epigraph, which is from Walter Benjamin, who may have had the story from Gershom Scholem, via Agamben's *The Coming Community*:

> The Hassidim tell a story about the world to come that says that everything will be just as it is here. Just as our room is now, so it will be in the world to come; where our baby sleeps now, there too it will sleep in the

91   Lerner 2014, p. 19.
92   Malm 2017b, pp. 3–4.
93   Freud 1977, p. 351.
94   Lerner 2014, pp. 133–4.

other world. And the clothes we wear in this world, those too we will wear there. Everything will be just as it is now, just a little different.[95]

In Lerner's novel this moment is parsed after seeing the totalled art, and then in the moment of walking across the Manhattan Bridge while contemplating the Brooklyn Bridge.[96] Here the shift in perception, the small but supposedly radical change, is registered as an aesthetic effect. Exactly how far this effect is supposed to extend, beyond the narrator and the reader, is left as a possibility.

This is only one moment in the novel, however, which does not pursue a sustained analysis of the commodity form. The novel remains in tension, not least due to the social position of its detached and quasi-autobiographical narrator. Forms of struggle are admitted into the novel, in the very literal form of the narrator letting an Occupy protestor stay over and use the facilities of his apartment. At this point, reflecting on the possibility of his having children, the narrator also muses on an alternative: 'What you need to do is harness the self-love you are hypostasizing as offspring, as the next generation of you, and let it branch out horizontally into the possibility of a transpersonal revolution-ary subject in the present and co-construct a world in which moments can be something other than the elements of profit'.[97] This, typically deadpan, invoc-ation of the revolutionary subject, is, however, folded into the later humanist epiphany of the narrator's success in guiding a young boy around a natural his-tory museum. It is the ability to, even temporarily, assume paternity that is seen as the mark of adulthood and maturity. It is, of course, also the classic trope of high modernism, especially in Joyce. Certainly not without irony, the 'warm abstraction' of paternity seems sufficient to displace the colder abstractions of the commodity-form.[98]

What interests me in Lerner's novel is how it plays with the tensions of E.M. Forster's humanist literary motto 'only connect', itself put under unbear-able strain in his contact with colonialism in *A Passage to India* (1924). In Lerner's novel to connect takes on different forms: the connections of the com-modity chain, of paternity, of heterosexual romance, of the writer and audi-ence, and of the revolutionary subject. In contrast to Clover's incendiary com-pression, Lerner's novel presents a space of anxiety that, finally, ends in vari-ous forms of success and relative stability. Placed together they are not simply broken halves that do not make a whole, but each indicates a relation and a

---

95   Lerner 2014.
96   Lerner 2014, p. 135.
97   Lerner 2014, p. 47.
98   Toscano 2008a, p. 56.

mapping, not only of the capitalist totality as the sublimity of capitalist power, but also of its struggles and contradictions. They suggest the difficulties that lie in categories like the suspensive or subtractive, the modern epic or the pocket epic. In this way they indicate the problem that remains still in the demand of the avant-garde and the epic, in very self-conscious reflections on those possibilities in the present moment. They also suggest the difficulties of imagining collective forms of life that precede and exceed capitalist totality, with forms of friendship and family (even if non-standard) playing the role of indicating a totality not consonant with capitalism.

4   The Commodity with an (In)Human Face

The classical avant-gardes inhabited a range of positions on the shock of capitalist modernisation. In a schematic fashion we could distinguish those projects which welcomed the opportunity to fuse or infuse life into the machine in an act of melding, such as Italian Futurism, elements in the Soviet avant-gardes, and British Vorticism, from those projects that aimed at re-enchanting the everyday world of the commodity, notably Surrealism or, in a more extreme fashion, the spiritual unifiers of the French avant-garde group The Great Game.[99] The first strand would find its echo in Jean-François Lyotard's libidinal inhumanism and, as I have done, can be articulated around the problem of accelerationism – the inhabiting of capitalist forces the better to accelerate and punch through the limit of capital.[100] My suggestion here is that commodity-chain fictions operate more by posing the second tendency, of re-enchantment, against the first tendency, of inhumanism.

   This is certainly a tentative and equivocal characterisation, which sketches an initial point of orientation. It does, however, speak to the form of contemporary work that at once echoes and ironises the ambitions of the avant-garde and the epic. The tendency here is to register the object as fading from any inhuman synthesis, the object or commodity as registration of failure that can then connect to our experience of failure. In this situation it is not only the surrealists, but more particularly Walter Benjamin who becomes the key figure. This is not so much the communist or messianic Benjamin, but the curatorial Benjamin, the image of Benjamin as collector and rag-picker, which often detaches these gestures from the implications Benjamin traces between these practices and revolutionary ambition.

---

99   Duncan (ed.) 2015.
100   Noys 2014.

The commodity-chain fictions I have indicated work, especially in the case of Lerner, by the attempt to put a human face on the inhuman commodity. Instead of the embrace of the inhuman, in the melding with the capitalist forces of production, in the fusion of living and dead labour, we have the replacement of the inhuman with the human, even if only in the form of the stunned consumer or spectator. Connections, whether positive, as in Lerner, or violent, as in DeLillo, promise at least some engagement with the abstract forms and forces that deliver the commodity to us and us to the commodity, at least a very particular us. This tense humanisation relies on some emergence of the human against the commodity, or in the revelation of its void. The result is the preservation of an exteriority reached through the traversal of the commodity, but one that leaves the commodity untouched or, as in Lerner, subjects it to a minor aesthetic shift that renders us, briefly, a utopian glimpse that is rapidly withdrawn. The notion of a totality exceeding and preceding capital appears to have disappeared, or been subsumed within capital itself.

The manifest inhumanity of capitalism, lived directly on the peripheries, '[t]he profound hypocrisy and inherent barbarism of bourgeois civilization ... assumes respectable forms [at home], [compared] to the colonies, where it goes naked',[101] but now, once again, returning to the heartlands, poses a problem of representation and figuration. Hence, we could note the resurgence of interest in the monstrous figurations of capitalism, from the work of Marx to the present,[102] with capitalism ranging from the Lovecraftian Shoggoth to the Zombie. Lenin, in 1916, remarked: 'Capitalist society is and has always been *horror without end*'.[103] At their extreme, as Steven Shaviro has explored, the full-blown horror of capitalism is that we are reduced and distorted into parasitic creatures desperately clinging to the body of capital.[104] The fear here is not only integration, but also abandonment. If living in the capitalist relation is impossible, then living without that relation is even more impossible. In terms of the petroleum complex we can recall the *Mad Max* films, with their vision of freedom through retention of the dwindling resource of petroleum.[105] Once again, the absence of the commodity, the withdrawal of capitalism, presents a feral vision of the state of nature, rendered as a civil war that is, in fact, already intrinsic to the capital relation.[106]

---

101   Marx 2019, p. 658.
102   McNally 2012.
103   Lenin 2008, 11.
104   Shaviro 2015, pp. 41–60.
105   Calder Williams 2010, pp. 21–6.
106   Tiqqun 2010, p. 60.

These representations risk a negative sublime. If the dream was once integration, disintegration now appears to be the mode, and a mode that can reinforce the capitalist relation as the only horizon of existence. While humanisation appears a problematic evasion, inhumanisation appears an equally problematic encoding of endless horror. I am, once again, tracing a failure. While this is a realism about the limits of narrative and non-narrative figuration, it can also simply be another celebration of failure that consoles our incapacities. That is why, while not providing a recipe book for restarting the avant-garde and/or the epic, here I have aimed to probe the conditions in which such gestures operates and the effects of the limits in which they, by necessity, find themselves. The failure here is not, I think, easily or magically convertible into a success, even into a success of a failure. Instead, the problem of the mapping and narrative of global capitalism in crisis is one which is unavoidable and not yet subject to solution. This intractability is a place to begin, but it is also a place to advance an understanding of totality that is not equivalent with capitalist totality. New forms of the avant-garde and epic, together and apart, confront this positive task.

CHAPTER 6

The Crisis of European Philosophy

It seems ironic that at the moment the unifying concern of Europe is how to put an end to Europe. In very different ways, with vastly different political and social forms, emerging out of heterogeneous formations, a range of discourses want to end Europe: discourses of radical right populism, perhaps best symbolised by Brexit, left critiques of Europe as neo-liberal form, decolonial critiques of the colonial form of Europe, no borders struggles against the European border security system, all want to put an end to Europe endless – the vision of Europe as a now permanent feature of the global system, in the form of the European Union.[1] To reiterate, and as I will unpack below, these are very different forms of Europe and very different forms of ending Europe to very different ends. It does seem difficult, however, outside of the realm of European Union functionaries, to find many who want to maintain Europe endless.[2] Even amongst those who want Europe to continue the desire is for it to end as it currently is.

That said, this problem of Europe endless and ending Europe perhaps speaks to something of that repeating discourse of the crisis of Europe, a discourse that predates significantly the global financial crisis of 2008 and the resulting regimes of austerity.[3] That global crisis does, however significantly inflect the crisis of Europe. In a telling moment, the British historian of art and former member of the Situationist International, T.J. Clark, justified his decision to vote to leave the European Union in these terms: 'I voted Leave, without enthusiasm, mainly because I had promised to do so in Greece last July'.[4] The financial waterboarding of Greece, which still continues, is not only a sign of the financial crisis but also a crisis of Europe that turns Greece into a sacrifice zone. This is particularly telling in this context due to the complex role of the exclusive inclusion of Greece in Europe in the philosophical imaginary.[5]

---

1   For a Marxist analysis of the project of European integration as class strategy see Sotiris and Sakellaropoulos 2018.
2   Weber 2009, pp. 71–2.
3   Jones 2010.
4   Clark 2016.
5   Karatani 2017.

If the crisis of Europe is a call to end Europe, it might also be a call to begin again. This, at least, is the claim of Franco 'Bifo' Berardi, who suggests that

> Europe is dead, because of the austeritarian rule. But we must build another Europe. Immediately and without delay, we must build a social Europe, a Europe of equality and freedom from wage-labour.[6]

Europe must be ended, but this time to the benefit of a new Europe. The desire to end Europe endless is also closely bound up with the desire to begin a new Europe. The crisis of Europe would force a passage to this rebirth. What is striking, both in these discourses and in actuality, is the difficulty in producing this ending. The delay in Brexit at least seems an empirical symptom of the difficulty of ending Europe, and even now it has been achieved it does not satisfy all its partisans.[7]

Europe might even appear here as what Hegel called a bad infinity, in which the infinite is separated from and dominates the finite as an 'alien force'.[8] The difficulty of realising Europe, of ending Europe endless, would speak to a conceptual failure in which infinite Europe is separated from actual Europe. The calls to re-invent Europe, of a Europe to come, to adapt Jacques Derrida,[9] translate Europe into an infinite and endless task to achieve aims that constantly recede. In the words of Rodolphe Gasché, echoing Husserl, this is Europe as 'the infinite task'.[10] For Gasché, such an idea of Europe can be rewritten beyond the Kantian regulative idea, but even this remains a Europe that still always only promises to live up to its openness and self-criticism.[11] Despite the attempt to go beyond Kant this Europe seems to remain pre-Hegelian, in the sense of an infinitely deferred task. Europe endless is valorised as the true state of Europe, which should never achieve the equality and freedom that it always promises. The promise is even a guarantee that we should not risk such a dangerous realisation, in a repeat of the trope of the various anti-totalitarianisms that were so crucial to post-war Western Europe. In this case, endless Europe is the perpetually deferred but always possible promise of

---

6   Berardi 2017. See also Berardi 2012, p. 50, for an earlier statement of a Europe that would 'embrace a future form of the international'.
7   Finlayson 2018.
8   Hegel 2010, p. 109.
9   Derrida 1992.
10   Gasché 2009.
11   Gasché 2017.

Europe. It might even be in response to such a Europe that we see the desire to end it, either to destroy any promise of equality and freedom or, finally, to bring it about.

What strikes me here also is a weariness with Europe, even a disgust, which again crosses the boundaries of various positions. Europe endless is a provoking prospect. Here I want to trace a philosophical discourse of Europe as a discourse of crisis and spirit. I begin with Nietzsche, as the European philosopher par excellence, with all the paradoxes, tensions, and violence, including colonial violence, which that entails. It is Nietzsche who exemplifies the notion of Europe as a site of crisis and tension that must be resolved in a new Europe. Then I move on to consider discourses of the spirit of Europe and crisis from the inter-war period (1919–39) in the figure of Edmund Husserl in particular. Here the spirit of Europe is one that must be maintained against irrationality but, being formed through a discourse of the life-world or community, always risks a particularism. Nietzsche is, again, in the background here. My aim is to sketch the relations of Europe endless to crisis and so to consider the delimitation of the future through and by Europe.

1   Good Europeans

It should be no surprise that the philosopher of Europe is Nietzsche, who self-describes as one of the 'good Europeans'.[12] In a remarkable moment, Nietzsche would even proclaim 'the economic unification of Europe is coming of necessity'.[13] Nietzsche as philosopher of the European Union almost seems as paradoxical as Nietzsche's provocation of Cesare Borgia as Pope.[14]

This good European is, however, suspicious of a good Europe, or of how good Europe currently is. To be a good European is to aim for the target beyond what Europe is (a Europe of Jesuits, democrats, and Germans, in Nietzsche's words). Existing Europe, certainly in the notes collected as *The Will to Power*, is the Europe of European nihilism. Europe suffers from a sickness, a narcosis, which is seemingly without end except for an end in catastrophe. Nietzsche writes that: 'For some time now, our whole European culture has been moving as toward a catastrophe, with a tortured tension that is growing from decade to decade: restlessly, violently, headlong, like a river that wants to

---

12   Nietzsche 1973, p. 14.
13   Nietzsche 1968, p. 396.
14   Nietzsche 2005, p. 64.

reach the end, that no longer reflects, that is afraid to reflect'.[15] Europe wants to reach the end, but while doing so it is inhabiting a soporific state that is, in fact, a state of tension. Beneath the appearance of tranquillity, if not tranquilisation, lies a rushing to catastrophe. In common with much of Nietzsche's clinical diagnostics of culture, in which the worst sickness presents itself as the best of health, or the healthy are seemingly sick, we find a site of reversibility and confusion in which Nietzsche's superior diagnostic skills are put to work. Certainly, Nietzsche belongs to the nineteenth-century discourse of decadence,[16] which is the shadow of the dominance of the notion of progress. Nietzsche is not original in this respect, but does stress the necessity of a transition through this illness, a surpassing or overcoming of the catastrophe.

This diagnosis of Europe as site of catastrophic nihilism gained empirical traction as Europe entered its own thirty-year civil war (1914–45). Of course, Nietzsche's diagnosis is not only empirical or not at all empirical but metaphysical, although the metaphysical and the empirical stand melded in this diagnosis, as the fate of Europe is a philosophical one. In all this Nietzsche stands as the good European, but not so good. Nietzsche describes how he is 'the first perfect nihilist of Europe who, however, has even now lived through the whole of nihilism, to the end, leaving it behind, outside himself.'[17] Nietzsche's advantage over Europe is to have lived its fate in advance. Whereas Europe is entering into nihilism, which is a spreading infection or drug, Nietzsche has already left it behind and is in recovery. The good European might then be the one who has transcended the crisis of Europe, in which crisis takes on the older meaning of a significant moment in the progress of a disease, the moment at which the patient will either die or recover. Nietzsche has survived that crisis, the fever of nihilism has broken, but Europe still has to confront that moment of crisis. Nietzsche has experienced inoculation or recovered from the addiction that is nihilism. At least that is Nietzsche's claim. The discourse of the bridge or the transition or overcoming speaks, however, to the difficulty of forcing this passage or break.

To refer back to *Beyond Good and Evil* (1886), the moment of European nihilism is not only a moment of exhaustion but of supreme tension, 'a magnificent tension of the spirit such as has never existed on earth before: with so tense a bow one can now shoot for the most distant targets'.[18] This might seem to

---

15   Nietzsche 1968, p. 3.
16   Nordau 1993.
17   Nietzsche 1973, p. 3.
18   Nietzsche 1973, p. 14.

be belied by the fact that Europe does not appear European, but as European Buddhism. The Platonic and Christian legacy of Europe ends in a self-dissolving nihilism as it undermines its own premises.[19] This is why we can speak of a developing European Buddhism, which has yet to match the 'Nothing' of original Buddhism.[20] Instead we have:

> The European form of Buddhism: the energy of knowledge and strength compels this belief. It is the most *scientific* of all possible hypotheses. We deny end goals: if existence had one it would have to have been reached.[21]

In this absence we confront 'the European form of Buddhism – *doing* No after all existence has lost its "meaning"'.[22] This state is the condition for the rebirth of an active and strong Europe, but only once this state has been transcended by new free spirits.

This diagnosis of European nihilism, of course, underpins Nietzsche's reactionary attacks on socialism, feminism, anarchism, and any other gesture of egalitarian dissent as nihilist.[23] In Europe life is declining and so also the norms it sets, which are reduced to the herd instinct. This is evident in *Beyond Good and Evil*, in which the herd animal is found in many forms, including 'anarchist dogs' and 'brotherhood fanatics who call themselves socialists' that usher in the 'new Buddhism'.[24] Here diagnosis reveals the virulence of its acceptance of nihilism in the contrast between a Europe to come, a Europe of higher spirits and hierarchy, which will overturn the misery of existing European nihilism.[25] The Europe endless of nihilism will be ended by a new Europe of a new caste imposing hierarchy,[26] the imprinting of new forms and a new gestalt, to use the Nietzschean terms of Ernst Jünger.[27] It is only after 'tremendous socialist crises' that new barbarians will arise to impose form on chaos.[28]

Of course, it is possible to see Nietzsche's Orientalism, his recognition of a European Buddhism inferior to actual Buddhism, as an act that de-centres

---

19   Nietzsche 1968, p. 16.
20   Nietzsche 1968, p. 21.
21   Nietzsche 1968, p. 36.
22   Nietzsche 1968, p. 37.
23   Losurdo 2019.
24   Nietzsche 1973, p. 107.
25   Martin 1995.
26   Conway 2009, pp. 42–7.
27   Jünger 2018.
28   Nietzsche 1968, p. 465.

Europe and destabilises the notions of Occident and Orient.[29] Within Nietz-sche's Orientalist use of concepts there lie moments of critique, such as the claim 'the Chinese is a more successful type, namely more durable, than the European'.[30] In this model, Orientalism would serve the purpose of disorienting Europe. Yet, these valorisations of the Orient are matched by Nietzsche's taste for scathing analogies, like 'the Buddhist type or the perfect cow'.[31] European Buddhism might be the fate of Europe, but it is one that must be traversed and left behind. Also, Nietzsche's valorisation of the Orient is one attuned to moments of hierarchy and caste. One Nietzsche sees in the Orient, or partly projects into the Orient, is a new hierarchical order. I do not think it is satisfact-ory to simply remark on Nietzsche's taste for paradox and provocation. Instead, Nietzsche's Orientalism is similar to his anti-anti-Semitism.[32] Just as Nietz-sche's opposition to some forms of anti-Semitism, those he sees as populist, socialist, and involving mass movements, does not involve any real sympathy or engagement with Judaism, so Nietzsche's Orientalism is not really the sign of any real sympathy with the Orient except as it serves his project of establishing a new caste order.

In both cases, this seeming identification or valorisation is more at the ser-vice of disruption than any positive engagement. Nietzsche regards Europe's others as the means to disrupt or shock Europe into awakening to its own des-tiny, which involves transcending European Buddhism and the Judeo-Christian to attain its true form. The Europe to come, for Nietzsche, is a martial and cultural power, triggered by 'Napoleon, by awakening again the man, the sol-dier, and the great fight for power – conceiving Europe as a political unit; Goethe, by imagining a European culture that would harvest the full inher-itance of attained humanity'.[33] This is the new Europe to come: hierarchical, violent, imposed from above, ordered, and Greek, in that inflection Nietzsche gives, which is to say aristocratic. It is the rediscovery of Europe as Southern, as Dionysian, 'to rediscover the South in one and to spread out above one a bright, glittering, mysterious Southern sky'.[34] It is also, ironically, the tourist Europe, although one, as with all reactionaries, that would have been lambasted by Nietzsche. So, Nietzsche's provocative remapping of Europe through its Others

29   Luisetti 2011.
30   Nietzsche 1968, p. 55.
31   Nietzsche 1968, p. 188.
32   Martin 1995, p. 143.
33   Nietzsche 1968, p. 66; on Napoleon in Nietzsche's thought see Glenn, 2001 and Dombow-sky, 2014.
34   Nietzsche 1968, p. 542; on Mediterranean fascism, see Bull 2014.

– the Orient, Judaism, the south, the Mediterranean – is one that absorbs and erases these sources into a new European synthesis of aristocratic free spirits imposing order on a slave class.

This new Europe is also potentially a global form. While Nietzsche can be critical of the petty imperialism of the late nineteenth century, which caused so much devastating suffering to colonised peoples,[35] his vision is finally of a strong Europe imposing its goals on the world. Petty imperialism would be replaced with Grand imperialism, in the same way in which a Nietzschean great politics would replace the trivial politics of democracy.[36] This is evident in this quote, which forms a precursor to Joseph Conrad's *Heart of Darkness* (1899), if much less equivocal than Conrad: 'What means one has to employ with rude peoples, and that "barbarous" means are not arbitrary and capricious, becomes palpable in practice as soon as one is placed, with all one's European pampering, in the necessity of keeping control over barbarians, in the Congo or elsewhere'.[37] While Europeans are pampered, they must become powerful to impose control over barbarity, in a classical imperialist trope. Here, as in *Heart of Darkness*, the threat lies in the violent means required by colonialism, Kurtz's 'exterminate all the brutes!', which awakens Europeans to hardness and threatens them with barbarity. For Nietzsche, this barbarity must be controlled and channelled so it can produce not only an imperial dominance but also dominance over the underprivileged internal to Europe as well. The workers, those other barbarians, must also be kept under control.

This discourse of European crisis and the traversal of Europe is another expansive vision of a Europe endless. As Timothy Brennan has detailed, and as we have traced, Nietzsche's apparent anti-European image is in the service of a new European spirit that is 'a mixed and stylistically novel fantasy of conquest and European triumphalism'.[38] While apparently lying in the self-critical notion of European thought, Nietzsche in fact re-forges a European hammer that will resolve the European crisis for Europe. The spirit of Europe emerges from and through crisis and then resolves that crisis for Europe on a global scale. To repeat this argument, in a different form, while seeming to end Europe in a radical way Nietzsche re-births the most dubious forms of Europe endless. A hierarchical, violent, and barbaric Europe is projected onto the world, or the image of the reality of this imperial project is given metaphysical dignity

---

35   Davis 2000; Hochschild 1998.
36   Nietzsche 2009, p. 89.
37   Nietzsche 1968, p. 487.
38   Brennan 2014, p. 1 95.

in Nietzsche's thought.[39] This violence is also endless because this vision can never be realised or achieved. Nietzsche remains a bridge and the overcoming remains contaminated by what it overcomes. Finally, the world (or Europe) cannot be broken in two, but rather a repeated violence tries to constantly remake Europe to achieve its real spirit. Spirit, in fact, is the word for this violent excess, this painful process of self-overcoming.[40] This difficulty of spirit is that this self-overcoming remains something to be overcome and spirit is the problem it purports to solve. In this way, Europe endless becomes endless violence and Nietzsche bequeaths this problem to the European spirit.

2   Europe-Problem

Jacques Derrida identifies a particular discourse of crisis and spirit that traces the outlines of Europe in the inter-war years: 'Here, too, one cannot overlook the common focus towards which, between 1919 and 1939, the discourses of worry gather or rush headlong: around the same words (Europe, Spirit), if not in the same language'.[41] In the middle of the European civil war, this discourse is particularly articulated, for Derrida, by Paul Valéry, in *The Crisis of Spirit* (1919), Edmund Husserl, in 'Philosophy and the Crisis of European Humanity' (1935), and by Heidegger, in the Rectoral Address (1933) and the *Introduction to Metaphysics* (1935). Derrida at once stresses the heterogeneity of these discourses and their disturbing congruences. While Derrida is locating spirit within a particular form of Western metaphysics and as a particular metaphysical concession by Heidegger, in yet another attempt to deal with Heidegger's intimate involvement with Nazism,[42] here I am more interested in this general move of identification of Europe and Spirit. In particular, I want to focus on Husserl's essay, which is saturated with the discourse of spirit.

Husserl begins the essay and the discussion of European spirit, like Nietzsche, with the issue of sickness: 'The European nations are sick; Europe itself, they say, is in critical condition'.[43] In a curious parallel to Freud, who in *Civilisation and Its Discontents* (1930) had inquired into the possibility of collective neurosis,[44] Husserl argues for the possibility of an inquiry into collective spir-

---

39   Lukács 2021.
40   Conway 2009, p. 50.
41   Derrida 1989, p. 61.
42   For a critique of Derrida's inadequacies on this point, see Rose 2017, pp. 65–87.
43   Husserl 1965, p. 150.
44   Freud 2002, p. 80.

itual illness. While Freud had doubted the possibility of a position from which to make the judgement of sickness, Husserl is much more cavalier. Husserl argues that 'our Europe-problem' has to be understood historically, out of the birth of the European spirit and how that spirit has come into crisis.[45] The sickness of Europe is self-inflicted.

This is, unsurprisingly, a story of the origin of philosophy, and particularly the Greek origin of philosophy. It is the story of the birth of the attitude of *theoria* and how that creates a particular form of infinite rationality that is, according to Husserl, particular and peculiar to Europe as a community. Husserl makes an explicitly racial discrimination of Europe as an 'environing world' (*umwelt*). This 'spiritual structure' of Europe is one to which 'belong the English dominions, the United States, etc.', i.e. white settler-colonial states, 'but not, however, the Eskimos or Indians of the country fairs, or the Gypsies, who are constantly wandering about Europe'.[46] Derrida notes that this 'sinister passage' indicates how discourses of spirit and freedom can be close to the worst.[47] Derrida also suggests that Husserl's preservation of English dominions implies the inclusion of India and so Indian people, which would not be strictly logical in a racist terms. It does not seem difficult to suggest, however, that this is a typical colonial and racist settler-colonial logic of tutelage and administration. This is reinforced by Husserl's remark that the people of India wish to 'constantly Europeanize themselves', while Europeans 'will never, for example, Indianize ourselves'.[48] Again, while being forcibly brought to the European ideal is acceptable, to depart from that is folly. It is not difficult to imagine what Husserl would have thought of European hippies travelling to India.

Husserl regards Europe as 'the unity of a spiritual life and a creative activity' that belongs to a particular community and life-world.[49] Despite recognising human history as a 'sea in which human beings, peoples, are waves constantly forming, changing, and disappearing',[50] Husserl stresses the singularity of the Greeks to a construction of Europe as 'the free fashioning of its being and its historical life out of rational ideas and infinite tasks'.[51] Europe finds its spiritual origin in Greece, which Husserl treats as a unity, as a 'nation'.[52] What originates in Greece, or in Husserl's Greece as nation, is an attitude that forms

---

45   Husserl 1965, p. 153.
46   Husserl 1965, p. 155.
47   Derrida 1989, pp. 120–1.
48   Husserl 1965, p. 157.
49   Husserl 1965, p. 155.
50   Husserl 1965, p. 156.
51   Husserl 1965, p. 156.
52   Husserl 1965, p. 158.

science and philosophy as an attention to the world in its infinite forms. This is a disinterested attitude that also aims at the universal. It is 'a spirit of free criticism providing norms for infinite tasks, ..., creating new, infinite ideals'.[53] Husserl argues that this attitude is sustained and exercised through European man who therefore has the 'role of leadership for the whole of mankind'.[54] While we might want to consider the singularity of philosophy in particular forms and consider the historical conditions of its emergence (for example, Alfred Sohn-Rethel's suggestion of philosophy as abstract universal emerges from the abstractions of money and trade[55]), Husserl simply asserts the unity of Europe with Greece, as origin, and the unity of its spirit with a singular community.

What, then, is the source of the European crisis? Husserl argues that this is a crisis due to rationality, but not a crisis of rationality *in toto*. Philosophy is the 'idea of an infinite task', but the risk is falling into the claim we have realised philosophy or limit it into a one-sided form.[56] In particular, the problem has been the domination of mathematical and objective knowledge of the world, which occludes spiritual knowledge. The result is that this objective and psychophysical notion of the human causes reason and the forms of spirit to fracture. Husserl's solution is that sciences of spirit must not mimic objective science, but return to themselves against 'naïve exteriorization'.[57] The resolution is Husserlian phenomenology, which through attention to intentionality recovers an 'absolutely autonomous science of spirit'.[58] Spirit is not subject to nature, but nature belongs to spirit. The ego is also not isolated but intimately related to other beings. The resolution is an extreme subjectivism in which the world is reduced to the subject before being rediscovered in these communitarian and nationalist forms.

The crisis of Europe can therefore be resolved by the turn to phenomenology, which would recover the spirit of Europe as an infinite task. In a very Nietzschean vein, Husserl declares that 'Europe's greatest danger is weariness'.[59] Husserl even cites Nietzsche's good Europeans. Europe must overcome its alienation from the reason and take up again the vital task of reason. Europe must embrace the 'mission to humanity', in which spirit will be reborn.[60] We see

---

53   Husserl 1965, p. 177.
54   Husserl 1965, p. 178.
55   Sohn-Rethel 1978, p. 67.
56   Husserl 1965, p. 180.
57   Husserl 1965, p. 189.
58   Husserl 1965, p. 190.
59   Husserl 1965, p. 192.
60   Husserl 1965, p. 192.

that an extreme subjectivism promises the resolution of crisis as a subjective matter, a matter of thought, detached from any objective dimensions of crisis, especially imperialism and the crisis of capital begun in 1929. Husserl's is perhaps the most explicit version of Europe endless, with Europe as the origin and bearer of philosophy as infinite task. It is also similarly problematic to Nietzsche's in a global projection of Europe, specified in a limited and racialised fashion. What Husserl projects out from and in doing so constructs is a limited life-world that polices its own borders. Husserl also adds a fear of the determination and realisation of spirit, in which spirit remains mere regulative Idea in the Kantian sense. In this way, spirit polices without ever really emerging or actualising itself.

This limitation of the life world is also evident in Husserl's *Cartesian Meditations* (1931). In the famous fifth meditation, which considers the other and transcendental intersubjectivity, Husserl deduces the life world as the open and transcendental relation to others. Yet, while this would seem the most open and global form of relation, at the same time this is also delimited. Husserl declares that products of spirit, 'all cultural Objects', 'carry with them ... the experiential sense of thereness-for-everyone' but only 'everyone belonging to the corresponding cultural community, such as the European'.[61] So, while it seems we should belong to a universal cultural world, in fact we live in 'concrete life-worlds in which the relatively or absolutely separate communities live their passive and active lives'.[62] We are historically rooted in a community, according to Husserl, and so this community is 'barred to anyone from another community'. While Husserl continues by suggesting the possibility of opening out understanding through sympathy, we can see again, as with the European idea, how a transcendental openness or relationality is radically delimited into a community. While resisting realisation of the universal, what is preserved is the particular.

To return to Husserl's essay, we find in its closing discourse of heroism and risk an embrace of the Nietzschean style. The problem of the realisation of reason is not addressed and reason is left as infinite and infinitely deferred. So, we have something infinite that is, at the same time, always preserved and limited to a particular community. Subjectivity is not replaced with objectivity, but with a higher (or grounding) subjectivity that is community.[63] Reason is surreptitiously confined to a particular group and left as a critical resource

---

61   Husserl 1977, p. 92.
62   Husserl 1977, p. 133.
63   Nancy 1991.

that can always find any realisation wanting, but at the same time is therefore unable to function effectively as a criticism. Sickness is diagnosed and heroism called for, but the disease is left fundamentally untouched so it can remain to constantly spur efforts to cure. The realisation of philosophy in a life-world is left vague and at the same time delimited to Europe. While Husserl cannot help but recognise the spread and displacement of this new attitude of philosophy, at the same time this also becomes another infinite task, rather than a series of transformations and instantiations. The notion of reason as global, as emerging across multiple spaces and engaging the world, is denied by a vision that simply extends reason from fantasmatic fusion of Greece and Europe. In Husserl's proclamation of European spirit, we find the full vision of Europe as infinite task and the foundering of that vision.

In this manner the crisis of philosophy is rendered as a permanent crisis, but this denial of resolution does not imply a weakening of philosophy. Instead, we are left with a philosophy that maintains itself as a radical subjectivism that is then incarnated in particular communities, while the crisis of philosophy is an internal matter to philosophy, even in its broader effects. The resolution of crisis can only be hinted at as a resolution by and through the subject and any objective elements of crisis, any sense of the actual life-world, is left as merely reflective of this philosophical crisis. While cast in the language of reason, which is its merit, Husserl's thinking of crisis, as we have argued, remains profoundly Nietzschean. The crisis of Europe is Nietzsche's crisis and this crisis is an internal matter for the resolution by a fantasmatic European subject – the good European with a vengeance.

3   Conclusion: Spirits of Crisis

Crisis now seems to have settled in to being a constant state, if that wasn't always the case. What Berardi calls austeritarian rule has not only settled in across Europe, and globally, but also taken on aggressive populist and potentially proto-fascist forms.[64] In this situation, Europe endless, Europe as the infinite task of rationality, as the spirit and promise of philosophical reason, seems both further away than ever (including the state of philosophy as an educational subject) and more desirable than ever (for some). In this situation ending Europe also appears more urgent than ever, including if we are to realise another Europe or a new Europe that would resolve or mitigate the global

---

64   Berardi et al 2018.

capitalist and ecological crisis, which are interwoven together.[65] We could add that philosophical considerations like this one might seem, precisely, luxuries we can no longer afford, in an austerity of thought that must engage the urgency and austerity of the moment.

While understanding all this, and agreeing with some, if not all, of these contentions, I have also made a claim to resist an austerity of thought. To collapse the problem of Europe endless, I have suggested, is to risk repeating it, rather than working it through, to use a convenient Freudian distinction. That said, it should be evident that I share a dissatisfaction with the Kantian form of the regulative idea of Europe as infinite task, even when that is cast in its best form: one that strives towards the open and the possibilities of transformation and displacement that have composed the history of philosophical rationality. The difficulty I have identified with this conception of Europe is its fear of actualisation and realisation, which chimes with those reactionary critiques of reason and revolution that have always feared and resisted the re-ordering of existence that such a realisation would demand.

There is also that risk of reading the particular crisis of capitalism, including the global crisis of 2007–8, as another crisis of Europe and the claims to a European civilisation. This is precisely the problem of treating Nietzsche as the philosopher of Europe at face value. The danger is that Nietzsche provides a way of reading capitalist crisis as presaging or realising the crisis of civilisation, treated as European civilisation, and so ushering in the potential for new hierarchical and imperial orderings on a global scale as the solution.[66] Nietzsche takes the problem of crisis away from reality and places it, instead, into a fantasmatic space in which crisis is made and resolved at the level of the subject or in the form of the transcendence of the subject in which that transcendence still departs from reality. This action is one that places the subject not only as the individual, but also as Europe itself, often violently delimited, as the global financial crisis is re-read as the crises of Europe.

The same problems would beset the Husserlian reading of crisis, which we have seen is indebted to Nietzsche. Nietzsche's own trans-national European project of domination remains secreted within the conceptions of European crisis and Europe as infinite task of realisation. As we have noted, Husserl's radical subjectivism is not so much a solution or displacement of crisis, which it claims to be, but another intensification and radicalisation of crisis away from objective reality. Of course, Husserl claims that this subject is the only way

---

65   Moore 2015; Malm 2015.
66   Losurdo 2019.

back to reality, particularly spiritual reality, but, as we have seen, such a return to reality is one limited to particular national or supra-national communities that create another level of subjectivity. Also, the resolution of crisis becomes another subjective matter, and the problem of crisis is both removed from reality and removed from any definitive resolution.

Even the critical re-readings of this project by Derrida and Gasché do not, I think, fully escape or work through these tensions. They try to explode the problem of subjectivity, but they do not significantly displace it. Instead, we are left with an intensification of the Husserlian and Kantian projects, with Nietzsche left lurking as the disturbing figure that impels much of the pathos of the narrative of crisis. That is because the dissolution of the subject, as in Nietzsche, can itself lead to an identification of the subject with reality and the subjectivation of reality itself.[67] The ultra-transcendentalism of Derrida and Gasché is valuable for trying to displace these elements and remaining with the legacy of the rational found in Husserl.[68] All this critical acumen, however, cannot break out of the notion of the realisation of Europe as an infinite task and cannot deal adequately with the problem of crisis and its impact on philosophical thinking.

Therefore, my conclusion is that we consider a discourse of spirit that is devoted to grasping the various shapes of consciousness and materiality in which spirit forms and develops. In short, the Hegelian account.[69] Spirit and the infinite do not stand above a fallen world, as judge and executioner, but work and sacrifice themselves in that world. Such a working of spirit is one that constantly realises itself and takes on particular material figures of that realisation. In Nietzsche and Husserl, we see the shaping of a neo-Kantian form that both incites and defers realisation. This is also an ideal of Europe rooted in hierarchy, in modes of community and in forms of realisation that have led to disaster. Alternative critical realisations of another Europe, still cast in the form of the infinite task, do not resolve these toxic legacies but risk repeating traces of them secreted in thought.

Instead, of course, any sort of internationalist realisation, of the type that communism first defined, seem farther away than ever, in Europe and elsewhere. Derrida states that: 'And communism was essentially distinguished from other labour movements by its international character. No organised political movement in the history of humanity had ever yet presented itself as geo-political, thereby inaugurating the space that is now ours and that today is

---

67   Klossowski 2007, p. 100.
68   Dews 2007.
69   Hegel 1977; Rose 2009.

reaching its limits, the limits of the earth and the limits of the political'.[70] This geo-political movement now seems to be dominated by capital at the expense of this other world. That such possibilities of realisation seem further away than ever, in Europe in particular, should be recognised. This might speak to one particular understanding of crisis, which involves a global dimension that cannot be resolved at the level of Europe. The retreat from Europe to the nation state would be another ironic effect of this global dimension and its intractability. In the face of global crisis, the retreat is to defend the nation-state against any opening. This must be resisted, of course, but to simply claim to relaunch the infinite task of European spirit, in whatever guise, is also inadequate. Instead, I suggest we recognise forms of the actualisation and realisation of rationality, collectivity, and freedom that could resolve the situation of crisis, in and beyond Europe. These include those realisations and actualisations that are global and would, again, displace or transform Europe and the global situation. The loss of Europe would then be a global task that resolves crisis in a moment of global transformation.

---

70   Derrida 1994, p. 47.

PART 3

Crisis and Communisation

∵

CHAPTER 7

Communisation and the Fabric of Struggles

Barely thirty years have passed since the collapse of actually-existing socialism and already we have witnessed the crisis of actually-existing capitalism, in its neo-liberal version, in 2008–9. The shrill capitalist triumphalism of the 1990s, embodied in Fukuyama's thesis of the end of history,[1] or the bellicose equation of capitalism with democracy that defined the 2000s war on terror, now rings more than a little hollow after the resulting frozen desert of burst financial bubbles and devalorisation. The commodities that make up the capitalist way of life have turned malignant, exposed as hollow bearers of debt servitude that can never be paid off. The cry 'No New Deal' goes up as wealth is transferred in huge amounts to save the financial sector.[2] We have lived another round of sacrifice as structural adjustment and shock doctrine return to the centre of global capitalism after extensive testing on its self-defined peripheries.[3] Whether this is terminal crisis, entropic drift, or merely the prelude to the creative destruction that will kick-start a new round of accumulation, still remains obscure.

In this situation new waves and forms of struggle have emerged in dispersed and inchoate forms. We have also seen a new language being used to theorise and think these struggles: the human strike, the imaginary party, clandestinity and, not least, the strange and spectral word communisation. The concept of communisation emerged from currents of the French ultra-left in the late 1960s and early 1970s, but has gained resonance as a way of posing the problem of struggle today. It draws attention to the exhaustion of existing forms of organisation that have tried to lead, dictate or pre-empt struggles; contests the tendency to affirm or adopt an alternative counter-identity (worker, militant, anarchist, activist, etc.); and challenges the despotism of capitalism that treats us as sources of value.

It is necessary to clarify the conceptual stakes of communisation, as both theory and as 'real movement'.[4] Here I focus on tensions, problems, and difficulties that beset this particular form of communism, while no doubt more

---

1   Fukuyama 1992.
2   Negri 2009.
3   Klein 2007.
4   Marx and Engels 2011, p. 26.

sympathetic accounts and uses of communisation exist.[5] It is not easy to define what the word communisation refers to, and it has often been used more as a slogan, a nickname, or even worse a brand, that forces together very different perspectives and analyses. What we find in communisation is often a weird mixing-up of insurrectional anarchists, the communist ultra-left, post-Autonomists, anti-political currents, groups like the Invisible Committee, as well as more explicitly communising currents, such as Théorie Communiste and Endnotes. Obviously at the heart of the word is communism and, as the shift to communisation suggests, communism as a particular activity and process, but what that is requires some further exploration.

Here I want to give some initial points of orientation by analysing the communising arguments that pose struggles as immediate, immanent, and as anti-identity. In each case I want to treat these points as sites of dispute, especially between the theorisations of the well-known contemporary French radical grouping associated with the journal *Tiqqun*, also publishing under the name the Invisible Committee (henceforth I will refer to them as Tiqqun for convenience), on the one hand, and the less-known but explicitly communising currents of Théorie Communiste and Endnotes, on the other.

What does it mean to say that communisation is or should be immediate? It suggests there is no transition to communism, no stage of socialism required before we can achieve the stage of communism, and so no need to build communism. It dismisses the category socialism and displaces or disavows the category of transition.[6] This, however, has a very different meaning in different hands. For Tiqqun, and others influenced by anarchist prefigurative politics, this immediacy means that we must begin enacting communism now, within capitalism. From the commune to commoning, from cyber-activism to new forms-of-life, in this perspective we cannot make any transition to communism but must live it as a reality now to ensure its eventual victory. On the other hand, Théorie Communiste and Endnotes give this immediacy a rather different sense, by arguing that communisation implies the immediacy of communism in the process of revolution. In fact, they are deeply suspicious of a prefigurative or alternative politics, regarding such forms of struggle as mired in capitalism and often moralistic. They critique Tiqqun and the Invisible Committee on this exact basis.[7] Instead, if anything, contemporary struggles can only be negatively prefigurative, indicating the limits of our forms of struggle and indicating only possible new lines of attack.

---

5   Clover 2016.
6   Toscano 2014.
7   Mattis 2011.

These differences also reflect on another key way of posing the problem of communisation in terms of immanence. The point here is that communisation requires that we start thinking communism from within the immanent conditions of global capitalism, but again this can lead in very different directions. Tiqqun regard capitalism as globally dominant, but also see it as leaving spaces and times through which revolt can emerge, or into which revolt can slip away from power. They regard capitalism as porous or, in Deleuze and Guattari's formulation, 'holey'.[8] Again, this kind of enclave theory is a familiar strategy, ranging from the Italian social centres, to squats, to communal gardening, communes themselves, and other practices of commoning. This kind of formulation appeals to struggles in progress, to activists, and so links with the claim for a prefigurative immediacy. Again, we might not be surprised to see that Théorie Communiste and Endnotes disagree. They too regard capitalism as dominant, but as a contradictory totality fissured by class struggles between proletariat and capital. There is no outside, or line of flight, but only a thinking through of this immanent contradiction and antagonism secreted within capitalist exploitation of labour to extract value.

In terms of the contesting of identity, Tiqqun develop a new clandestine or invisible identity of the militant that escapes capitalist control and capture. Refusing the old identity models of Marxism, the working class or proletariat, as well as the new models of identity politics, they instead prefer the language of contemporary theory: whatever singularities, or post-identity models that intimate new forms-of-life. In contrast, Théorie Communiste and Endnotes retain the classical Marxist language of the proletariat, but insist that this is not an identity, but rather a mode of self-abolishing. We cannot reinforce a workers' identity, or try to replace this with another identity. Instead, the negativity of the proletariat consists in the fact it can only operate by abolishing itself.

If there are analytic disagreements over the forms that the struggle should take, there seems to be initial agreement about what communisation opposes: capitalism. Again, however, this is actually a point of contention. Many in the communising current adopt a variant of Marx's distinction, from the unpublished sixth chapter of capital, the 'Results of the Immediate Process of Production',[9] between formal and real subsumption. Formal subsumption is the general form of capitalist domination, and involves capital subsuming an existing form of production as it finds it. For example, peasants may still work in

---

8   Deleuze and Guattari 1998, pp. 413–15.
9   Marx 1990, pp. 1019–38.

the fields in the way they always have but now they are compelled to take their goods to market to realise value. In this mode of subsumption, Marx argues, capital generates absolute surplus-value, and can only do so by demanding extension to the working day. So, surplus-value can only be generated by forcing work beyond the amount necessary for self-reproduction, although this compulsion does not tend to happen directly but through economic functions, i.e. you need to produce a surplus to generate income to live, rather than to pay off a feudal lord. This stands in contrast to real subsumption, in which capital revolutionises the actual mode of labour to produce the specifically capitalist mode of production. Here the compulsion can increase relative surplus-value by the use of machinery, the intensification of labour and the remaking of the production process. We could see the transformation of agriculture to modern mechanised farming, with its extensive use of mechanisation, fertilisers, and mono-cropping, to extract as much value with intensified use of labour, as an instance of real subsumption.

Within communisation, and especially for Théorie Communiste, Marx's distinction is taken as a model of historical periodisation. While Marx, and others like Endnotes,[10] see formal and real subsumption as intertwined processes that have developed with capitalism and take different forms, the periodising argument suggests that we have shifted from formal subsumption to real subsumption. In the argument of Théorie Communiste this shift is linked to cycles of struggle. In the initial phase of capitalist accumulation, we have formal subsumption, and class struggle expresses itself in the affirmation of a precapitalist identity and moral economy.[11] With the advance of real subsumption, in the industrial form of the factory during the latter half of the nineteenth century, we see a new antagonism of the worker versus capitalism, which reaches its apogee in the Russian Revolution. In this new cycle of struggles central is the independent workers' identity, and Théorie Communiste call this form of struggle programmatism.[12] Here the forms of struggle actually become internal to capitalism, as the relation becomes mediated through unions, social welfare, and other forms of Keynesian control. These revolutions tend to reinforce capitalism, encouraging the passage from formal to real subsumption through socialist accumulation, and lead to the theology of labour and the oxymoron of the workers' state. This form comes into crisis with the struggles of the 1960s and 1970s, which indicate the crisis of programmatism. Workers now

---

10   Endnotes 2010.
11   Thompson 2013.
12   Théorie Communiste 2008.

abolish their identities, and flee the factory and other forms of social control. The extension of real subsumption over life, what Italian Operaists and Autonomists called the social factory,[13] generalises struggles. In the capitalist counter-attack, however, we witness a second phase of real subsumption; a re-making of the world in conformity to capital and the crisis of the identity of the worker. This re-making was, of course, central to the project of neo-liberalism.[14]

Such an analysis is shared by Jacques Camatte, Antonio Negri, and many other post-Autonomists. It could seem to imply the pessimistic conclusion that resistance is futile, that capitalism is a monstrous alien subject that vampiric-ally draws all of life within itself (to mix Marx's gothic metaphors). Such a position was visible in the Frankfurt school's positing of a totally-administered or one-dimensional society.[15] It is taken today by certain currents of primitivism or anti-civilisation anarchism, which desperately try to recover the remaining fragments of non-capitalist life.[16] Communisation, in contrast, regards the passage to the dominance of real subsumption as requiring new forms of struggle and antagonism, and the abandoning of the affirmation of the worker and workers' power. New conditions call for new modes of struggle, and new conditions limit or make futile past forms of struggle. We confront new landscapes of class and class struggle that we must read beyond the limits of programmatism.[17]

Again, differences emerge at this point. Negri and the post-Autonomists tend to argue for the emergence of the power of the multitude,[18] which is always ready to burst through the capitalist integument and install communism; Tiqqun stress new singularities, new forms-of-life, which escape or flee or declare war on the forms and structures of real subsumption; Théorie Communiste argue for new self-abolishing relations of struggle as the contradictions sharpen and the proletariat is no longer a viable identity in capitalism and so communism only really becomes possible now; Gilles Dauvé and Karl Nesic prefer to see communisation as an immanent possibility of struggles across the history of capitalism, an invariant of the capitalist mode of production;[19] Endnotes accept the diagnosis of the crisis of programmatism, but reject the

---

13   Tronti 2019, pp. 12–35.
14   Foucault 2008.
15   Marcuse 2002.
16   Camatte 1995; Perlman 1983; Zerzan 1998.
17   Neel 2018.
18   Hardt and Negri 2000.
19   Dauvé and Nesic 2008. This is similar to Badiou's theory of communist invariants, see Badiou 2013, p. 43.

bluntness of the periodisation of subsumption by Théorie Communiste and others. While different in expression and consequences, what we can see is that communisation demands a reformulation of modes of struggle that are equal to contemporary conditions.

Without wishing to collapse these important differences, we can see the emphasis on the horizon of capitalism as dominant, even in the moment of crisis. It is capitalism that forms the terrain and fabric of struggles which communisation tries to engage with and theorise. It is also class struggle and capitalist responses to that struggle that have re-posed the crisis of the workers' movement and pose the need to create new modes of thinking contemporary struggles. That said, how we think and understand the form and history of capitalism is a crucial point of debate to develop forms of struggle against it, and different understandings lead to very different conclusions. While, at times, currents of communisation can seem to suppose that the riddle of history has been definitively answered by the emergence of capitalism as fully real subsumption, historical and critical problems remain.

I want to baldly state some of the (interconnected) problems that seem to immediately face communisation as a theory. The first is that the final collapse of actually-existing socialism in 1989, and the widespread disenchantment with social democracy, unions, and other forms of traditional affirmations of the worker as means of resistance, does not seem, as yet, to have led to any rebound to a self-abolishing model of proletarian negativity or the multitude, or whatever singularities, or other new modes of struggle. While programmatism is obviously in crisis, a replacement is not evident.[20] Of course, it could always be argued that these forms of struggle are still emerging,[21] still nascent, or that their lack of appearance is a sign of a transition beyond programmatism, but in the context of capitalist crisis, and capitalist-induced ecological crisis, this does not seem to offer much reassurance.[22] While the workers' states were often terrible and bloody failures, not least for the working class, the emergence of an alternative real movement is hard to detect to say the least. Even the austerity of the Théorie Communiste position, which prefers to only negatively trace emergent forms of struggle and their limits, still depends on a minimal teleology of possible revolution, and so still has to confront this problem.

A second problem, which I have already noted in passing, is that the triumph of real subsumption, which integrates the reproduction of the proletariat to the self-reproduction of capital, seems to allow very little space, or time, for

---

20   Elliott 2008.
21   Clover 2016.
22   Malm 2017b.

resistance. Even if we do not think in terms of real subsumption, but rather the global dominance of capitalism or Empire, we still have to confront the issue of whether it can be defeated, and how. The ways in which capitalism permeates and modulates the whole of life (what Deleuze called 'the society of control')[23] leaves us with little leverage to resist. It appears that we can think capitalism as a totality, but that we lack any thinking of a totality of life and existence that lies beyond (and before) capitalism.

In particular the end of the workers' standpoint, the end of the classical proletariat, seems to deprive us of an agency to make the mass changes communisation would require. While Théorie Communiste insist on the proletariat as conceptual marker, they have to struggle with its empirical non-emergence. This leaves us with a question: 'How can the proletariat, acting strictly as a class of this mode of production, in its contradiction with capital within the capitalist mode of production, abolish classes, and therefore itself, that is to say: produce communism?'[24] The alternative articulations of possible agents of change, such as immaterial workers or whatever singularities, by other currents of communisation, are very thinly specified and seem more hopeful than real. We need to rethink the problem of totality and the problem of agency together, beyond the contours of the totality of capitalism and its 'automatic subject'.

This leads to a third problem. While communisation insists on immediacy and the abandonment of debates about transition or teleology, i.e. debates on what we are aiming to achieve, it is hard to see how it can coordinate or develop such moments of communisation globally across the social field (as it would have to, to destroy or counter a global capitalism). This is true for those who emphasise communising now, in which case how do such moments come together and avoid remaining merely alternative? It is also true if we regard communising as intrinsic to revolution, because then we must answer how the process of communising can be coordinated in a revolution that will be geographically and temporally striated, dispersed and differential? Franco Fortini posed the problem in this way: 'But the only possibility of an initial world-scale communist victory still remains subordinate to the capacity of internationally coordinating those united by social antagonism against the general mechanism of exploitation'.[25]

Théorie Communiste do ask: 'How can a "unity" arise, in a general movement of class struggle, that is not in fact a unity but an inter-activity?'; their answer is rather unsatisfactory: 'We do not know ... But class struggle has often showed us

---

23   Deleuze 1992.
24   Théorie Communiste in Endnotes 2010, p. 152.
25   Fortini 2013, p. 52.

its infinite inventiveness'.[26] Pending proof of this inventiveness, there is a risk that communisation becomes a valorisation of only fleeting moments of revolt, of small chinks in which the light of revolution penetrates capitalist darkness; or that it become the promise of a total revolution that will achieve its aim in process, without any substantial account of how that might take place.

This is not to call for a simple return to the party form, although critical redevelopments of that form have emerged,[27] and a rethinking may well be necessary. It is also not to simply rehash debates concerning Leninism, although these debates might remain more important and resonant than we think.[28] Rather, it is to suggest that the difficulty in specifying agents of change can also flow into the difficulties in specifying the contents of change. Certainly, communisation was right to critique the formalism of the left, what Théorie Communiste calls its programmatism, which often seemed to suppose the correct form (Leninist party, workers' councils, etc.) guaranteed communism would unfold. What is as yet unclear is what forms of struggle will make 'the poetry of the future'.[29]

These are, of course, not only problems for communisation, but for any attempts to make radical change. What I want to stress is the acuity with which communisation allows us to pose these problems, and the stress it places on engaging with them, rather than presuming they will be dissolved in some rush to praxis. Communisation as a problematic links together issues of the current state of struggle, and their seeming disappearance in traditional forms, the nature of capitalism and the possible agents who might resist this social formation, and the strategic or tactical forms that resistance might or will take.

In his story 'The Two Kings and the Two Labyrinths', Jorge Luis Borges describes the competition between two kings to construct the perfect, and so impossible to escape, labyrinth or maze.[30] The first king uses the traditional method of constructing a highly complex series of tunnels, resulting in a terrible labyrinth which the second king only escapes from by the intervention of God. In his turn the second king lays waste to the first king's lands and casts him into a labyrinth impossible to defeat: the desert. The impossibility of this labyrinth lies not in the choice of paths, but the absence of any paths. For Tiqqun we are living in a 'desert that incessantly deepens', the neutralisation of

---

26   Théorie Communiste 2009.
27   Dean 2018.
28   Malm 2020; Heron and Dean 2022.
29   Marx 2019, p. 483.
30   Borges 1999, pp. 263–4.

means to orient ourselves and escape the labyrinth of capital.[31] This may over-state the case. Capitalism is not a featureless terrain or 'smooth space',[32] but it certainly is proving to be a labyrinth that is hard to traverse. I do not want to suggest that communisation is our compass or that it exhaustively maps the desert. Many other paths are possible; in fact, in the desert we face not so much a garden of forking paths but the infinite multiplicity of paths we cannot even yet trace. Communisation does pose the question of what paths there might be, refusing to accept the capitalist desert as natural phenomenon and beginning to detect the struggles and thinking required to re-make this terrain.

---

31   Invisible Committee 2016, p. 7.
32   Deleuze and Guattari 1998, pp. 474–500.

CHAPTER 8

Communisation and the End of Art

There is no obvious reason why communisation theory – the theory of revolution as immediate communist measures, developed out of the French ultra-left of the 1970s – should necessarily have anything to do with the practice of art. There are contingent reasons for this encounter: the interest and involvement of artists in recent protests and movements, the reflections by artists on that experience, and the emergence of communisation theory (in various forms) during the moment of capitalist crisis. Here I want to explore the deeper links that might help to develop this convergence. Crucial to my discussion is the question of impossibility: for communisation theory, this is the suggestion that the limit of contemporary struggles lies in the fact they can no longer affirm the identity of the worker, whereas for artistic practice, this lies in the encounter of artists and art theorists with the limits and ends of art and the identity of the artist.[1]

I want to explore this fairly abstract statement of a possible convergence through the fault line or fracture that runs through the problem of struggles at the present moment. First, I will sketch the way communisation theory, particularly the form of that theory articulated by Théorie Communiste, poses the problem of our present moment. This is the thesis of the crisis of the identity of the worker, or what they call the end of programmatism, as characterising contemporary struggles. This analysis can be linked to the problem of art practice through the reflections of Roland Simon, a leading theorist of Théorie Communiste, on the attempt by the Situationist International to hold together the critique of the workers' movement and the critique of art. Then, I want to consider how we have inherited this tension in the current conjuncture and how we might think together communisation and the practice of art.

A few caveats and cautions are necessary from the beginning. First, speaking of a singular communisation theory is intensely problematic. I will largely be referring to the analysis of Théorie Communiste and related groups, but at points I want to draw out other strands or approaches that have linked themselves to communisation (see Chapter 7). The risk here is homogenising a disparate and conflicted space. Much the same could also be said about my

---

1   Noys 2019.

discussion of art and artistic practice. Here I will be concerned predominantly with attempts by artists to take on or develop a political practice of art and how that might be affected by communisation. Finally, I should make it clear from the beginning that I do not agree with every element of communisation theory. What interests me and what I want to develop is the way certain forms of communisation pose a rigorously negative conception of practice and struggle at present. Therefore, what follows is a preliminary attempt to trace the emergence and convergence of a common problematic.

1   The End of Programmatism

What characterises many forms of contemporary communisation is a belief in the persistence of forms of class struggle, but also the decline or crisis of the traditional forms these struggles took. This thesis is articulated by Théorie Communiste as the end of programmatism. In the words of Théorie Communiste, programmatism refers to 'a theory and practice of class struggle in which the proletariat finds, in its drive toward liberation, the fundamental elements of a future social organisation which become the programme to be realised. This revolution is thus the affirmation of the proletariat, whether as a dictatorship of the proletariat, workers' councils, the liberation of work, a period of transition, the withering of the state, generalised self-management, or a 'society of associated producers''.[2] Programmatism, as a particular form of practice, assumes that class struggle depends on the assertion of the autonomy of the proletariat. Théorie Communiste argue that this assertion of autonomy, ironically, links the proletariat to capital and leaves it within the form of capitalist reproduction as the necessary support of capital.

In the historical account of Théorie Communiste, the decomposition of programmatism takes place as this relational link between capital and labour comes apart under the twin shearing pressures of class struggle and capitalism's recomposition. Beginning in the 1970s, a new phase of real subsumption takes place as capitalism penetrates further into all areas of life and, at the same time, workers struggle against the imposition of work. The result is that the identity of the worker can no longer form an internal antagonistic pole – both included and somehow autonomous from capital. The decomposition of programmatism can be read in the collapse of so-called workers' states, the decline of unions, and the crisis of various social democratic forms of welfarism.

---

2   Théorie Communiste 2008, p. 155.

The conclusion drawn by Théorie Communiste is that today, struggles have to take place at the limit of any reproduction of the worker. In the case of workers' struggles, this 'rift' (*l'écart*) is indicated in suicidal struggles, which register the limit that class identity forms.[3] The result is the burning down of factories, attempts to claim as high a redundancy payment as possible, and other exits from work.[4] Crashing against the limit that capitalism itself can no longer sustain, which is the worker's identity, this means that the tragedy and possibility of struggle today lies in a rift from this identity and the confrontation with class as an exteriority. In this moment there can be a fleeting de-essentialisation of labour, and it is this moment that is negatively prefigurative of a communising process.[5] That is, the revolution emerges on the horizon as an immediate process of communising measures due to the impossibility of any sustained alternative or autonomous form of identity that could be posed against capitalism. The impossibility of the identity of the worker as a sustainable identity produces or incites the possibility of the negation of that identity.

If we take the parallel Alain Badiou draws between the political avant-garde of the Leninist Party and the artistic avant-garde of the 1920s in *The Century* (2005),[6] we could suggest that both forms have been hollowed out. If the political avant-garde of programmatism is exhausted then, we could add, so is the programme of the avant-garde: small groups, privileged artists, the manifesto, etc. If we can no longer affirm the critical autonomy of the worker, then neither can we continue to affirm the critical autonomy of the avant-garde. In *Logics of Worlds* (2006), Badiou argues that our present situation is characterised by a 'democratic materialism' that reduces life to the atomised state of 'bodies and languages'.[7] I would combine this diagnosis with the argument of *The Century* to suggest that the 'passion for the real' of the short twentieth century,[8] concentrated in the party and programme, has now fragmented to splinters of the real, localised in individual bodies. In fact, Badiou's exemplar for this situation is postmodern art and its theorisation by Antonio Negri, which revels in its tracking of the 'manifestness of bodies', which leaves us with a 'materialism of life'.[9] The present moment would then be one of an experience of fragmentation in

---

3   Bernes 2020.
4   Simon 2011, p. 119.
5   Simon 2011, p. 120.
6   Badiou 2007.
7   Badiou 2009b, p. 1.
8   Badiou 2007.
9   Badiou 2009b, p. 2.

both art and politics, and the question or problem of recomposing forms of struggle and creation. In Badiou's case, he argues that we need to reinvent the earlier moment through extracting its 'subtractive moment' – exemplified by Malevich's painting 'White on White' (1919) – to guide a subtractive practice of art and politics that can disrupt the supersaturated regime of democratic materialism.[10]

Of course, declarations of the death of the avant-garde and calls for a reinvention of the avant-garde are commonplace to the point of banality; even the proposals of relational or post-production art by Nicolas Bourriaud borrow this trope.[11] The difficulty lies in what kinds of possibilities and functions of art and artistic practice might operate in the wake of the end of the programme of the avant-garde. Badiou does not endorse a radically new situation, but rather explores a qualified fidelity, which tries to redraw possibilities and lessons from the tensions of the original avant-garde and communist projects.[12] To anticipate, communisation theory will pose a less programmatic solution to this problem, preferring, in the case of Théorie Communiste, a more rigorously negative and non-prefigurative politics that explores the tensions and contradictions of the present moment, rather than offering a subtractive exit.

2   Exploding Programmatism

To consider the implications of communisation theory for artistic practice, I now want to turn to the critique offered by Roland Simon, a leading theorist of Théorie Communiste, of the ultra-left practice of the Situationist International. From the beginning, in 1957, the Situationist International tried to hold together the critical practice of art and that of politics. In their practice of revolutionary urbanism, détournement (the reuse of existing images turned to radical ends), and film, the Situationist International attempted the realisation and suppression of art in revolutionary practice. This involved an acute awareness on the part of the SI of the tensions of this position. In his last film *In Girum Imus Nocte et Consumimur Igni* (1978), Guy Debord, de facto leader of the Situationist International, reflected on the adventure of the group. In his commentary, Debord stated: 'Avant-gardes have only one time; and the best thing

---

10   Badiou 2007, p. 56.
11   Bourriaud 2002; 2005.
12   Noys 2009.

that can happen to them is to have enlivened their time without outliving it'.[13] Despite this awareness of finitude, according to Simon, Debord and the Situationists remain in an uncomfortable tension. On the one hand, they are able to trace out the end of art and work, and the impossibility of proceeding in terms set even by an ultra-left programme (primarily the form of workers' councils). In this sense, they come close to the realisation of the end of programmatism and the theorisation of communisation. On the other hand, they have nothing to replace this programme with, and so fall back on nostalgia or practices that invoke the old models that they have rejected, again workers' councils or, in art, the gesture of Dada and the negative avant-garde. In Roland Simon's formulation, 'I think the Situationist International led programmatism to its point of explosion'.[14]

While the Situationist International aimed at a dialectical supersession of art through its suppression and realisation in revolutionary practice, they tended to remain split between the aesthetic and the political. In the first aesthetic moment, the constructed situations of the early Situationist International presage revolution in the forms of enclaves or moments within the reign of the spectacle.[15] They are affirmative counter-possibilities, and this belief in a counter-art remains close to the belief in an affirmative proletarian identity found in council communism by the Situationist International. The aesthetic Situationists continue to make art as they continue to make revolution. In 1962, at the prompting of Guy Debord, most artists and elements of the artistic avant-garde were expelled from the group. This might seem to indicate the termination of the attempt to integrate art and politics and so the politicisation of the Situationist International. The aesthetic, however, continues to find a role in the later Situationist International, often in the form of nostalgia for past adventures and possibilities.

For Roland Simon, it is the penetration of real subsumption – the dominance of capitalism that reworks the production process to capitalist ends – that signalled the end of the prefigurative and artistic possibilities embodied in the first phase of the Situationist International. The end of this possibility, along with the end of an alternative working-class identity, means that no such moments of aesthetic construction of situations or artworks can be realised under the dominance of capital. In contrast, following through on the rigorous negativity of revolution, the suppression of art and the politicisation of

---

13   Debord 2003, p. 182.
14   Simon and riff-raff 2006.
15   Situationist International 1989, pp. 17–25.

the Situationist International indicates a recognition that art can only take place within the revolutionary process – within communisation. Therefore, constructed situations might better describe the process of revolution – qua communisation – than the pre-revolutionary and prefigurative process of triggering revolution.

In the case of the Situationist International, this rigorously negative formulation keeps relapsing into ambiguous gestures. The so-called pessimism of the later Debord can be seen as a sign of the difficulty in holding on to this rigorous negative gesture and overcoming the desire for a positive form of art now. This can be seen in his tendency to project back a nostalgic perception of the possibilities of the past that have become lost in the present; whether a lost Paris, lost comrades, or the decline of the quality of alcohol, moments of the aesthetic recede into the past.[16] Debord and the Situationists indicate the tension or contradiction of the explosion of programmatism: between the hollowing out of the programme and the difficulty of a recomposition that can grasp the negativity of an artistic and political activity not beholden to a positive identity. In many ways, I would argue, we have inherited this tension or contradiction. The contemporary theorisations of communisation explore, rather than resolve, the contradiction of an empty identity of the proletariat and the artist. In doing so, they try to respond to the negativity that is inherent in both identities.

3   Burning Down the Gallery

The communising position implies that with the evacuation of proletarian identity and the avant-garde, and the evacuation of the potential fusion of both in some passion for the real, we must abandon all aestheticising models and prefigurations of revolution. In these terms, the positive vision of the first phase of the Situationist International as regards aesthetics is not merely outdated but, strictly speaking, impossible. It also means that the remnants of aesthetics in the later phase of the Situationist International need to be subject to a critique to pose the contradiction of the end of programmatism in all its consequences. This bears some resemblance to the thesis of the death of the avant-gardes, but it does not imply a welcoming of this death as the opportunity for some new positive modes of practice or reinvention – from the relational to the reconfigurative, we might say. Instead, the cri-

16   Debord 1992.

tique of Théorie Communiste implies the futility and necessary nullity of any affirmative revolutionary art. All that we can have is the rift that exists at the limit.[17]

If I risk transferring terms like the rift into art, then we could say the identity of the avant-garde is the limit the artist confronts. If the worker, today, confronts the impossibility of affirming their existence as worker in relation to capital, then, today, the artist cannot affirm their identity as artist in relation to capital.[18] To continue to be an artist is the problem, an unsustainable identity. The rift would lie here with the de-essentialisation of art, which would now be posed as a limit we can no longer practise. The rift or swerve from the identity of the artist results in a making of art detached from the content of art as mandated by that identity. In this sense what emerges is a making and a material without the legitimation of artist and art.[19] The tension lies in what might be produced in the absence of these dual legitimations and the relation to those legitimations when placed in crisis.

To take one, controversial, example we could say that this situation is already implicit in the practice of Andy Warhol. On the one hand, his work belongs to the moment of programmatism, with the discourse of the factory, Warhol's studio and production space, and the model of serial industrial and media proliferation as production. This renewed and estranged discourse of alienated labour is doubled by the nihilism that inhabits the practice of art as impossible. Programmatism is haunted by the rift that emerges at the point of explosion. In his essay 'Theatrum Philosophicum', from 1970, Foucault registers this equivocally subversive function. Describing what he calls 'the greatness of Warhol' as a play of equivalences, Foucault detects something happening within this apparent monotony: "How stupid this stupidity!" But, in concentrating on this boundless monotony, we find the sudden illumination of multiplicity itself – with nothing at its centre, at its highest point, or beyond it – a flickering of light that travels even faster than the eyes and successively lights up the moving labels and the captive snapshots that refer to each other to eternity, without ever saying anything: suddenly, arising from the background of the old inertia of equivalences, the zebra stripe of the event tears through the darkness, and the eternal phantasm informs that soup can, that singular and depthless face'.[20] Warhol's stupidity stages a mute multiplicity unfolding within and against its

---

17   Bernes 2020.

18   Noys 2019.

19   Mansoor 2016.

20   Foucault 1977a, p. 189.

mimicry of the commodity form. In this case, according to Foucault, we have a certain stupidity that leads to an emergence of the phantasm out of the old inertia of equivalences. While Foucault would not put it in these terms, we can see here a crisis of making and of art that reveals a multiplicity of making detached from art and the artist.

While Warhol was a relentlessly affirmative artist, and would have nothing to do with gestures of negation and rift, we can follow Foucault in tracing the negative prefiguration of a limit in this monotony. All that remains is the contradiction of eternal production that itself becomes a kind of event in its registration of contradiction. The obvious tension of Warhol's success as an artist, his embrace of both business and celebrity, suggests how a negative possibility can fold within the continuity of value production. Much the same could be remarked about an artist such as Jeff Koons.[21] The deliberate choice to function as something like a symptom of the art market, all the while benefitting from that market, suggests that the nihilism of this kind of position inhabits contradiction to the benefit of the artist qua nullity. The challenge of someone like Koons to communisation, or discourses of the end or hollowing out of art, would be the dialectical inversion he performed to recreate himself as an artist. In this case value is accrued within the rift or hollowing out of identity that remains within equivalences and the generation of value as speculative proposition.

There is also the problem of temporal displacement and time lag, which we already saw with the Situationist International. Why should the most resonant artistic experiments in regard to communisation, at least which feature in discussion, such as The Artists Placement Group, Duchamp, Warhol, Santiago Sierra, and others, come at the wrong time, i.e. within programmatism? We could hazard an interpretation from within the communising problematic. While these ruptures with the regime of art and the artistic are chosen gestures, the end of programmatism might be said to make them necessary. If the end of art was an act, such as Duchamp's quitting art in favour of chess (equivocal as that was), now, the artist faces the necessity of such gestures as they cannot self-reproduce as an artist.

However, that does not explain why all or most art of the present moment does not seem to take this negative form. In fact, as we will see, the present moment seems more dominated by the desire to turn the negative into new forms of positivity – most notably new objects and new materialities. This, we could say, is the condition of making, and even attempts to embody the

21   Foster 2014.

negative retain an essential equivocation.[22] Therefore, the problem of period-isation, as acute as it already is for the characterisation of the present in terms of real subsumption, is also acute for artistic practice as well. Lags, prefigura-tions, regressions; the unfolding narrative is hardly stable. In fact, the instability appears to be the narrative, and it is perhaps not surprising that we have seen a shift away from the moment of communisation in art towards movements like accelerationism, which stress the possibility and necessity of making within a technological regime of possibility.[23]

The emptying out of art, however, in its truly negative form, is registered by another strand of contemporary communisation, which is pursued by the post-Tiqqun milieu. In 'A Fine Hell' (2013), Build the Party argue that 'aesthetics, therefore, is imperial neutralisation, whenever direct recourse to the police is not possible'.[24] This echoes the poet Sean Bonney's statement: 'police violence is the content of all / officially sanctioned art'.[25] Build the Party unequivoc-ally condemn aesthetics as originating as a counter-revolutionary strategy in Schiller and have no time for any artistic communism out of early Marx or the 'Oldest Programme of German Idealism'.[26] Instead, aesthetics is synonymous with the aesthetic regime of empire, with the aesthetic performing an infernal synthesis on any antagonism. In common with their Agambenian roots, they regard aesthetics as a house to be burnt down;[27] or, in the case of Claire Fon-taine, an art gallery to be burnt down (after a 2013 incident in which an art gallery was allegedly damaged after an accident during the installation of the Fontaine piece 'burnt / unburnt', which consists of fifty thousand matches in the shape of the United States).

The alternative to the aesthetic is 'the materialist obviousness of forms-of-life'.[28] The only art is the art of inhabiting our determinations rather than trying to escape them. In this traversal, we must practise 'an apprenticeship in the art of tying and unbinding'.[29] Art is impossible; installation art can only make 'little portable hell[s]'.[30] Instead, we have an (anti-)political practice that views art as technique to form and find the dispersion or chaos of forms-of-life. This is a col-lective elaboration, a sharing or force they call communism. Here art seems to

---

22   Taussig 1999.
23   Noys 2014.
24   Build the Party 2013.
25   Bonney 2015, p. 12.
26   Hartley 2017; Martin 2009.
27   Agamben 1999, p. 115.
28   Build the Party 2013.
29   Build the Party 2013.
30   Build the Party 2013; Bishop 2012.

coincide with political practice as an unworking of various imperial identities, including that of the artist. We might link this unbinding to the notion of the rift, with tying the possibility of new forms-of-life and new materialities emerging in the wake of the rift with the identity of art and the artist. In general, and in line with the thinking of Tiqqun, the Invisible Committee, and Claire Fontaine,[31] we might suggest that this mode of communisation is less rigorously negative than the suggestion of Théorie Communiste. Instead, we have a sense of a renewal of an activist art, although the question remains of how inventive or different these new forms-of-life and materiality will be.

The difficulty, which seems to me to afflict communisation generally, is the uncomfortable tracing of limits and rifts. These rifts are at once prefigurative, but also not. They indicate possibilities, but the realisation of such possibilities can be understood in very different ways. In the case of Théorie Communiste, the only prefiguration is negative. The crashing into the limit of class identity is all there is and so the artist could only crash into the identity of artist as well. The rift here makes sense of a new making only really in relation to a revolutionary situation and the possibility of new modes of making emerging in the process of revolution. For Tiqqun, and others, there is something of a traversal within these determinations that promises a reformulation of forms-of-life. This vitalist interpretation suggests an excess of life encrypted within and against, as a force or capacity of life that can realise certain modes of communism now that will form and develop within the interstices of empire. Such moments, however, also only make sense in the context of a wider revolutionary moment that would serve to link and sustain them. For the artist and the making of art the question or problem remains of what can or should be made now and under what legitimation, if any.

4   Expressive Negations

What does this clarify about our situation? To return to the story of the Situationist International, one of the ironies is that this story is often told today as an aesthetic story. Communisation suggests the necessary termination of this story, so why should it persist? Why, to use a phrase of Johanna Isaacson, has the legacy of the Situationist International been thought in terms of lineages of expressive negation?[32] That is to say, the Situationist Interna-

---

31   Fontaine 2013.
32   Isaacson 2011.

tional has tended to be mined for aesthetic gestures of negation that would somehow express, here and now, precisely a sense of revolutionary possibility. An exhaustive account would be beyond the limits of time and patience. What I would suggest is that these lineages of expressive negation have dominated much of the reception of the Situationists: from Greil Marcus's *Lipstick Traces* (1989),[33] with its lineage of negation from the Situationist International to punk, to McKenzie Wark's *The Beach Beneath the Street* (2011),[34] with its recovery of the artistic wing of the Situationist International, the tendency has gone precisely in the opposite direction from that indicated by communisation.

The difficulty then remains of how we should account for the error of these readings. If Debord and the Situationist International could not hold on to a negative reading and thus had to persist in nostalgia, we might say the limit of reading today turns the Situationist International itself into an object of nostalgia. Marx's 'poetry of the future' seems as distant as ever.[35] We could argue that this is one sign of the current limit of class identity and the blockage that forces us back into nostalgia for expressive negation at a moment that is, to say the least, unconducive to such forms. The additional irony is that such negations are often justified and retained precisely because of their positive forms. It is the fact that they seem like existent possibilities, rather than the austere path of the resolutely negative, that lends them a certain heft in the weightless experience of capitalism. I would suggest that it is precisely the paradoxical positivity of these expressive negations that at present exerts attraction and fascination.

In fact, we could suggest that these expressive negations become attractive, as positive alternatives, in the moment of the dominance of affirmative art. The consistent emphasis of present practice on materialities, networks, and relational density seems, to me, stifling. This intrusive atmosphere of 'warm abstractions', to borrow Alberto Toscano's phrase,[36] seems to demand rupture and violence. The difficulty is that this is sought through nostalgia for the past and reactivations of past negations don't seem to construct real alternatives but are relocated within this affirmative moment. The vitalist turn, in certain forms of communisation, aims to outbid this positive moment by a greater degree of positivity. The detachment of the worker and artist from value production, due to their abandonment by capital, is recoded as a force or excessive power

---

33   Marcus 2011.
34   Wark 2011.
35   Marx 2019, p. 483.
36   Toscano 2008a, p. 56.

that can posit itself as an alternative. The risk here, which is why I have some sympathy for Théorie Communiste's more negative critique, is of the aesthetic performing a consolatory function.

5   Making It with Communisation

Can we then make anything out of communisation? In a response to a ques-tionnaire on Occupy sent by the journal *October*, Jaleh Mansoor, Daniel Marcus, and Daniel Spaulding argue that 'art's usefulness in these times is a matter less of its prefiguring a coming order, or even negating the present one, than of its openness to the materiality of our social existence and the means of proving for it'.[37] This is a useful attempt to flesh out what art might do within the context of communisation, and one that suggests the absence of affirmative practice. Instead of an affirmative alternative or an empty negation, the practice of art offers access to the matter of materials we have to work with (and against), rather than some kind of guaranteed practice.

They go on to unpack that statement by arguing that art registers the falsity of the capitalist universe and insist that bodies and things cannot be captured: 'At best, art beckons from beneath the present state of things, showing us – sometimes brilliantly, sometimes naively – the world composed of objects and bodies alone'.[38] My difficulty with this formulation is the modelling of capit-alism as the capture of pre-existent forms, objects and bodies (we can note commodities are missing). It also seems to echo Badiou's description of demo-cratic materialism, with its reduction of the world to bodies and language.[39] This 'beneath the present state of things', their metaphor, seems in danger of returning to the problematic metaphor of the May '68 slogan 'beneath the cobblestones, the beach'. Problematic, because it seems to suppose merely tear-ing off the skin of capitalist society is enough to reveal a vital and repressed power beneath that will resolve all difficulties.

There is a tension of lurking vitalism, I find, which seems to fall away from the probing of art and labour, including the failure of labour. We return to formulations close to those of Build the Party. Perhaps this vitalism emerges from the very rigour of the negative, as its flipside and affirmative moment. In that sense, it might form a necessary supplement, but even so problematic. We remain split between a negativity that leaves nothing and an accompanying

---

37   Mansoor et al 2012, p. 48; see also Mansoor 2016.
38   Mansoor et al 2012, p. 50.
39   Badiou 2009b, p. 12.

vital materiality that enchants the materiality of the world beneath or beyond value. This returns us to the tensions and problems of the Situationist International, between their negativity and nostalgia, and suggests that the end of programmatism, or the cusp of that end, remains less clear cut than we might imagine.

In fact, what is registered is a tension in the contradictory position of art and labour at present. On the one hand, we can have a rigorously negative modelling in which we can explore the material of art as the site of a contradiction that lacks resolution within the horizon of the present moment. In this case, the fracture or tension of artistic identity opens a kind of neutrality of the material that is unhinged from articulation as art, or puts its articulation as art under pressure. We could call this the communisation of contradiction. On the other hand, what I have called the vitalist moment of communisation registers this unhinging as not merely the site of contradiction, but also separation and departure. In this case, the fracturing of artistic identity, and the identity of labour, renders the possibility of an emergent force of life that has experienced its detachment from capitalism. This would be a vitalist communisation.

The discussion by Jaleh Mansoor, Daniel Marcus, and Daniel Spaulding registers these two possibilities. In terms of making a choice, if that is an appropriate word, I have already indicated my distrust of the vitalist option and preference for the negative formulation. However, it is also important to recognise the tensions of those negative moments, which seem to leave us in the unsatisfactory position of merely exploring negative prefigurations: limits, ruptures, suicidal activities, identifications with capital, and aesthetic regressions. Of course, working with negativity is one of the definitional traits of the avant-garde, so this activity is not so unfamiliar. The difficulty remains that such negative formulations, what I have called the communisation of contradiction, might well generate the positive or vitalist forms as a necessary supplement. What I am suggesting is that these gestures go together, as the austerely negative and the romantic form reactions to the difficulty of grasping capitalism in a dialectical way.

I want to conclude by noting the problem of lags and delays in the formulation of the demise of programmatism, which may be more drawn out than certain formulations of communisation suggest. These forms have not simply disappeared, but as more satisfactory discussions of communisation suggest, they have to be explored to their limits – precisely to the point of explosion that the Situationist International prefigured and inhabited. What I consider the essential element of communisation is that it can be useful as a kind of therapy, in the Wittgensteinian sense, for our prefigurative and ruptural desires. Therapy is, or should be, painful; in Freud's famous formulation, we hope to pass from hysterical misery to common unhappiness.[40] In the context of communisation, we could rework this to suggest moving from an oscillation of hysterical misery and elation to everyday misery. That is to say, to begin from where we are.

What we must also do, however, is to overcome this oscillation and this might take a new thinking of the relation to capitalism as a totality and the totality of existence, of life, which preceded, remains, and will need to exceed the totality of capitalism. Here, as communisation theories struggle to record, art may well have its role in grasping and presenting these relations and these tensions. The formulations of real subsumption risk over-stating forms of capitalist domination while also neglecting the ways such modes of domination enter into bodies and materials before they become art. What may be required is a revision of these forms of analysis and a revision of what art, in all its forms, can do as a representation of the objective forms of capitalism. We do not yet know what art can do.

---

40   In Breuer and Freud 1974, p. 393.

CHAPTER 9

War and Communisation

You can have a proletarian insurrection on the condition that the others hold their fire. If they dump two tank battalions on you, the proletarian revolution is as good as nothing.

ANDRÉ MALRAUX[1]

· · ·

The crowds could only enter the squares to claim their desire for liberation and change because tanks did not appear across from them or on other streets. With a few machine guns one can hold onto a town. Crowds and armies can only stand side by side when, tacitly or not, an agreement has already been sealed somewhere.

MICHEL HENRY[2]

· ·
·

In regards to the events of 2011, the use of the language of acceleration, resonance, excess, and saturation to describe the various forms of protest has been ubiquitous. Implicit in these characterisations has been the suggestion of a politics of time. The Arab Spring, the *indignados*, and the Occupy movements were often taken as incarnating a new politics of time that evaded and accelerated beyond any capture by the state and capital. In an appropriately resonant characterisation, Gastón Gordillo used the work of Spinoza and Deleuze to suggest that these forms of protest produced 'nodes of acceleration, which shoot out high-speed resonances in all directions and make millions of bodies fight oppression in myriad places at the same time'.[3] He went on to suggest that the movements of the Arab Spring in particular were the sign of 'an epochal clash

---

1 Qtd. in Virilio 2006, p. 115.
2 Henry 2014, p. 2.
3 Gordillo 2011.

between new revolutionary velocities and the old supremacy of the state in controlling means of speed-creation'.[4] Here velocity is revolutionary insofar as it outpaces any attempt at control.

My approach to this politics of acceleration, saturation, and expansion is more cautious and critical. Instead of analysing the actual events, I want to consider different theorisations of practices of resistance and revolution.[5] My focus will not be on the obvious, which is to say the Deleuzian (or Deleuzo-Guattarian) and Negrian approaches that have become the lingua franca of contemporary theorisation and activism: multitudes, lines of flight, resonance, minor politics, etc.[6] Rather, in the interests of critical displacement, I want to consider two lesser-discussed critical perspectives: the 1970s work of Paul Virilio,[7] and its convergence with the work of communisation theory. My reason for doing so is not only that both resonate in terms of contemporary struggles, but that they also pose crucial questions around the possibilities and limits of what Virilio calls popular defence.[8] They remain attentive to the exhaustion of past forms of struggle, while also suggesting the limits of contemporary struggles. What I also want to trace in this convergence is an attention to the emergence of the military question as a problem of reflection, analysis, and practice.

Occupy obviously has a military connotation. It is a counter-discourse and counter-practice to not only the various military occupations (Iraq and Afghanistan), but also to the everyday occupation of space and time by capital and the state. Despite this reference, the military question – the question of the role, power, and the lethal nature of military intervention – has not been particularly central to the debates over the strategy of occupation. Of course, the question has been critical for those protests in the Arab Spring: from the initially equivocal role of the army in Egypt to the militarised repression found in Bahrain and Syria, and on to the ambiguous military struggle in Libya by the resistance, with United Nations support. Gordillo notes that a politics of acceleration would also have to confront the fact that 'The state still counts on powerful weapon systems that allow it to destroy resonant bodies at high speed'.[9] Within the protest movements, and notably the occupy movements, in countries like the United States, the Britain and Spain (Greece would be a different case), the

---

4   Gordillo 2011.
5   Nunes 2012; Nunes 2021.
6   Hardt and Negri 2000.
7   Adams 2012.
8   Virilio 1990.
9   Gordillo 2011.

military question has tended to be raised via the militarisation of policing. In the case of Britain, the deployment of tear gas and baton rounds as responses to the student protests and rioting 'for the first time on the mainland' refers to the colonial experience of Ireland and the military-police-secret-services fusion that was already tried in this laboratory for counter-insurgency. Questions of violence have, certainly on the side of the protestors, remained at a relatively low level.

I want to suggest that a critical consideration of the politics of acceleration as mode of resistance requires a parallel consideration of the military capacity to destroy at high speed; therefore, this will be the optic through which I consider the question of the politics of temporality. One brief remark before beginning this task; it is notable that often reflections on the military question can slip into a techno-fetishism, machismo, or replication of the nihilism of pure war.[10] In a review of Karl Marlantes's fictionalised account of his Vietnam experience *Matterhorn* (2010), Jackson Lears noted the implication of 'war as authentic experience: this is the nihilist edge of modern militarism, unalloyed by moral pretension'.[11] Such a nihilism was evident in earlier reactionary thinkers of war, especially Ernst Jünger.[12] This nihilist edge often takes the form of aesthetic awe at the destructive power of military force and its technical means. I doubt whether I can entirely avoid this problem in what follows. I do, however, want to suggest that the military question be confronted without, as far as possible, conceding to this fetishisation.[13]

1   Endo-colonisation

In his work of the 1970s Paul Virilio offers a startling account of the emergence of state and capitalist power in terms of military power. While indebted to Marx or, more precisely Engels, who researched military questions in detail,[14] Virilio's narrative offers significant departures from the more familiar Marxist account. Originating in his work as an urbanist, Virilio became fascinated by the spatial dimension of war and its role in crystallising the forms of contemporary power.[15] He rethinks the proletarian condition in military terms. His

---

10   Virilio 1990, p. 68.
11   Lears 2013.
12   Jünger 2003.
13   Noys 2015b.
14   Virilio in Virilio and Lotringer 1983, p. 105.
15   Virilio in Virilio and Lotringer 1983, pp. 1–3.

analysis proposes that the proletariat is produced through semi-colonisation by the military class, which seizes goods and value to support their own indolent and parasitic existence.[16] In response, the proletariat forms itself into a counter-war-machine, militarising itself in the compact formations of the march and the violence of sabotage to seize the streets and engage in retention of the instruments of violence. In this model the forms of the traditional workers' movement – notably parties and unions – become alternative armies to counter this military domination.

For Virilio this path will eventually lead to failure, as the absolute violence of nuclear war signals the end of the proletariat: 'In this sense, the proletariat's determining role in history stopped with the bombing of Hiroshima'.[17] Military hyper-power renders any proletarian counter-power ineffective, as there is no longer an available territory on which to ground resistance. The result is 'a kind of absolute colonization',[18] in which the military class finally eliminates any localisation or ecology of resistance. This is what Virilio calls endo-colonisation: a colonisation internal to the modern state in which the people are colonised by military power. If this endo-colonisation is successful then the people are reduced to domesticated animals, to the status of the 'human commodity'.[19] The aim of military occupation is to 'reduce [...] a population to the status of a movable slave, a commodity'.[20] In fact, 'One now colonizes only one's own population. One underdevelops one's own economy'.[21] This collapse of the possibilities of ecological resistance is visible in the passage from the desperate holding on of the Vietnamese against the ecological destruction of their territory, to the disappearance (in the 1970s) of the Palestinians from any territory into the final deterritorialised space of the media. Confronting the reduction of status to mere commodity, the Palestinians launch a suicidal popular assault, as popular defence is no longer possible.

Virilio implicitly tracks the rise of neoliberalism by exploring the withdrawal of the state from sustaining reproduction and its intrusion globally as a military force through a doctrine of security permitting intervention anywhere.[22] In the face of the terrorism of the 1970s, the state evolves a new modelling of power as 'a world-wide police chase, a fearsome blend of military and judicial

16   Virilio 1990 pp. 45–6.
17   Virilio 1990, p. 29.
18   Virilio 1990, p. 32.
19   Virilio 1990, p. 65.
20   Virilio 1990, p. 54.
21   Virilio in Virilio and Lotringer 1983, p. 95.
22   Virilio 1990, p. 57.

violence'.[23] This characterisation obviously resonates with the dominance of neoliberalism and the instantiation, in the 2000s, of the war on terror. Virilio presciently captured the sense of new forms of asymmetric warfare and the hostage-holding function of military control in contemporary mediatised societies. In this situation, traditional forms of popular resistance and what Virilio calls ecological struggles, 'the simple freedom to come and go, as well as the freedom to remain, to stay put',[24] become put into question.

This ecological struggle, the right to stay put, obviously speaks to the situation of Occupy, which attempts to place a limit on the intrusion into what remains of public space. It tries to establish a new figure of subjectivity – the 99% – to find a grounding of resistance. In this way, implicitly if not explicitly, it tries to refigure the situation of the people from this status as movable commodity into immovable protestor. Similarly, the protests of the squares also pioneered this resistance to military domination, in direct confrontations with their own militarised ruling classes. And yet, these movements and protests also have to confront the accelerative problem of what Virilio calls the delocalisation of the military class. The emphasis on speed and saturation of process is intended to outpace the forms of military and capitalist power without succumbing to a suicidal popular assault. In this way the protests restate the right of resistance.[25] Yet the tensions of this ecological resistance remain in the disappearance of protests and occupations, not least under the pressure of police and military surveillance and re-occupation of contested spaces.

Virilio's pessimistic conclusions concerning the erosion of ecological resistance have not simply been disproved by the events of 2011. Rather, while the right of resistance is restated in these struggles, the accelerative forms of this new resistance also have to confront effects of dissipation and exhaustion. This is the key problem that confronts the new forms of accelerative mobilisation. It is in this way that Virilio's analysis gains its power as both predictive and critical in advance of these new forms of struggle.

2   The End of the Worker

In a rather uncanny way Virilio's analysis also dovetails with that of the Marseille-based group Theorié Communiste and their announcement of the end of programmatism. In this thesis, capitalism and the workers' movement re-

---

23   Virilio 1990, p. 63.
24   Virilio 1990, p. 91.
25   Caygill 2012, p. 19; Caygill 2013.

mained locked in a duel in which the capitalist negation of the proletariat generated the affirmation of the workers' identity. Programmatism refers to this affirmation as a programme to be realised, and one structured by the capital-labour relationship.[26] Théorie Communiste offer a periodising hypothesis based on Marx's distinction between formal and real subsumption.[27] In formal subsumption we witness the subsumption of workers by capital, but they still produce externally to capital. For example, peasants would still till their fields, but they would have to bring their produce to a capitalist market to realise its value. Real subsumption is the process by which the act of producing is brought under capitalism, such as in production-line work or, in the case of agriculture, through the rise of mechanised agri-business. While Marx regards these as parallel processes, Théorie Communiste periodise a transition from formal subsumption into real subsumption.

The period of formal subsumption draws to an end around 1917, with the emergence of a new cycle of struggles around real subsumption that involve affirming the worker's identity. This programmatism comes into crisis with the second phase of real subsumption, beginning in the early 1970s, and a new cycle of struggles that suggest the limit of this identity. Capital's abandonment of the worker, and workers' struggles of absenteeism, sabotage, and wildcat strikes, open new lines of flight that hollow out the traditional formations of programmatism (unions, parties, etc.) Under these twin shearing pressures, the affirmative forms of worker's identity would be hollowed out. Rather than this simply being the sign of defeat, Théorie Communiste argue that it signals a recomposition of struggle with the proletariat as the pole of negation, structured within and against a capitalist system that no longer required the working class as mediator.

In the analysis of Théorie Communiste this cycle of struggle does not simply end the proletarian condition ('we are all middle-class now'), but reconfigures it to suggest the necessity (rather than the choice) of the proletariat as the self-abolishing class. They argue that: 'Communization is prefigured every time the existence of the proletariat is produced as something alien to it, as an objective constraint which is externalised in the very existence of capital'.[28] The appearance of communisation is one at the edge or limit of struggle in which class itself 'appears as an external constraint, a limit to overcome'.[29] In this historical model these shifts in struggle put communism as communisation on the agenda, shorn of previous workerist illusions.

---

26   Brown 2011, p. 22.
27   Marx 1990, pp. 1019–1038.
28   Simon 2011, p. 95.
29   Simon 2011, p. 95.

The comparison between Virilio and Théorie Communiste becomes clearer if we consider the 1973 occupation and self-management by workers of the Lip watch factory in Beçanson.[30] At the time several on the French far-left, primarily Maoists, regarded this act of occupation as the signal that workers no longer required the guidance of parties or militants to direct their struggles. This, at least, was the conclusion of Jacques Rancière.[31] A similar conclusion was drawn by the former Maoist militants Guy Lardreau and Christian Jambet:

> We came to realize at a certain point that the masses had gotten all they could out of us, that intellectuals had nothing left to give them. Everything we had done had passed over into the masses themselves. Witness the events at Lip. It was becoming clear that there was no longer any sense in militancy.[32]

There were, however, dissident voices. The French ultra-left journal Négation argued that the workers of Lip had reached a limit – the limit of self-management.[33] The Lip workers had been unable to go beyond their own factory and were limited to restarting a capitalist enterprise. So, while recognising this was a struggle, for Négation it was limited by its failure to go beyond the limits of the workers' identity as workers. It is this point, as we have seen, which is taken up in more detail by Théorie Communiste.

In the case of Virilio, his point is similar. With more sympathy, Virilio regards this struggle as the attempt to hold on to an ecological niche of struggle. He remarks that 'the trade unions knew what they were doing when they ordered the workers to carefully maintain their tools of production. It's as if, in their minds, these tools were the last representation of the original environment, the guarantee and mainstay of their entire legal existence'.[34] While certainly, in a fashion somewhat similar to Négation, Virilio sees this struggle as outpaced by the delocalising forces of the State and capital, he also refuses to simply condemn this attempt at attachment. Virilio sees the struggle as quixotic but also necessary as an attempt at ecological struggle.

In both cases, however, the recognition is that the traditional ground of resistance has been abolished. It is not that the struggle at Lip was the cutting-edge of struggles, suggesting a new militancy beyond programmatist forms, but it was the exhaustion of those forms and their collapse.

---

30   Reid 2018.
31   Rancière 2011, p. 90; Brown 2011, p. 20.
32   Qtd. in Starr 1995, p. 91.
33   Négation 2007; Brown 2011, p. 20.
34   Virilio 1990, p. 54.

Certainly, the events of 2011 might provide confirmation for this diagnosis. They have been widely taken as signalling the end of previous forms of struggle, notably those centred on class, party, and union, and the birth of new forms of struggle organised around the fluid gathering of the multitude or the people. In fact, as Rodrigo Nunes has pointed out, the evidence is more equivocal than that.[35] Certain forms of so-called traditional organisations retained and developed key roles in the seemingly acephalic spreading of protests. We can, of course, say, however, that the very changes in these forms of organisation might well indicate their obsolescence. The question remains, how do we respond? We have seen that Virilio stresses the continuing, although vanishing, possibility of resistance. In contrast, Théorie Communiste insists that the current situation suggests, in its limits, the necessity of new configurations of revolution.

3   Resistance or Revolution?

The tension of resistance and revolution encompasses many contemporary movements of struggle.[36] In fact we could read acceleration as the solution to this tension in that it supposes the reaching of a critical tipping point in which speed would lead to a qualitative transformation of resistance into revolution. We have seen that Virilio remains sceptical about this possibility, preferring to insist on the reinvention of resistance. He concludes that the dispersion of military power across space and time puts an end to the traditional right of resistance, which was grounded in a particular territory and the preservation of means of violence. In fact, 'deprived of their productive arsenal, they [the proletariat] stop being privileged economic partners in the pact of military semi-colonization'.[37] The collapse of the place of the pact between the military and civilians means that: 'From now on, military assault is shapeless in time and orgiastic participation is no more than the irrational support of a *techno-logistical supra-nationality*, the final stage of delocalization, and thus of servitude'.[38] This disappearance means that we cannot locate a moment of resistance, and so it enters into dissolution.[39]

---

35   Nunes 2012.
36   Caygill 2012.
37   Virilio 1990, p. 53.
38   Virilio 1990, p. 72.
39   See Schmitt 2007.

The pessimistic conclusion of Virilio is that revolution is over and only revolutionary resistance remains,[40] but as we have seen this seems largely ineffective or threatens to disappear. In typically hyperbolic fashion he concludes:

> We can all drop dead. In any case, they no longer need us: robots and computers will take care of production. War is automatized, and along with it the power of decision. They no longer need men, soldiers or workers, only means of absolute extermination, on the commercial level as elsewhere.[41]

While this registers capital's abandonment of labour, as also registered by Théorie Communiste, it extends it to a vision of annihilation that falls outside the still-remaining moving contradiction of capital's need for labour. In this vision there is only a desperate clinging on to the last remaining ecological niches of resistance.

On the contrary, Théorie Communiste argue that new forms of suicidal struggle by workers register the limits of this delocalisation, while continuing to contest it. In these struggles workers no longer try to hold on to a wage labour that has failed, but instead are forced into a rift with that identity. The result is the burning down of factories, attempts to claim as high a redundancy payment as possible, and other exits from work.[42] These struggles have an equivocal status, indicating both the tragedy of workers deprived of the identity of the worker and the fleeting prefiguration of a de-essentialisation of labour.[43] Contrary to Virilio's sense of the exhaustion of the proletariat under the threat of extermination, Théorie Communiste suggest that the rift of proletarian self-abolishing can lead to the possible emergence of a new communising process of revolution.

While Virilio tends to an apocalyptic pessimism, Théorie Communiste's evasion of the military question produces some moments of seemingly remarkable optimism concerning the communising process of revolution: 'The confrontation with the state immediately poses the problem of arms, which can only be solved by setting up a distribution network to support combat in an almost infinite multiplicity of places. Military and social activities are inseparable, simultaneous, and mutually interpenetrating: the constitution of a front or of

---

40   Caygill 2012; Caygill 2013.
41   Virilio in Virilio and Lotringer 1983, p. 102.
42   Simon 2011, p. 119.
43   Simon 2011, p. 120.

determinate zones of combat is the death of the revolution'.[44] This statement relies on proliferation and dispersion to make a challenge to the compact military body of the transnational ruling class. While this may be possible, or even desirable, the means and capacities to engage in this infinite combat seem problematic, to say the least. They problematically converge with American military doctrine of the world as global battlespace and models of liquid warfare.[45] Elsewhere, Théorie Communiste concedes that there may be 'the possibility of a multitude of small, barbaric wars'.[46] While this is less sanguine, it still supposes that wars will be small scale and that mobility and multiplicity will win the day.

The hope of Théorie Communiste is that the very speed of the communising process will outpace the military and logistical capacities of the capitalist class: 'It [the revolution] permits the abolition to an ever greater extent of all competition and division between proletarians, making this the content and the unfolding of its armed confrontation with those whom the capitalist class can still mobilize, integrate and reproduce within its social relations'.[47] It is the rapid expansion of the proletarian condition, no longer tied to the usual organisational and wage forms, which will permit an overcoming, it is claimed, of the fraction of the military (and its capacity for destruction) still integrated in capital. Therefore, they stake communisation on an effect of acceleration: 'This is why all the measures of communization will have to be a vigorous action for the dismantling of the connections which link our enemies and their material support: these will have to be *rapidly destroyed*, without the possibility of return'.[48] Of course, it is again not easy to see how these connections, the logistical chains of capital and state, will be dismantled at a sufficient pace.

A similar trope occurs in the communising text by the two groups Rocamadur and Blaumachen on the London riots of 2012. They conclude: 'The dynamic of class struggle today can never be victorious, because it will keep finding class struggle itself as its limit, up to the point when the multiplication of rifts will become the overcoming of class belonging (and therefore of class self-organization), as a revolution within the revolution, as communizing measures, that will either de-capitalize (communize) life further and further or be crushed'.[49] Of course, the question is whether the speed invoked by Thé-

44   Théorie Communiste 2011, p. 56.
45   Demmers and Gould 2018.
46   Simon 2011, p. 138.
47   Théorie Communiste 2011, p. 56.
48   Ibid., my italics.
49   Rocamadur / Blaumachen 2012.

orie Communiste, the spread of communisation in the process of revolution, will de-capitalise life further or be crushed. It is, to me, the rather sanguinary tendency to not take seriously the second possibility that seems problematic.

This is Virilio's question. He notes the disappearance of the military from their own war-machine. Remarking on an incident during the conflict between Britain and Argentina over the Falkland or Malvinas Islands, Virilio points out that the Captain of the British Guided Missile Destroyer HMS Sheffield had no time to react to an Exocet missile launched from an Argentine Super Etend-ard aircraft, whose pilot obeyed the injunction of Fire and Forget.[50] The ship was destroyed. Beverly Silver has also pointed out that against the great citizen-armies, which allowed workers to then make a claim on the States which had unleashed them in war, the response has been to professionalise, privatise, and minimise the role of workers in war – in line with the general tendency of cap-italism to replace variable capital with constant capital.[51] In the jargon of the US military in regards to drones, the aim is the compression of the kill chain – the removal or minimisation of human involvement from destruction. It is per-haps not hard to imagine these hardwired moral drones regarding proletarian revolution as an immoral act.

The tension here is that the forms of capitalism which for Théorie Commun-iste condition the possibility of self-abolishing and the rapid and contagious emergence of revolution as communising process also involve the elimination and restriction of labour from sites of production and military power. The con-tradictory forms of these tendencies – which involve complex national and transnational processes, both spatially and temporally – make rapidity and res-onance a more complex and risky strategies than I think Théorie Communiste and other theorists of contemporary movements admit. Of course, they can argue that these comments are only referring to an actual process of revolution that has yet to emerge, but if that process is to be successful we might further consider the tensions of acceleration.

4   The War of Time

Banking on speed and movement is precisely the ground of the war of time that Virilio identified as the problem of the military class. The war of acceleration turns on new technologies that push humans out of the domain of choice and

---

50   Virilio in Virilio and Lotringer 1983, p. 18.
51   Silver 2003.

control, in favour of an autonomous and automatic deterrence. It also, as we have seen, operates along the vectors of the accumulation of capital that operate by similar effects of technological displacement. Of course, for many this is the great virtue of these forms of the new forms of protest, resistance, and struggle. They engage with the actuality of capitalist and state technologies to re-tool and re-deploy them against power.

This was already evident in the strategic theorisations of the possibilities of internet technologies. Galloway and Thacker, for example, have suggested that the power to overload the system lies in the speed and resonance of 'the exploit', a hacking strategy that can have wider application for subverting networked forms of power.[52] In a similar vein, Harry Halpin argues that the ontological capacity for invisibility developed by the hacker group Anonymous also suggests a new mode of struggle that saturates and exceeds the control networks of the internet.[53] In these cases it is the explicitly military technology of the internet, originally developed as a mode of dispersed communication to counter nuclear war, that provides new possibilities as modes of struggles that can then be realised on the streets. They both also owe a debt to the Invisible Committee's theorisation of an insurrectional politics premised on anonymity and evasion, which could create new spaces for forms of life in the rifts created by contemporary state and capitalist power.[54]

In this modelling, the war of time can only be successfully waged on the same terrain of networks, nodes, and their forms of acceleration. This is, of course, the fundamental point made by Marx: 'if we did not find concealed in society as it is the material conditions of production and the corresponding relations of exchange prerequisite for a classless society, then all attempts to explode it would be quixotic'.[55] The question is where exactly do we identify these material conditions, and how far do we accept them as they are? My suggestion is that the affirmation of acceleration implies of mimicry and replication of state and capitalist relations that is insufficiently critical.[56] The adoption of online strategies of subversion by the extreme right have suggested, in fact, the equivocal nature of such online forms of resistance. In particular, what the acceleration of bodies neglects are the processes of the incorporation and elimination of labour as the mechanism of capitalist power.

---

52   Galloway and Thacker 2007.
53   Halpin 2012.
54   Invisible Committee 2009.
55   Marx 1973, p. 159.
56   Noys 2014.

In some enigmatic passages Paul Virilio turns to the metaphysics of metem-psychosis – the transmigration of souls – to suggest the tension of the loading of the soul on to various metabolic vehicles. He argues that we find the soul as 'plural, multiform, fluidiform, coagulated here and there in social, animal or territorial bodies'.[57] In the philosophy of the military class weak souls are tied to their environments, imprisoned within the body. This military philosophy is a Gnostic philosophy, which presumes that the powerful soul is deterritori-alised – the fluid transferable soul of the gyrovagues (wandering and itinerant monks) which can smoothly move from vehicle to vehicle. Acceleration is pre-dicated on the power to escape or move from body to body, and in this way to exceed any territorial capture. This accelerative politics is in close proximity to the politics of resonance and saturation, which also stresses a contagion that exceeds territorial grounding.

For Virilio, of course, this deterritorialisation is not to be lauded. It incarn-ates the nihilistic politics of pure war. We can find a resonant figuring of this thanatopolitical acceleration in Thomas Pynchon's novel *Gravity's Rain-bow* (1973). Set during the Second World War, Pynchon explores the ways in which in which 'the War has been reconfiguring time and space into its own image'.[58] This reconfiguration takes its terminal form in the human passenger that is integrated into a remaining Nazi v-2 rocket, in an experiment staged by the rocket crew following the Nazi defeat. With tongue somewhat in cheek, Pynchon suggests that 'secretly, [the war] was being dictated instead by the needs of technology ... by a conspiracy between human beings and techniques, by something that needed the energy-burst of war'.[59] In this way war and technology become forces demanding acceleration and the integration of the human into the suicidal war-machine. In Pynchon's pessimistic and conspirat-orial view, the emergence of great systems of control operate precisely through energy and acceleration.

Virilio's insight into the boarding of metabolic vehicles, reinforced by Pyn-chon's provocation, suggests the metaphysical desire for integration and dis-persion of human and machine at work in the dynamic of technology, military power, and capitalism. The resulting tension is that the reading of contempor-ary protest and struggles in terms of endorsing this integration and dispersion becomes problematic. The metabolic vehicles, which is to say living bodies, risk being occluded by an assimilation of struggle to the same dynamic by which

---

57   Virilio 2006, p. 96.
58   Pynchon 1975, p. 257.
59   Pynchon 1975, p. 521.

capitalism insists that we are endlessly transferable and mobile labour. Communisation theory also suggests the importance of labour and the body, even in the moment of its rift and evacuation as a category. While such a theory can be read as promoting an entirely new mode of struggle transcending the limits of programmatism it is also, I contend, a thinking of how we might engage with these limits and rifts.

In terms of the logic of struggle, the war of time is coded as one between the elimination and minimisation of labour from the processes of warfare and production, which will then be countered by a superior force of escape and flight. In response to this conflict, I would suggest two symmetrical risks. In the case of the minimisation and elimination of labour and bodies from warfare and production, we could adopt an overestimation of the powers of the trans-national military class, and thereby engender our own stasis, if not even the reification and fetishisation of military power (a risk run by Virilio). This might result in a technofetishism or nihilism that celebrates the awesome power of military technology as means of destruction. The American withdrawal from Afghanistan, completed in 2021, suggests some of the limits of this hyper-power. The second risk is that by relying on the superior speed of revolution and resistance we could ignore the effects of military and capitalist power that operate along similar, or the same, vectors. Here we could say the risk is a fetishism of struggles, in the suggestion that the process of struggles, praxis, will always find a solution if only we go further. In many ways, this fetishism is strangely close to the first, almost an inversion, as instead of fetishising military technology what is fetishised are the technologies of liberation as technologies of speed.

Here, my main concern has been with this second risk. While those who theorise contemporary movements of struggle often, and rightly, insist on the embodied nature of this acceleration and resonance,[60] my concern is that this embodiment repeats the fluidiform ideology of pure war identified by Virilio. Of course, Occupy and related struggles are, or were, heterogeneous formations that often aimed to break outside of this kind of ossification. It could be argued that, if anything, they try to break exactly the framing I am suggesting, by positively refusing the discourse of pure war, especially as it was replicated in traditional forms of struggle. Obviously, this seems to be an essential task. Similarly, the tendency of communisation theory both to pose these problems and then suppose their solution within the solvent dynamics of revolution only displaces the issues. The difficulty that I am suggesting is that in supposing escape

---

60   Gordillo 2011.

and evasion from these problems, in supposing a flight from both labour and the territorialising effects of power, they do not fully consider the new forms of deterritorialised power. While the aims were laudable, it might be that a politics of dispersion, resonance, and acceleration will have to confront not only the inertial effects of the practico-inert, but also the militarised forms of the capitalist State that deploy and engage with exactly these new forms to produce their own de-localisation and localisation of power.

PART 4

Critical Figures

∴

CHAPTER 10

The Masses Make History: On Fredric Jameson

Fredric Jameson's *Allegory and Ideology* (2019) is a book of collectives.[1] It is not only a book swarming with figures, texts, debates, examples, emotions, and levels, but also a book of the masses. Jameson notes that the 'underground theme' of the work is 'the pressure of population on form and thought'.[2] In Jameson's recent work, population displaces the masses to refer to a new demographic reality emerging as a result of decolonisation and the globalisation of capitalism.[3] In *Allegory and Ideology* population is inflected towards Jameson's concern with making a liveable earth. Jameson calls this 'terraforming of the earth',[4] in a provocative formulation derived from Kim Stanley Robinson.[5] While these are vital concerns, here I want to make a more traditional reading by returning to the level of collectives or the masses as makers and unmakers of history. This question offers us a way to read this text and Jameson's intervention more widely, not only as a form of ideology-critique, but also in that insistent utopian dimension that structures all Jameson's critical work.

The masses appear in *Allegory and Ideology* and also reveal themselves as the subject of the text. To make this appearance apparent is a matter of reading, of reading allegorically, of reading the levels, and of reading for the masses. It is that reading, beset with difficulties and possibilities, which I want to make. Raymond Williams remarks: 'There are no masses; there are only ways of seeing people as masses'.[6] This is no doubt true to an extent, and my text is vulnerable on this count and others to the accusation of projection. If, however, we do not see people as masses at all, that is also a problem in that it makes the masses disappear. The risk of seeing people as masses is one I want to run here as a way of grasping the peculiarities of Jameson's monumental text. This is also a way to place the masses again on the stage of history, with all the tensions that involves.

---

1 Jameson 2019.
2 Jameson 2019, p. xx.
3 Jameson 2009c, p. 515.
4 Jameson 2019, p. 37.
5 Robinson 2012.
6 Williams 1958, p. 289.

At one point in *Allegory and Ideology*, Jameson notes how Aijaz Ahmad accused him of surreptitious Maoism in his text on the Third World and national allegory, reprinted here with a commentary. This was related to Jameson's use of the slogan of Lin Biao: 'The contemporary world revolution presents a picture of the encirclement of the cities by the rural areas'.[7] For Ahmad this was a sign of an orientation to the peasantry, and Jameson admits to a liking for the desire expressed in the peasant revolutions of the twentieth century.[8] As an aside, more could be written about this relationship among left intellectuals and Marxists to the peasantry – to the tragic role it played in communist revolution, and to its ongoing disappearance due to capitalist agriculture. We find this left turn to the peasantry in Jameson, especially in his discussion of the peasant utopia in Platonov's novel *Chevengur* (1972, written in 1928);[9] Brecht's taste for peasant cunning and wisdom;[10] John Berger's critical and fictional writing;[11] and across T.J. Clark's art-historical interrogation of modernity.[12] To return to the masses, which are also the peasant masses, Jameson could be said to carry the traces of the Maoist 'mass line': Mao's corrective emphasis on the creativity and potentials of the masses, even if this emphasis could result in the worst forms of voluntarism. We could also recall Althusser's encrypted reference to Mao in *Essays in Self-Criticism* (1974), with the statement 'the masses make history'.[13] The masses intrude into the seemingly impregnable structuralist fortress of Althusserianism. They also intrude into this in-many-ways strange book, although here they are welcomed, even if that is not always obvious.

The masses appear as a pressure within Jameson's text, itself at once a 'loose baggy monster' (as Henry James described the Victorian novel) and an attempt at a rigorous modelling of texts as particular and peculiar structures. This tension, between event and structure, repeats itself in the pressure of the masses on and within this text. The pressure of the masses is not only evident in the use of Mao, but also in Jameson's references to Gilles Deleuze, here and elsewhere in his writing. This is the Deleuze of *Cinema 2*, who writes of the invention of a 'people to come'.[14] For Deleuze, the people are not simply formed or given by cinema, but given a place in which to appear, or even invented (which is where

---

7   Jameson 2019, p. 188.
8   Jameson 2019, p. 189.
9   Jameson 1994, 2000.
10   Brecht 2016.
11   Berger 1992.
12   Clark 1999; Clark 2018.
13   Althusser 1978.
14   Deleuze 1989; Jameson 2019, p. 297.

projection can enter with a vengeance), in this case by Third World cinema. An art work does not show the people, but rather the very absence where they could appear. Deleuze's concern with the people and with their appearance, or better, clearing a space for their appearance, echoes in Jameson's text. The aim is not so much a direct rendering of the masses, vulnerable to the kinds of projection detailed by Raymond Williams, but of making a space for the masses within the text.

We could also add here the collectives that appear in Kafka's texts in the reading by Deleuze and Guattari.[15] This work famously refers to the minor and to the issue of the minorities in relation to the textual space of Kafka's writing. The seemingly hermetic and sealed modernist text is, in fact, overrun with collective forces. For Deleuze and Guattari, the minor is a mode of writing that is political and collective – as they write, 'literature is the people's concern'.[16] So, the minor is not opposed to the masses, it is even the very language of the masses, but one constricted and constrained by the major. Finally, Jameson's consideration of imperial texts, or texts concerned with empire, especially Dante and Spenser, indicates a pressure of the people and an enlargement that orients towards the group, even if in the mode of domination.[17] This may connect with the Kafka of that strange formation the Austro-Hungarian empire, and also to the tensions that emerge in both Deleuze and Guattari, and explicitly thematised with Jameson, concerning national-liberation struggles. A whole range of potential and contradictory collectives emerges out of the experience of the masses.

The masses are not simply outside these structures or merely some intrusive and vital force, as in some variations of Maoism in which voluntarism and vitalism go together, or in some contemporary theorisations of the multitude.[18] If the masses make history they do not, to allude to Marx, make it under circumstances of their own making.[19] These conditions include the 'practico-inert', as described by Sartre and redeployed elsewhere by Jameson: the congealing of activity and the turning of activity into structure and ideology.[20] In fact, as is evident in this work's use of allegory to suture structure and event, in many ways Jameson is still worrying at the problem of history and structure that preoccupied Sartre in the failed synthesis of The Critique of Dialectical Reason

15   Deleuze and Guattari 1986.
16   Deleuze and Guattari 1986, p. 18.
17   Jameson 2019, p. xvi.
18   Hardt and Negri 2000.
19   Marx 2019, p. 480.
20   Jameson 2008.

(1960). Jameson writes self-consciously and with awareness, in the wake of
Claude Lévi-Strauss's devastating critique of Sartre's attempted totalisation.[21]
Jameson, then, constantly tries to restore and rework the problem of totality
through the integration of structure and dialectic.

In Jameson's terms in this book we have the structure of the text, which
is formed by historical conditions, and then the reading of that structure
which can also reveal how those historical conditions have been made. Reading returns structure to the historical process that formed it, both in the text
and in history. The structure is based on the four levels of traditional allegorical reading proposed by Origen: the literal (what narrative the text tells),
the allegorical (the relation to other sacred texts, typically between the New
Testament and the Old Testament for Christians), the moral (the individual's
soul), and the anagogical (concerned with the afterlife and the future). For
Jameson, obviously, these levels can be secularised and rendered as a complex and contradictory structural form. To risk a translation of Jameson's multiple and singular readings of texts through these different levels here and
elsewhere, we could propose a modern (or postmodern) rendition: the ideological or mythic (the literal), in the Barthesian sense of everyday myths or what
Althusser called 'spontaneous ideology';[22] the initial interpretive level or the
kind of interpretive reading the text poses regarding itself, for example Margaret Atwood's *Handmaid's Tale* (1985) as a conscious critique of the alliance
of anti-pornography feminism with the religious right (allegorical or mystical);
the individual in the psychoanalytic sense of the divided self (moral); and the
masses making history and being made by history (anagogical). This is a simplification of Jameson's four-fold schema, which not only distinguishes these
levels but traces their overlaps and interrelations, hence Jameson's preference
for the Greimas square.[23] The collective, my concern here, is not limited to the
anagogical level, but can appear elsewhere in Jameson's readings. In terms of
a general schema, however, this forced translation captures something of the
masses as they surge through the book, even as that might not be apparent at
first sight. The masses appear as the condition of history and of the future as
their afterlife.

The revelation of the role of the masses is a matter of reading. Allegorical
reading is a reading that reveals the multiple and contradictory structure of
the text in its production, including the levels or dimensions of history and the
collective. Allegorical reading is an 'interpretive virus' or 'dangerous contagion'

---

21   Lévi-Strauss 1972, pp. 245–69.
22   Barthes 1973; Althusser 1990.
23   Jameson 2019, pp. 349–60.

that multiplies levels of reading within the textual host.[24] Allegory and allegorical reading find their enemy in 'the unity of the living symbol',[25] which supposes an equation between the text or textual element and a symbolic level. The
second enemy, less discussed in this book, is that concrete realism that denies
the multiple levels of allegorical reading.[26] The enemy is also within allegory, as
the symbolic reading is close to those kinds of allegory that imply an equation
between one level and another. As Jameson puts it: 'The two-level system is
the mark of bad allegory'.[27] An example would be those readings of Orwell's
Nineteen Eighty-Four (1948) as supposedly really about the Soviet Union or
totalitarianism, equating the world of the text with one referent, something
implied, I think, by Orwell's own text. For Jameson 'the ideology of the symbol
[is equivalent] to the language of dualistic or two-level, point-to-point allegor-
ies, as distinguished from the multileveled systems we are about to confront'.[28]
Hence the insistence on the four levels of allegory, as against two or three, and
the insistence on the transversal relations between these levels. It is a matter of
structure and event, or event in structure or structure as event. In that sense –
and again echoes of Althusser might be detected – we have a mode of reading
that tracks and reveals the form of these levels and how particular texts encode
moments of crisis in trying to renovate or explicate these levels.

If this is the complexity of the text, in its four levels, we also have different
further possible allegorical levels. In addition to the largely canonical texts discussed in *Allegory and Ideology* we have the allegorical reading of those texts
that reveals their allegorical structure. What this then reveals is the ways these
texts engage and transform the allegorical social forms we live with and their
points of crisis – allegory as social structure. Text, reading, and social form, all,
we might hazard, operate in the mode of allegory. Many of Jameson's chosen
texts in this book, if not all, are texts of crisis. It is in the moment of crisis
that the four levels become visible, structure and history start to appear in the
moment of their rending, and the necessity for an allegorical reading becomes
evident.

The role of the critic as reader is the mapping of structure and interpretation,
which find their conditions in 'a differentiation of the various senses and other
phenomenological levels of "experience" and a mobile and seemingly random
yet properly transversal play of attention back and forth, which seems to dwell

---

24   Jameson 2019, p. 1, p. 2.
25   Jameson 2019, p. 2.
26   Jameson 2013a.
27   Jameson 2019, p. 6.
28   Jameson 2019, p. 10.

in turn and without any particular order on point-to-point relations between individual strands'.[29] This is specifically with reference to Dante, but I think it can stand for something like the mode of attention generally required to read allegorically, in Jameson's sense. This is how Jameson reads, and, by implication, both how we should read Jameson and how we should read in general. It bears some resemblance to the free-floating attention of the psychoanalyst who should, if sufficiently skilled, be able to move through the levels of the story the analysand tells, understand their suffering, use psychoanalytic concepts to read this experience, and also be aware of how those concepts themselves can become bad allegory. A good analyst is not one who simply declares 'say Oedipus!', which is why, I think, Deleuze and Guattari exaggerate the violence of Melanie Klein's mode of analysis.[30] A good analyst is able to feel their own concepts come under pressure, grasp the possibilities of their own countertransference, and to offer interpretive possibilities that develop new forms of relation.

The texts of modernity, by which Jameson means many of the texts discussed in *Allegory and Ideology*, are 'precious fever charts, of a disease as yet unidentifiable (let alone curable)'.[31] This is a strange and problematic concession of weakness, even if metaphoric. Psychoanalysis and medicine might seem to place us in the moral domain of the individual soul, now translated into psyche and soma. This would seem to exclude the masses, a problem psychoanalysis stumbled over, while in medicine the vital field of public health and epidemiology is split from the 'moral' relation of doctor and patient. These metaphors for reading indicate the difficulty – reading seems to be a solitary and singular operation between us and the text. This is also true for the critic who, as Deleuze noted, repeats the clinical gaze.[32] The text enters the consulting room and is diagnosed and cured or, as Jameson suggests, used for its indicative or curative properties. The risk is that the allegorical reading will become a moral reading.[33] The treatment of reading as a moral matter is at the heart of that collective endeavour that is literary criticism. While collective, the aim is the formation of individual taste and discrimination and this is on the model of the priestly and theocratic.[34] Jameson's explicit turn to the theological model of allegory is homeopathically designed to counter such a triumph of the moral and the sacred in literary criticism.

29   Jameson 2019, p. 260.
30   Deleuze and Guattari 1983, p. 45.
31   Jameson 2019, p. 328.
32   Deleuze 1998 and Foucault 1973.
33   Jameson 2019, pp. 198–9.
34   Williams 1958; Jameson 2019, p. 89.

Certainly, however, the practice and experience of collective reading appears to have declined. Think of Dickens' *Our Mutual Friend* (1864) and the orphan child Sloppy who reads the newspaper to his ward Mrs Higden. She states, 'you mightn't think it, but Sloppy is a beautiful reader of a newspaper. He do the Police in different voices'.[35] T.S. Eliot would consider 'He do the Police in different voices' as a title for what became 'The Waste Land', lending a modernist recoding to this practice of reading aloud. One is also reminded of Walter Benjamin's essay 'The Story Teller', and its reflections on the shift away from oral tale-telling.[36] The reading of newspapers and radical pamphlets aloud to illiterate workers was a staple of the communities that formed the English working class, as E.P. Thompson has detailed.[37] These are collective practices of reading or listening unlike, for example, the current audio-book, which remains a largely individual relation of listening symbolised by the use of headphones. Elements of this collective reading persist in the reading group or, technologically mediated, in online forums and forms, which often turn on collective practices of interpretation and, of course, misinterpretation.

All this is not simply to romanticise past modes, nor necessarily to share the Benjaminian confidence, inspired by Brecht, that cinema or other technological forms might reinvent new modes of collective expression for the masses (all this given a more muted form in the work of Marshall McLuhan).[38] It is to note the problem of the collective and its pressure emerging within the act of reading and its institutional mediation. In literary criticism the sign of this difficulty, but not its resolution, was found in reader-response criticism. While largely liberal in orientation, responding, in part, to the extension and massification of education in the 1960s and 1970s, this current was also responding to the newly-radicalised reading publics of that moment. This was a particular pressure of population or the masses. Today, we could argue that this pressure of the uneven experience of massification in literary education is felt in the turn to digital humanities and online teaching. These technological modes of mediation of collective experience in a largely individualised form are predicated on skills and the appeal of science and technology as the real material of our world.

The collective not only traces a negative pressure on the act of reading but more definitely within texts themselves. In that sense Eliot's integration of the oral within the text of 'The Waste Land' is a sign of both loss and gain:

---

35   Dickens 1997, p. 198.
36   Benjamin 2019.
37   Thompson 2013.
38   Benjamin 1968, pp. 239–41.

the loss of collective reading or enunciation; the gain of the integration of voices within the text. Modernist collage is the practice of the collective in the text despite or perhaps because of the well-known 'fear of the masses' present in modernism and linked to the imperial moment.[39] This is evident in Conrad, and we should add in other writing of that moment, with H.P. Love-craft's pulp weird fiction demonstrating the anxiety provoked by the racialised mass as monstrous.[40] Modernist collage and parallel gestures at once integrate the masses but also control or try to control them within or through the gaze of the modernist. This is something like a version of the thesis of Bakhtin on carnival and carnivalesque, in which the living experience of carnival as social practice is translated into the carnivalesque of voices within Rabelais and later the novel.[41] The result, problematically, is a seemingly endless series of debates as to whether such moments are liberation or confinement, the carnival being the model of temporary transgression and restored order.[42] Similarly, as I have suggested, is modernist integration of the oral and the collective to be understood as neutralisation or politicisation? It would be possible (schematically, it is true) to read modernism itself as an expression of these two lines, a right and left modernism, each trying to tear itself from the other.

I want, however, to displace this debate and return to the tensions of allegory in terms of the tensions of the masses as makers and made, producers and produced, within the allegorical levels themselves. I also want to return to the problem of bad allegory, the point-to-point allegory, for which Jameson's example is Albert Camus's *The Plague* (1947) as allegory of the French resistance against Nazi occupation or more broadly for the human condition. Jameson regards the novel as a lapse from 'found freshness ... into sheer moralising'.[43] The tension that had sustained Camus's previous work, between the moment of happiness and the absurd, has here slackened. This is dual allegory with a vengeance. The temptation is given from the start, with the quotation from Daniel Defoe announcing: 'It is as reasonable to represent one kind of imprisonment by another, as it is to represent anything that really exists by that which exists not'.[44] The potential movement implied by this statement is, however, limited. Tony Judt's afterword to the Penguin English translation is telling in this

---

39   Jameson 2007, pp. 152–69; Carey 1992; Balibar 1989.
40   Miéville 2005.
41   Bakhtin 1984.
42   Eagleton 2009.
43   Jameson 2019, p. 8.
44   Camus 2013.

regard, saving the novel from the limitation of being about Nazi occupation and French resistance by claiming it is targeted at general dogma or compliance.[45] The allegorical reading is expanded but only to one other level, the human condition, and that in the most loose of terms.

Instead, I want to suggest that *The Plague* is perhaps more successful as what Jameson calls 'a realistic representation' of plague infection in Oran.[46] In this sense we could read it non-allegorically as a book about the plague, about disease, quarantine, struggles between duty and fear, profiteering and heroism.[47] As Jameson notes, it is political since it concerns the collective, although largely with the exception of the Arab population.[48] The politics turn not so much on political as virological resistance, those politics of plague and quarantine that make fleeting appearances in Foucault's readings of madness and the prison.[49] This is the possibility of a biopolitical reading of Camus, which would also include the biopolitics of his exclusions. In Foucault's words, while leprosy involves 'separation' and the project of exclusion, the plague involves 'segmentations' and the problem of order.[50] Camus's *The Plague* would be a novel of this problem of order, of segmentations, in relation to the disorder of the masses, more particularly within the urban, as Oran becomes city-as-prison.

Dr Rieux, the narrator of *The Plague*, announces: 'But when an abstraction starts to kill you, you have to set to work on it'.[51] Certainly, the novel displays that dislike and distrust for abstractions that runs through Camus's thought and fiction. This is also true of the taste for the concrete in the phenomenological tradition, which, as Adorno pointed out, can often take on a deeply abstract form.[52] The novel aims at abstractions as something deadly, but then the presence of the plague can also attract another sense of the concrete. This is the form we have called the biopolitical, and the work on the abstractions is practical in orientation, with particular credit being given to the daily record-keeping and organisation by the civil servant Grand. The forms of the plague and the responses to them in the novel involve material organisation and planning. Such materialities seem to defy or complicate the distinction Camus operates between the concrete and the abstract. They demonstrate that Camus's concept of the concrete is highly abstract and another concrete can be sought

---

45   Judt in Camus 2013, p. 246.
46   Jameson 2019, p. 8.
47   Rose 2020.
48   Apter 1997.
49   Foucault 1989, pp. 1–5; Foucault 1977b, pp. 195–8.
50   Foucault 1977b, pp. 197–8; Foucault 2003, pp. 44–52.
51   Camus 2013, p. 69.
52   Adorno 2002.

in grasping these segmentations and organisations. In this case, the biopolitical might yield another potential reading of the abstract as the diagram that takes concrete form in the quarantine, regulation and ordering of the city-space by the civic and other authorities.[53]

Of course, we have here the risk of another grand one-to-one allegory, with Camus's novel becoming an allegory of the disciplinary project of modernity. This would be the case if we simply tried instantiating the biopolitical level as singular; that is to say, biopolitics as the fundamental explanatory schema and totalising understanding of modernity. It is a risk run by Foucault and, even more so, by Giorgio Agamben.[54] Yet, reading Camus as biopolitical suggests the multiplicity of the biopolitical, which cuts across Camus's text and also, as we will see, Camus's own ideological commitments as they structure his texts. It is not a matter of replacing the Nazi occupation or the human condition with biopolitics, but instead unfolding biopolitics as this particular moment of disease and responses to the measures for the individual and the collective. This is a complex situation within the novel. Quarantine is not to be taken as some negative imposition on the vital forces of the masses, with the plague as 'collective festival' opposed to 'strict divisions'.[55] This vision, courted by Foucault, perhaps another instance of what Carlo Ginzburg calls his 'black populism',[56] needs to be resisted. In fact, in the heroism of organising and sustaining the quarantine as a necessary act we see something of the dissolution of this political myth of the anarchic masses opposed to segmentation and discipline, which recurs even within the sobriety of Foucault's texts. The masses align as a collective, not simply with 'resistance' to quarantine and its regulations but as the need to make these survivable for the masses. It is a matter of collective life and death refracted through Camus's range of characters.

The biopolitical reading of Camus, which I sketch here as a possibility, would be a realism that engages with the text contrary to the allegory of the Resistance or of the human condition. It would make it a more practical, if not prosaic text. Such a treatment would allow us to question Camus's own 'Mediterraneanism', an ideological form that celebrates the uniqueness of Mediterranean space and nature at the expense of political understanding of the violent exclusions that structure this space that mediates East and West.[57]

---

53   Deleuze 1988, p. 34.
54   Agamben 1998.
55   Foucault 1977b, p. 198.
56   Ginzburg 1980, p. xviii.
57   Bull 2014.

The setting in mercantile Oran and the impositions of the plague-quarantine block the celebration of sun and sea that translate the Mediterranean into a numinous reality (as we see in *The Outsider* (1942)).[58] On the contrary Oran, a city Camus disliked, is presented as hot, dusty and smelling of seaweed.[59] The denial of this ideological form, or its torsion, suggests how a biopolitical realism might work against this ideological moment. Certainly, the text does not particularly engage with its own exclusions, but traces of another biopolitics are possible.

The realism we are proposing is not the collapse of reality and symbol that Jameson finds in Auerbach's reading of Dante, which plays a Thomist realism against allegory. That would be a realism of the one-to-one, which fuses reality with the religious in a moment of enchantment. This biopolitical realism denies such a fusion. It would move beyond the numinous as the reality of realism, including that Mediterranean numinous that preoccupies Camus. It would also move beyond the Occupation and the human condition. Instead, we would have a realism of the quarantine forms of biopolitical power, an engagement with the nonhuman virus mediated through spatial forms of power, the possibilities and limits of collective responses to those forms, and the ideological forms of collective expression in biopolitical crisis. This would be a retooling of Camus's text, which remains problematically sententious, and also of biopolitics, which remains within a discourse of modernity that is in denial of the fundamental connection with capitalist modernity.[60]

The problem of realism and Jameson's sensitivity to a theology of the material is valuable, especially at a moment in which the material is valorised as some kind of automatic resistance to transcendence and the religious. Nothing could be further from the truth. We can hazard that what Jameson is suggesting is that realism does not simply collapse all the levels into one – 'reality' – but that it embeds all the levels into reality, which itself becomes the problem. This would be something like Lukács' distinction between naturalism, which reproduces and therefore renders reality ideologically, and realism, which can create an internal critical fracture in 'reality' and envisage a totality.[61] In the case of Camus, we can see how such religious formulations can take secular forms, in this instance the Mediterranean ideology. We can also see a biopolitical realism of the nonhuman that resists such theological or mystical moments of numinous realism.

---

58   Apter 1997, p. 510.
59   Camus 2013, p. 130.
60   Jameson 2013b.
61   Lukács 2007.

More widely, we might refer to the predominance of the thinking of Heidegger in the interpretation of the key texts of modernity, a point made by Jameson.[62] A staging remains to be made of the conflict between Heidegger's four-fold (gods, mortals, sky, earth) and Jameson's four levels of allegory. The sacred reading of texts proceeds in the absence of allegory, precisely by a series of theological or mystical fusions of word and reality. In the case of Heidegger, his own gathering of simulacral and mystical collectives would stand as a central example of the false appearance of the masses. This mystical naturalism of the masses translates the most speculative and metaphysical forms into the most brutally banal appearances – Germany, 'the land of the middle', the whole 'peasant ideology', in the most negative sense.[63] Heidegger abolishes history in the name of historicity and stands as the inversion of that Marxist interest in the peasantry that we noted at the beginning of this essay. Jameson's text seems to me to offer some tools for the dismantling of the Heideggerian naturalist mysticism of the mass and of language, while not always being clear about this possibility.[64]

Underlying these issues is the threat of the loss of the four levels and the arising of strict correspondence of the kind X = Y, or 'X really means Y'. This is a problem I have already raised with dystopian fiction; what Y is X dystopian text an allegory of or how does X dystopian text compare to the Y of the present? Such would be bad allegory. In a sense, Jameson's longstanding concern has been with trying to render allegorical texts, thinking of his work on science fiction,[65] away from this kind of bad allegory and towards the complexity of levels he details here. We could add that this is obviously a political matter and relates to the masses, which are often squeezed out or constrained by one-to-one allegorical structures. The mysterious place of the 'proles' in *Nineteen Eighty-Four*, which are source of both hope and utter despair, is indicative of this constrained presence of the masses.[66] The result in *Nineteen Eighty-Four*, as many critics have noted, is that the novel becomes a seemingly middle-class affair. In terms of politics we should add that Jameson has always been concerned with resisting the depoliticising effects of moral and ethical readings that find their structure in the opposition good/bad.[67] Bad allegory is not

---

62   Jameson 1994, p. 89.
63   Badiou 1999, pp. 53–4.
64   Jameson 2016.
65   Jameson 2006.
66   For critical discussion see Williams 1991 and Deutscher 1969, pp. 35–50.
67   Jameson 2002.

something moral, but the disabling of transversal readings between levels, pre-cisely the kind of oscillation we saw in the Bakhtinian carnival, which can only swing between subversion and containment.

On Jameson's own analysis of postmodern texts operating between the min-imal and the maximal, it would seem surely obvious that *Allegory and Ideology* is a maximal text. In fact, this productive excess runs through Jameson's work here and elsewhere. One thing Jameson certainly takes from Brecht is his pro-ductivism, and it is this that perhaps makes Jameson a somewhat unusual West-ern Marxist. Certainly, the very justification for Marxist reading is itself cast in terms of a maximum of productivity: 'the advantage of a Marxist criticism, far from being 'reductive', lay in the fact that it includes more, it expands the phenomenon of the text to greater and more multiple dimensions of both ref-erence and signification, making of the literary work an act in history and time as well as an inert and static objective structure'.[68] The four levels of allegory are the drivers of this production, proliferation and complexity. The blending and clashing of the four levels in the multidimensional space of the text, to paraphrase Barthes,[69] result in this productive structural tension that expands the text.

While this certainly involves all the productive forces, something Jameson has been insistent upon against the nervousness of many Western Marxists who emphasise the destructive results of those forces, it also involves the masses. The masses gain their organisation and coherence through these forces; they do not stand outside the forms of capital, nor are they simply an internal rupture. That said, again as in Mao, the relations of production and their relation to the masses making history are central problems that remain before us as well as embedded in singular texts. In that sense part of Jameson's work has been in exposing hermetic and singular texts – perhaps especially those of high modernism, but also those like the works of Raymond Chandler, which start to look more like those of high modernism – to the pressure of the masses as well as the mutations of the capitalist mode of production.

The utopian, as usual with Jameson, is correlated with the desire and the expression of the collective. In this study the utopian makes relatively few appearances, which is strangely similar to the few direct appearances of the masses. I want to suggest that these are correlated, and that the pressure of the masses I have traced in Jameson's book is also a pressure of the utopian. What form does that pressure take? I want to conclude with one strange and to me

68   Jameson 2019, p. 276.
69   Barthes 1977, p. 146.

moving and comic moment of the intrusion of the masses onto the stage of history and the pressure of the utopian. This occurs in a parenthetical statement by Jameson in the chapter on Dante. Jameson is discussing the fate of the sinners in Canto x of *The Inferno*, who are in the sixth circle of hell, that of the heretics; specifically, in this Canto, the Epicureans, who believed the soul dies with the body and are punished by being eternally locked in red hot coffins. Also, while they have sight of the future they do not know the present. We could say, using Jameson's terminology, that this is a punishment of the impossibility of cognitive mapping or traversing the levels of time. Eventually they will be locked in the coffin and have no sight at all. In this way, they are deprived of the possibility of mapping continuous time, which comes to finite humans, according to Jameson, through ancestor-worship or concepts of immortality. This is Jameson's comment, aside, or addition: 'There must have been much celebration in ancient Egypt on that memorable day on which immortality was extended to the dead of the common people!'[70]

While extended suggests a passivity, we might recall Rancière's notion of the radically disruptive inclusion of the 'part of no-part',[71] or Marx's insistence on the negativity of the proletariat as the condition of its redemption of the whole of society. We could also bring together Benjamin's anxiety that even the dead would not be safe from fascism, which was proved correct,[72] and his interest in the notion of apokatastasis, generally attributed to Origen, that all shall be saved.[73] This includes Satan, who shall be saved last. This moment in Jameson's text, my favourite line in the book, suggests to me a claim to immortality on behalf of the masses that can, as Benjamin agreed, be realised on earth. In her book *Second-Hand Time* (2013) on the collapse of the Soviet Union, Svetlana Alexievich interviews many witnesses, including those workers or now-retired workers who recall how they used to name streets after workers.[74] While attentive to all the crimes of that social formation, these moments themselves stand out as a certain claim to immortality of the masses now being erased in new re-namings under capitalism. I see a short-cut or jump between these two moments and also how this strange textual monument to allegory traces the utopian desire of the common people to immortality. The masses not only enter history, they also enter immortality.

---

70   Jameson 2019, p. 266.
71   Rancière 2004.
72   Benjamin 1968, p. 255.
73   Benjamin 2019, p. 67.
74   Alexievich 2016.

CHAPTER 11

Conjuncture and Crisis: On Gregory Elliott

The plural ends of Gregory Elliott's title *Ends in Sight* (2008) ostensibly refer to the various forms of the end of history thesis canvassed at the close of the twentieth century by Francis Fukuyama, Eric Hobsbawm, and Perry Anderson.[1] There is really only one end, however, in question here: the end of socialism. The large thesis of this brief work is that we have witnessed the end of any kind of systematic alternative to capitalism for the foreseeable future. Elliott's provocative contention is that communism can no longer claim to be a 'real movement' grounded in the historical tendencies of capitalism, but instead has retreated into being a utopian idea; Marxism has succumbed to Marx and Engels' condemnation of 'critical-utopian socialism': at best offering 'valuable materials for the enlightenment of the working class', at worst merely painting 'fantastic pictures of future society'.[2] The charge of utopianism is, of course, a common trope of anti-Marxism, both right and left. Elliott, however, insists that rather than abandoning Marxism *tout court*, or embracing a utopian Marxism in the style of Bloch or Jameson, we must think Marxism in light of its historical weakness and crisis. To summarise Elliott's relation to Marx we could give the more idiomatic version of his repetition of Domenico Losurdo's definition of his relation to Marx: 'can't live with him, can't live without him'.[3]

The adoption of such an ambivalent and pessimistic position might not appear obvious from Elliott's previous intellectual and political trajectory. He is probably best-known for his work *Althusser: The Detour of Theory* (originally published in 1987 and reissued in 2006),[4] an intellectual biography characterised by a fine balance of criticism and sympathy towards its subject, especially considering the passions aroused by the Althusserian project, not least in Britain. Also, Elliott has done continuing and highly valuable work as a translator, and rightly gained a reputation as an eloquent and acerbic commentator, especially on the French intellectual scene.[5] He has always retained an independence of judgement, and a refusal of the usual see-sawing of enthusiasm

---

1 Elliott 2008; Fukuyama 1992; Hobsbawm 1994; Anderson 1992b.
2 Marx and Engels in Marx 2019, p. 90.
3 Elliott 2008, p. xi.
4 Elliott 2006a.
5 Elliott 2006b.

followed by renunciation that has often characterised British left intellectuals' engagement with Continental Marxist theory. He is, to return a judgement of Elliott's from a review back to sender: 'an author mercifully free ... of the phobias and philias about French intellectual life'.[6]

1   Displacing Marxism

The clue to the origin of *Ends in Sight*, I think, lies in his intellectual biography of Perry Anderson, *Perry Anderson: The Merciless Laboratory of History* (1998), to which it might be regarded as a pendant. In the concluding balance sheet of the biography Elliott noted Anderson's loss of 'confidence in the theory of historical trajectory – cornerstone of "scientific socialism" – of which he had been an indefatigable partisan'.[7] The result was not the abandonment of Marxism by Anderson, but rather its displacement from expressing a movement of social transformation to the explanation and criticism of the existing state of affairs, coupled to 'a quasi-Pascalian wager' on the future abolition of capitalism.[8] Elliott finished by expressing qualified admiration for Anderson's waiting game. In a strange moment of identification between biographer and subject, *Ends in Sight* adopts the position Elliott ascribed to Anderson wholesale.

The effect of this political identification profoundly shapes Elliott's work, but the permeating influence does not stop there. Anderson is not merely one of the figures discussed, but *primus inter pares*, as Anderson's own earlier discussions of Fukuyama and Hobsbawm guide Elliott's work.[9] There is also a more nebulous stylistic link. The often-remarked 'Olympian tone' of Anderson's work, which has attracted so much ire from the left,[10] is given a sharper and more urgent edge in Elliott's writing. A notable stylist in his own right, Elliott combines the combative polemical edge of Anderson's early work, which he had commended in his biography of Anderson, with the serene dismissiveness of Anderson's more recent surveys of intellectual life. Elliott contrasted the 'habitual iconoclasm' of Anderson's earlier work with the 'studied prudence' of his later work, concluding 'the most innovative, original Anderson is the intransigent freelance intellectual'.[11]

---

6   Elliott 2006b, p. 145.
7   Elliott 1998, p. 241.
8   Elliott 1998, pp. 242–3. On Pascalian Marxism see Goldmann 2016.
9   Anderson 1992b, pp. 279–375; Anderson 2005.
10   Linebaugh 1986.
11   Elliott 1998, p. 109.

Elliott's *Labourism and the English Genius* (1993) might be said to be his own exercise in mimicry of the iconoclasm of the early Anderson.[12] In the case of *Ends in Sight*, however, the result, however, is considerably more compressed than Anderson's work; this whole book is probably shorter than Anderson's essay on Fukuyama. It consists of a series of profiles reworked from articles and papers given from 1995–2004, and this perhaps accounts for the occasional repetitions and, more problematically, variations in tone and conclusions.

The first chapter, on Marx, is pivoted around the 150th anniversary of the Communist Manifesto (in 1998), and more particularly the faith that text placed in an historical dialectic that although proceeding 'by the bad side' could ground the necessary emergence of the revolutionary proletariat from the internal contradictions of capital. Elliott notes it was this faith that was essential to the workers' movement of the twentieth century, and he refers to Gramsci's remarks on the providential 'religion of the subaltern'.[13] For Elliott it is not possible to simply dismiss or ignore this grounding faith and its mobilising power: 'the ideological formation that was historical Marxism – the official party Marxism of the Second, Third and Fourth Internationals alike – was no mere betrayal of [Marx's] thought'.[14] Elliott is keen to stress, against the attempts to recover a pure or true Marxism, that historical teleology remains crucial to Marx (and Marxism). While the Marx of *Capital* and the *Grundrisse* would considerably complicate the teleological model of history, not least with his concept of the tendency, as would the critical Marxism of figures such as Lukàcs and Althusser, without some historical grounding that can be given or identified, communism risks being merely utopian. The severing of the dialectic between capital and its future gravediggers means, in short, that history is not on our side.

The next two chapters, on Fukuyama and Hobsbawm, pursue this theme in a more indirect fashion. In both cases Elliott is concerned to identify the problem of the collapse of systematic alternatives to liberal capitalism, which he regards, following Anderson,[15] as the 'rational kernel' of Fukuyama's thesis.[16] Hobsbawm mitigates this conclusion by a consoling insistence that the self-identified Marxist regimes, and social-democracy, provided a civilising balance to untrammelled capitalism in the twentieth century. For Elliott, such retro-

---

12   Elliott 1993.
13   Elliott 2008, p. 33.
14   Elliott 2008, p. 31.
15   Anderson 1992b.
16   Elliott 2008, pp. 55–9.

spective consolation neglects the internal contradictions of capitalism, minimises the crimes of Stalinism, and, fatally, allows Hobsbawm to leave his enlightenment Marxism intact despite the depth of its defeat. And yet, for Elliott, the recognition of the historical defeat and failure of actually existing socialism and social democracy also entails noting that this has not rebounded to the benefit of alternative formulations of socialism and communism. If we cannot console ourselves with the past record, neither can we console ourselves with future hopes; we might again rephrase Elliott's relation on Marx: couldn't live with actually existing socialism, can't live without it.

2   Realism or Resignation?

Again it appears that Elliott has adopted the same position he had previously analysed in Anderson, this time of Deutscherite form. The Deutscherite position, named after the great historian and biographer (notably of Trotsky) Isaac Deutscher, hoped for reform, either from above or below, of the actually-existing socialist countries and a recognition of their function as a bulwark or, in the language of theology, *katechon* ('restraining force') against capitalism.[17] With the dashing of these hopes in 1989 the pessimistic registration of historic defeat might appear as the only option.[18] Such a registration is, however, avoided by Elliott through invoking Andersonian lucidity, the lynch-pin of the whole work, and the subject of chapter four.

The chapter pivots around Anderson's editorial for the re-launch of the *New Left Review* in 2000, 'Renewals', in which he argued that in the face of the virtually uncontested consolidation of neo-liberalism the left has tended to adopt one of two positions: accommodation with the existing order, or the consolation of inflating the possibilities of opposition.[19] In a footnote Anderson courted a third option – resignation, 'a lucid recognition of the nature and triumph of the system, without either adaptation or self-deception, but also without any belief in the chance of an alternative to it'.[20] Even the disavowed notation of such an option in a footnote was enough to attract the usual charges of pessimism. For Gilbert Achcar, the editorial embodied an 'ultra-pessimism',[21] while for Boris Kagarlitsky, in a more intemperate style, it was a sign of 'uncon-

---

17   Davidson 2004.
18   Elliott 2008, p. 107.
19   Anderson 2000, pp. 13–14.
20   Anderson 2000, p. 13 n. 5.
21   Achcar 2000.

ditional capitulation'.[22] Despite his reputation for pessimism Anderson's own preference, at least as regards the *New Left Review*, was for the adoption of a stance of 'uncompromising realism' that would refuse accommodation and the consolation of understating the power of capitalism.[23] Elliott sympathetically and convincingly reconstructs this position of realism. Instead of drawing on dubious compensations from the past à la Hobsbawm, or inflating contemporary possibilities, Marxism can find its place in the unremitting criticism of the present coupled to a scanning for signs of resistance and refoundation.[24] Of course one could dispute whether Anderson meets this standard, and Elliott notes his high-handedness when it comes to analysing instances of resistance, but this necessity to ground Marxism in the conjunctural identification of the tendencies of the present, negative and positive, certainly offers a promising model for left thinking.

The difficulty with Elliott's reconstruction of realism, however, is how this sits with his prefatory remarks, reiterated in the first chapter, that socialism is condemned to 'become utopian once again'.[25] Such a utopian positioning would seem to leave Marxism, as Marx and Engels indicated, fatally detached from historical conditions and from a philosophical commitment to reality, and hence incapable of a realism that could critically assess reality, as we (ideologically) find it. This self-undercutting of his own proffered realism is further undermined by the full-blown pessimism of Elliott's conclusion. Lambasting the limitations of the rebirth of resistance against neo-liberal capitalism signalled by the emergence of the *'Il popolo di Seattle'*, Elliott can only conclude that no significant resistance, comparable to historical socialism, is in sight. The result is that he is drawn irresistibly to embracing Anderson's option of resignation, in a gesture *plus royaliste que le roi.*

That said, the conclusion is probably the most consistently amusing part of this work, dishing out brickbats with a mordant glee. Hardt and Negri are condemned for a 'mutant Browderism'.[26] Earl Russell Browder, General Secretary of the Communist Party USA from 1934 to 1945, was known for his slogan 'Americanism is Communism'. Elliott is mocking Hardt and Negri's philo-Americanism, and their faith that capitalism is already embryonic communism simply waiting for the multitude to step into power. For his support for Hardt and Negri, Slavoj Žižek is described as the 'artisan of a quasi-Third Period Marxism-Lacanism',

---

22   Kagarlitsky 2000.
23   Anderson 2000, p. 14.
24   Anderson 2007.
25   Elliott 2008, p. 25.
26   Elliott 2008, p. 118.

chiding the swings of Žižek's position and its likeness to extremist Stalinism.[27] Elliott is visibly frustrated with the claims for historical optimism that seem to ignore current weaknesses and fail to engage with past and present difficulties.

It would also be difficult to dispute Elliott's verdict that we have yet to see anything like a substantial enough institutional instantiation of the 'movement of movements' that could rival historical socialism. One can share Elliott's frustrations at the *bien-pensant* platitudes of the radical left, which risk verbally parlaying real defeats into the mirages of future victories. In fact, this might help explain the inconsistency of tone and position noted above. The bitterness of Elliott's conclusion would then be the result of a deliberate choice to bend the stick to a deep pessimism as the means of correcting the tendency to consolatory optimism on the contemporary left. In true Maoist fashion it might then be possible to achieve the correct line between these two deviations of the uncompromising realism Elliott elsewhere seems to favour.

This may, however, be a refusal to take Elliott at his word. If so, then his endorsement of resignation is deeply problematic, and not as coherent as he supposes. What Elliott appears unable to countenance is Anderson's suggestion that no one on the left is immune to consolation, nor can they be since political movements must motivate their adherent during periods of defeat.[28] Following Anderson, we might suggest consolation is a *necessary* 'illusion' for left politics, which precisely must balance itself between a recognition of structural constraints and the recognition of the ability to change those structures. Lacking that moment of change, resignation threatens to tip-over into renegacy, and the puncturing of illusions into the 'passing of an illusion' (to echo François Furet's adieu to Marxism). This is all the more disappointing as Elliott's careful extrication of Anderson's work from such charges promised a powerful re-orientation to a realism that would not neglect the organisational, structural, and agential questions so often elided in invocations of a socialist or communist future.

It might also appear that Elliott's confident judgement that there is currently no end in sight for capitalism is vitiated by the financial crisis that emerged almost in parallel with this work. And yet Elliott's pessimism would still stand because, as he notes: 'It would be a false consolation (not to say a defective argument) to infer from the existence of capitalist crisis some anti-capitalist resolution of it'.[29] While there has been a general agreement on the necessity

---

27   Elliott 2008, p. 119.
28   Anderson 2000, p. 14.
29   Elliott 2008, p. 56.

for 'financial regime change',[30] and concomitant shifts in political and intellectual regimes, the nature and form of that change remain as yet undefined.
To again quote Elliott: 'The cruces of an alternative – agency, organisation,
strategy, goal – that could command the loyalties and energies of the requisite
untold millions await anything approaching resolution'.[31] It may be that capitalism as we knew it had ended, but whether that truly signals its 'final ending' is
still very much in question.[32] We can choose to chide Elliott for the underestim-
ation of the factor of class struggle in these internal contradictions of capital,
but it would be difficult refute his thesis regarding the unlikeliness of the resolution of such contradictions in a Marxist, communist, or even social-democratic
direction, without the material bases of alternative agency.

3   The Ending of Marxism

At issue in Elliott's pessimism is his deliberate choice to conflate two ends:
the end of historical socialism with the end of Marxism as a scientifically and
historically-grounded theory. The collapse of the first, which is beyond argument, would not seem to necessarily cause the collapse of the second. Elliott's
blunt conflation, however, makes a more refined point: while he is at pains
not to deny the ability of Marxism to analyse the irrationalities of capital, his
emphasis falls on the seeming inability of this critique to find material grounding for its alternative socialist or communist vision, without which such visions
remain chimeras. In this sense his diagnosis of Marxism almost exactly conforms to the charge of 'critical-utopianism' levelled by Marx and Engels in the
Manifesto. While Marxism may offer the most persuasive diagnosis of capitalism, as the rush to Marx in the current crisis indicates,[33] it has been less
persuasive on predicting the transition out of capitalism. If the Communist
Manifesto could provide ideological fodder for the bourgeois triumphalism of
the 1990s, then, no doubt, *Capital* and the *Grundrisse* could provide consolation
for the current crisis. Lacking the guarantees of scientific socialism, Marxism
risks 'melting into air'. Elliott's question to any refoundation or reformulation
of Marxism is in what sense would it offer 'a plausible socialist prescription to
complement the diagnosis and prognosis for capitalism'.[34]

---

30   Wade 2008.
31   Elliott 2008, p. 111.
32   Elliott 2008, p. 127.
33   Brown 2009.
34   Elliott 2008, p. 124.

Underlying this question, and only implicitly sketched by Elliott, is the question of the motivational power of Marxism as a political discourse: the broken link between Marxism as science and Marxism as practice. The paradox of historical socialism was that although its confidence in the march of history may have been misplaced it was this confidence that led to its material success. Gramsci noted that belief in mechanical determinism, belief that 'the tide of history is working for me in the long term', was a source of resistance in the face of defeat.[35] His conclusion, however, was that this was a weak form of resistance, requiring transformation into the sense of an active will. The difficulty Elliott appears to be indicating is that the problematisation of such teleological and providential conceptions, and he approvingly refers to Althusser for just such a problematisation,[36] causes a crisis of faith in the efficacy of Marxism. Although, like Gramsci, Elliott dismisses such teleological conceptions he appears more doubtful about what might take their place. To remain in the religious register, a Pascalian Marxism of the kind suggested by Anderson might, like the Jansenism it borrows from,[37] be a Marxism for intellectual elites, unable to reach out to the masses who demand something more than the emptiness of the wager. It would also be a Marxism that lacked realism and the sense of a philosophical justification for its own existence in the world and the world to come.

What is omitted in Elliott's retention of a classical and strict division between scientific and utopian Marxism is the tension of the circularity of human practice, in which belief, no matter how false, can make itself true. The problem of Gramsci's formulation of the 'religion of the subaltern', reproduced by Elliott, lies in the way this motivating function is rooted in social practice and retrospectively legitimated by its success. Here we have the danger of a Nietzschean Marxism, in which the justification for communism becomes its future success and its galvanising power is purely mythic. This would be a Sorelian Marxism that has detached itself from reason and rationality. It also takes an elitist form, supposing these myths for the masses and the true enlightenment for the leaders. Against such a conception, we should agree with Elliott's Althusserian injunction against 'telling lies' and the need for a properly democratic mode of communist knowledge.

The point still remains, however, that the reality and realism of Marxism is neither mythic nor necessarily lost by the setbacks that currently surround us. The problem here is that a fully-disabused realism merely comes to reproduce

---

35   Gramsci 1971, p. 336.
36   Elliott 2008, pp. 52–3.
37   Goldmann 2016.

ideological reality. If we have a cynical manipulation of Marxism as mythic in the religion of the subaltern, then we can have a cynical realism that valorises ideological norms and worships intellectuals of the right as having superior insight. This is the problem that Lukács identified in literature by contrasting a critical realism, which could grasp the seeds of future transformation, with literary naturalism, which reproduced the ideological image of the world around us and so led to hopelessness and a modernist sense of despair.[38] Cynical realism is best understood as a naturalism that revels in a sense of despair and mimics bourgeois thought and reactionary ideologues out of a sense of envy.

It is the immense merit of Elliott's work to point to this tension and to challenge the current fashion for the emphasis on the utopian, the conjunctural, and the contingent as the virtues of Marxism. In posing the question, however equivocally, of how we might historically ground the possibility of socialism or communism in the absence of a faith in scientific socialism (or at least in its old teleological and providential form) *Ends in Sight* remains vital reading. Admirable in its uncompromising critical verve, if not always consistent or convincing in its conclusions, at its best *Ends in Sight* makes a powerful case for us to sharpen our thinking and to embrace an uncompromising realism that remains true to the flexibility of Marx's own conjunctural thinking. Such a path, however, might also need to consider issues of philosophical grounding and of the forms of objectivity that can grasp the persistent necessity of Marxism against the temptations of mythic manipulation and cynical despair.

---

38   Lukács 2007.

CHAPTER 12

Catastrophe and Culture: On Francis Mulhern

Books, libraries, houses; these are the tropes which Francis Mulhern identifies as lying at the heart of the new generic form he wishes to identify: the condition of culture novel. In a compact and provocative essay, an essay, no less, in 'Marxist formalism',[1] Mulhern identifies this new genre as a site of meta-cultural reflection, in which 'the principle of 'culture' speaks of itself and its general conditions of existence'.[2] These novels focus on questions of qualification, admission, and access to culture, not only for their characters, but also for their readers. Such a reflection culminates Mulhern's work, which has focused on the tradition of cultural criticism as it emerged in Britain in the twentieth century. Such a tradition often has a peculiar relation to Marxism – a companion in criticism of bourgeois society, but unlike Marxism articulating an elitist disdain for the masses inspired by Nietzsche. The Nietzschean tones of this tradition articulate a sense of cultural crisis and a critique of culture,[3] but one with very different commitments to the apparently similar Marxist tradition. Mulhern's interventions allow us to undertake the necessary work of teasing apart these very different understandings of crisis and culture.

Figures of Catastrophe (2016) is the most recent in Mulhern's reflective series of analyses of the mutating modes of cultural criticism. It is focused on the novel, rather than critical works, and it is focused on how novelists engage with a particularly and peculiarly English problem: the access of the working class to culture, with culture figured as a social whole or totality. The ominous title *Figures of Catastrophe* is the result of these novels suggesting that the access of the working class to culture can only have a catastrophic effect. For Mulhern we can read these novels as signalling a particular set of anxieties and fears that haunt the national formation of capitalism, and its opposition, in Britain.

We can locate Mulhern's project, in descending order of capaciousness, within the frame of Marxist cultural criticism, the specific British or English form of this tradition, and within Mulhern's own trajectory. The first two frames can be synthesised by bringing together two diagnoses made by Perry Anderson: the first is that Western Marxism has, problematically, shifted the ground of Marxism from the economic and political towards the philosophical and

---

1 Mulhern 2016, p. viii.
2 Mulhern 2016, p. viii.
3 Carey 1992.

cultural.[4] The second is that '[d]riven out of any obvious habitats' in British culture, the thinking of totality found refuge in literary criticism.[5] In terms of post-war British Marxists, this is confirmed by the fact a dominant historical mode of thinking is accompanied by an attention to cultural and literary matters. If one were to suggest a scale, from most historical to most cultural or literary, it might run like this: Eric Hobsbawm, Perry Anderson, E.P. Thompson, Raymond Williams, Stuart Hall, and Terry Eagleton. All have devoted significant attention to literary and cultural matters.

The implication is that the turn to culture bears a particular national specificity in the case of England. This is the tradition in which Mulhern locates his analysis in *Figures of Catastrophe*: the condition of England novel. It also links to what Patrick Keiller has called, with tongue somewhat in cheek, 'the problem of England'.[6] This problem was brought into focus by Perry Anderson and Tom Nairn (in what became known as the Nairn-Anderson theses) as the problem of the particular development of capitalism in England: at once far ahead, as England was the first capitalist country or one of the first, but also far behind, as England lacked a bourgeois revolution that would have secured a modern capitalism.[7] In cultural terms, developed by Perry Anderson, British culture lacked a mature consideration of capitalism, particularly in its lack of any development in sociology, and so the contemplation of capitalism as a totality led a fugitive and fragmented existence.[8] This would also result in a working class that had developed a positive class culture, but one that was not notably antagonistic, but rather corporatist in Gramsci's language.[9]

This diagnosis attracted dissent, notably from E.P. Thompson, who stressed the force and capacity of working-class tradition in England, as against the national nihilism of Nairn and Anderson.[10] It would also later be disputed by the historical work of Robert Brenner and Ellen Meiksins Wood, who both stressed the modernity of British capitalism in its agrarian origins and aristocratic form, against arguments of retardation, prematurity, and decline.[11] The problem of the peculiarity of the English, however, remains an issue of concern, even with these disparate framings. Patrick Keiller's film work explicitly confronts the problem; developing the Nairn/Anderson theses in his *London*

---

4   Anderson 1976.
5   Anderson 1992a, p. 97.
6   Keiller 2014, p. 6; Toscano and Kinkle 2015, pp. 218–26.
7   Anderson 1992a, pp. 14–57; Nairn 1964 and 1988; Lukács 1962.
8   Anderson 1992a, pp. 48–104.
9   Anderson 1992a, p. 36.
10   E.P. Thompson 1965.
11   Robert Brenner 1976; Brenner 1982; Meiksins Wood 1991.

(1994), while his later *Robinson in Space* (1997) took note of the argument of Meiksins Wood.[12] Paul Gilroy's *There Ain't No Black in the Union Jack* (1987),[13] was also a vital intervention in stressing the postcolonial impact of Empire on British culture, including its omission within Marxist accounts. The minor tradition of reflection on the problem of England shows no signs of dying, not only with Mulhern's essay but also with Owen Hatherley's *Ministry of Nostalgia* (2016), a critique of austerity aesthetics.[14]

Francis Mulhern's own work is located in the matrix of the *New Left Review*, and so with the work of Nairn and Anderson. Mulhern first published in the *New Left Review*, with a piece on Christopher Caudwell, sometime bête noir of British cultural Marxism, in 1974. His most recent contribution was a 2015 review of Kristin Ross's book *Communal Luxury* on the Paris Commune. His first book, *The Moment of 'Scrutiny'* (1979), was published by New Left Books and *Figures of Catastrophe* is published by Verso. With *Culture/Metaculture* (2000), anomalously published by Routledge in their 'New Critical Idiom' series, these form what Mulhern calls an 'informal trio' that composes 'a critical history of metaculture'.[15] In addition, there is also a 1998 collection of Mulhern's essays, *The Present Lasts a Long Time*.

The Moment of 'Scrutiny' was a study of the journal of that name, which was published between 1932 and 1953. The journal articulated a particular and peculiar anti-Marxist cultural politics, and its leading figure was the literary critic F.R. Leavis. Mulhern's detailed study, developed from his doctoral thesis, located *Scrutiny* within a European project that opposed culture to civilisation, with culture the bearer of humane values against the corruption of civilisation. For Mulhern *Scrutiny* did not only articulate cultural values, but also the value of culture itself. His summary of this treatment of culture by *Scrutiny* is the core that will be expanded upon by his two later works: 'Ever 'above' and 'beyond' politics itself, 'culture' was a permanent meta-cultural sanction, the tribunal before which all politics stood judged, in the name of the "human"'.[16] This notion of culture as a 'meta-cultural sanction' would be central to his next work, *Culture/Metaculture*, and to *Figures of Catastrophe*.

The conclusion of *The Moment of 'Scrutiny'* set out briefly the key implications of this tradition for the left. While the critique of civilisation could appear to share themes in common with the left critique of capitalism this was an

---

12   Keiller 2014, pp. 93–95; Toscano and Kinkle 2015, p. 221, p. 223.
13   Gilroy 1992.
14   Hatherley 2016.
15   Mulhern 2016, p. viii.
16   Mulhern 1979, p. 99.

illusory appearance. The dialectic of culture and civilisation in this tradition effectively suppressed and even dissolved the problem of politics.[17] This negation of politics rendered cultural criticism null and void as an ally. What could be learnt from was the organisational model of *Scrutiny* as a cultural strategy, a model of 'peerless militancy' that could be adapted to the return of politics.[18] It is not hard to imagine that Mulhern had the *New Left Review* in mind.

Mulhern's *Culture/Metaculture* develops the need to locate projects such as *Scrutiny* synchronically in a European-wide perspective on the tradition of 'Kulturkritik' (cultural criticism). Hence, much of the book is composed of a survey and comparative analysis of this tradition in the early twentieth century. The polemical point of this second work of the trilogy was not only to broaden reflection on the tradition of cultural criticism, but also to suggest that the new discipline of cultural studies, which primarily emerged in the 1970s, had not broken free of this discourse. This is a qualification of his earlier judgement, in *The Moment of 'Scrutiny'*, that 'the analysts of 'popular culture' and teachers of 'media studies', were *not* the 'continuators' of this tradition'.[19] Now, they do continue this tradition, but in inverse form. While expanding culture beyond the constraints of the opposition to civilisation, while posing populism against elitism, cultural studies still maintained culture as final arbiter. In this way cultural studies remained the secret sharer of cultural criticism and shared in its impasses: the dominance of culture undermining a credible concept of politics, as cultural politics simply reanimated culture as the primary object.

Figures of Catastrophe shifts away from the synchronic analysis of *Culture / Metaculture*, and back to the peculiarities of the English. The concern is with an English tradition of novels that belong to the metacultural discourse 'in which culture reflects on its own generality and conditions of existence'.[20] The keynote text of this genre is E.M. Forster's *Howards End* (1910).[21] The epigraph of the novel, 'only connect', is symbolic of the aim of the condition of culture novel to repair the cultural fabric by inclusion. The conclusion of the novel signals the limit of this project when confronting the working class. The lower-class Leonard Bast, an insurance clerk, after struggling for inclusion within upper class house and family of 'Howards End', is killed by being crushed under a falling bookcase, in symbolism both striking and bathetic. Attempting to enter into culture, Bast can only meet his death under the very form of that culture.

---

17   Mulhern 1979, p. 330.
18   Mulhern 1979, p. 331.
19   Mulhern 1979, p. 330.
20   Mulhern 2016, p. 7.
21   Mulhern 2016, p. 5; Mulhern 2000, p. 35.

Mulhern will construct for this novel and each of his major examples a Greimasian square, the formalism element of his Marxist formalism, to map the conflicts and contradictions of each of the novels. This formalises an impasse, of the entry of the working class into culture, which undergoes a series of historical shifts across the twentieth century and up to the present moment. For Mulhern this tradition is functionally and often explicitly conservative. It is concerned with preserving culture in the British ideological myth of continuity, bound up with notions of property and power. These attempts, strained and contradictory as they are, register the seismic shifts in relations of class power across the period.

Mulhern identifies 'the aristocratic fix' in Evelyn Waugh's *Brideshead Revisited* (1945), and works by Virginia Woolf and Elizabeth Bowen. These works emphasise the point, already evident from Forster, that 'at the heart of the matter of culture is the house'.[22] The preservation of the aristocratic country house, as symbol and reality of cultural continuity, is a means of resisting the encroachment of the middle and lower classes. Mulhern notes that 'it is the sentimental charge of inheritance that spiritualizes the material facts of survival and conveyance, rendering the house so potent as a trope of continuity'.[23] Evelyn Waugh, eyeing the emergence of the welfare state with horror, considered buying a house in Ireland to escape 'the Attlee terror'.[24] It would be the post-war rise of Labour that would displace this tradition of the old regime, but the fugitive literary form would find its substitute houses elsewhere.

If these novels register a sense of aristocratic decline and the desire for continuity, in the novels of the 1960s and 1970s this turns to horror. Mulhern's analysis of John Fowles's *The Collector* (1963) and Ruth Rendell's *A Judgement in Stone* (1977), reveals that now the working class kills for culture, or just kills culture. In these novels the working-class subject turns violent and deadly in the face of their exclusion from culture. Between these two works lies the global insurgency of 1968 and, more importantly for Britain, the miner's strike of 1974 which toppled the Conservative government. An insurgent working class threatens the middle- and upper-class idyll with a fatal rupture of continuity.

Mulhern then has a longer chapter on 'end-states', tracing what he sees as the decline and fall of the genre. Here lie the important postcolonial interventions of V.S. Naipaul and Hanif Kureishi, with his novel *The Black Album* (1995),

---

22   Mulhern 2016, p. 36.
23   Mulhern 2016, p. 126.
24   Mulhern 2016, p. 144, n. 38.

which while remaining within the anxieties of the condition of culture novel inflect the desire for continuity which remains its persistent core. The real terminus, if we like, is Martin Amis's *Money* (1984), in which the class ambition to enter culture is replaced by that form and signifier of equivalence from which the novel takes its title. There is time for one reprise, in Zadie Smith's *On Beauty* (2005), a strained re-writing of *Howards End*.

The importance of these works does not simply lie in tracing the history of one strand of British conservative culture, literally the attempt to conserve culture. For Mulhern, as we have seen, the condition of culture novel registers the seismic shifts of class struggle as well. This very English tradition can be read as a history of the fortunes and misfortunes of the working class, especially that form of class culture that formed in Britain as 'labourism'.[25] For Mulhern 'the condition of culture novel has for a century and more persisted as a complex of narrative conventions by or through which, across a variety of social identifications, a literate middle class could frame or crop, acknowledge, consider and (more often than not) resist the active historical presence of the working class'.[26] Mulhern's Marxist formalism allows us to read these ideological gestures of framing, cropping, and resisting the presence of the working class.

Within this narrative Mulhern implies not only the crisis of the condition of culture novel, but also the crisis of labourism.[27] These novels offer various 'figures of catastrophe' because they cannot imagine a reconciliation of the working class with culture, except in a deadly or catastrophic form. If the working class should manage to integrate or connect with culture, then, for these novels, that culture is rendered sham and corrupt. This constitutive double-bind takes on a charged dimension as the crisis of culture overlaps with the crisis of labourism.

Mulhern concludes that culture, in the form of continuity that can be conserved, has failed. The late condition of culture novels are 'all ... nihilistic in their different ways – examples of what culture is reduced to, once its enabling conditions have disintegrated'.[28] The key text here is Martin Amis's *Money* (1980), which reveals that: 'This wholesale transmigration of souls from literature to signage is one form of the final subsumption of culture under capital, a process whose teasing visible effect is that the streets of a post-literate metropolis come more and more to resemble the venue for some great book festival,

---

25   Hoggart 1958.
26   Mulhern 2016, p. 147.
27   Elliott 1993.
28   Mulhern 2016, p. 99.

or a library of sorts'.[29] The thesis of postmodernism, the replacement of reality with signs, is historicised to suggest this is a result of 'the final subsumption of culture under capital'.[30]

Mulhern does not unpack this statement in detail, but it is possible to detect a periodising hypothesis. If the condition of culture novel initially charted the crisis of conservative cultural continuity under the impact of working-class claims, now it appears to register the final crisis of capitalism as a subsuming force. This registers for working-class identity, which no longer takes the secure form of social-democratic claims to entry into culture. If we speculate, we could suggest Mulhern's argument brings him into convergence with those who periodise post-war capitalism as entering into new forms of real subsumption. In particular, the work of Antonio Negri and the work of those associated with communisation have suggested that since the 1970s working-class insurgency and capitalist counter-offensives have broken the previous arrangement, which stabilised the working class as a counter-pole to capital.[31] This crisis of the working class is, for Negri, with Michael Hardt, the positive possibility of developing a new figure of the 'multitude' to refer to a pluralised subjectivity that contests the regime of capitalist labour.[32] For the theorists of communisation a negative possibility emerges, as class identity becomes a limit to be struggled against and dissolved. Whether we accept these particular diagnoses it is certainly true that capitalism has achieved a significant global dominance, even in crisis, and that so-called traditional forms of struggle appear to reached their limits.

The termination of the condition of culture novel would register this termination of working-class identity, although from an upper- and middle-class position that registers the termination in the emergence of violent and lumpen forms of class identity.[33] Significant here would be Martin Amis's vicious caricaturing in *Lionel Asbo: State of England* (2012), which merits a, rightfully, dismissive footnote from Mulhern.[34] Here the working-class subject is identified with the 'ASBO': the 'anti-social behaviour order', a legal punishment belonging to the long list of disciplinary measures for working-class subjectivity. A parallel case could be made for the surprising absence of Ian McEwan's *Saturday* (2005), an explicit condition of culture novel. In that novel the read-

---

29   Mulhern 2016, p. 124.
30   Mulhern 2016, p. 124; Jameson 1991.
31   Negri 2003; Simon 2011.
32   Hardt and Negri 2005.
33   Jones 2016.
34   Mulhern 2016, p. 148, n. 41.

ing of Matthew Arnold's poem 'Dover Beach' placates the savage beast of the neurologically-ill working-class intruder. Sarah Brouillette has pointed out that this novel considers and critiques the question of access to culture, not only for the working-class other but also for its upper-middle class hero, the neurosurgeon Henry Perowne.[35] In the case of both these novels, as Mulhern formulates, the working class appear as the 'yob army of capital'.[36]

What these examples suggest is that figures of catastrophe have not simply ended, but now take fraught and violent forms that reverse the stakes of the 1970s novels. If those novels of the 1970s expressed horror at an insurgent working class, today's condition of culture novels express horror at a working class left to figure, in an ironic inversion, the capitalist subsumption of culture. The working class is still left to carry the burden of a lack of culture, although now culture is hollowed out by capitalism on a global scale. True to the Nietzschean roots of this mode of criticism, the working class is not only the pathologised carrier of nihilism, but also treated as a biologically inferior caste, beyond human sympathy. In an exemplary instance of blaming the victims, the arbiters of contemporary cultural value treat an immiserated working class as the barbarians at the gates.

This conclusion raises a number of questions. Can we imagine a new condition of culture novel that would engage with the Negrian multitude or communisation's stress on the limit of class identity, or other figures of contemporary struggles? Could we reverse the condition of culture novel, or could such a novel be written, which would start from contemporary forms of struggle? Here Ben Lerner's *10.04* (2014) offers a reflection on aesthetic autonomy in light of the impact of Occupy and various contemporary politicisations of the commodity.[37] This suggests, in a problematic fashion, the possibility of such a form of the condition of culture novel. Alternatively, is the condition of culture novel reduced to registration of the violent effects of capitalist real subsumption? Here we might suggest the prescience of Brett Easton Ellis's *American Psycho* (1991), set amongst the hyper-affluent financiers of Manhattan and with its ironic references to *Les Miserables* (of course, the musical not the novel). In this case, cultural access shifts from a stigmatised working class to a psychotic ruling class, adrift amongst the financial abstractions that generate and maintain value (both monetary and cultural).

These two examples are American, reflecting the shift of power of the novel from Britain to the United States. This shift is enough to satisfy the most vulgar

35   Brouillette 2014, pp. 175–99.
36   Mulhern 2016, p. 148.
37   Lerner 2014; Katz 2017.

of materialists. It also suggests the possibility of reading Mulhern's intervention as both specific to England and as located with a wider frame of global capitalist culture. Certainly, if Mulhern is correct, we might not rue the end of the condition of culture novel. A particular form of conservatism and a particular form of class culture might well be over and good riddance to it. Mulhern's thesis, however, also implies the crisis of the present and locates the crisis of the novel, a hackneyed trope, within a specific crisis of capitalism. The global dominance of capital, the depth and range of subsumption, suggests the difficulty of extracting culture from politics and the necessity of a politicised practice of the novel.

Mulhern's brief but powerful intervention is a provocative figuring of a particular catastrophe and this wider crisis. It intimates the formal limits the novel will be forced to confront and on which it may be wrecked. Mulhern also allows us to tease out the Nietzschean reading of crisis, with its emphasis on nihilism, the crisis of culture, and a violent rejection of the subaltern, from what might compose a Marxist cultural criticism sensitive to an historical understanding of crisis that does not repeat those tropes. In this way, Mulhern's work poses the problem of not just how we read (or write) the novel in these cultural conditions, but also the tensions that persist from the tradition of cultural criticism given its most vehement forms by Nietzsche. If we must reject the condition of culture novel then we must also reject those Nietzschean projects of cultural criticism that gave those novels their animating tropes.

CHAPTER 13

Crisis and Capitalist Realism: The Antinomies of Mark Fisher

The shifting fault-lines of contemporary criticism have thrown up some strange cases of the critical impulse at work. At large, there has been a small but significant resurgence in criticism inspired by or drawing on Marx and Marxist thought in the literary academy or, more precisely, sometimes on the precarious, fractally-multiplying and frayed edges of academia (the name academia itself is often a precarious reification of vastly different work patterns, life experiences, and modes of education). We could remark on recent work on literature, debt, finance, and crisis, inspired and informed by the crisis of 2008, particularly emerging in the United States.[1] There are also a number of projects, such as the Marxist-Feminist *Blind Field: A Journal of Cultural Inquiry* (begun in 2015) or the longer-running *Mediations: Journal of the Marxist Literary Group* (begun in 2007), which have renovated and renewed critique in a hostile literary and cultural environment. Similarly, in art history, the project of Hal Foster has retained a defence of the necessity of critique,[2] while in a different mode the work of Jaleh Mansoor has insisted on the material and formal legacies of Italian Marxist thought and art practice,[3] and Gail Day has explored the possibilities of the dialectic and negativity in art-historical practice.[4] These scattered signs do not amount to anything as substantial as a movement, more a tenacious holding on, but also demonstrate innovation in the face of a doxa that remains hostile to Marxist thought.

Here, rather than survey this scene, I want to turn to a more marginal and yet also global case – the project of blogger and writer Mark Fisher, also known as K-Punk.[5] Fisher's writing inhabited an exemplary edge space of precarity in relation to academia and, with the publication of *Capitalist Realism* in 2009, became globally resonant. His death in 2017 left Fisher's project, especially the planned volume on *Acid Communism*, incomplete. Here I want to consider

---

1 Nealon 2011; Clover 2011; Kornbluh 2014 and 2019; Isaacson 2016; McClanahan 2016; Bernes 2017.
2 Foster 2017, pp. 115–24.
3 Mansoor 2016.
4 Day 2010; Noys 2012.
5 Hammond 2019; Colquhoun 2020.

Fisher's work in relation to crisis, austerity and the regime of capitalist realism that he described. I will focus on perhaps his best-known work, *Capitalist Realism* (2009), but I also want to consider Fisher's work as an integral project, including his writing on cultural politics in *Ghosts of My Life* (2014),[6] the posthumous book *The Weird and the Eerie* (2016),[7] and the collection of his blogging and other writings that include a fragment of the uncompleted project *Acid Communism*.[8] My aim is a critical survey, although one that I hope is sympathetic to the tensions that structure Fisher's project, especially between what we could call Continental Philosophy or Theory and Marxist elements.

Part of the sympathy here is that I share some of the same cultural formation with Fisher, a parallel if very different engagement with Continental thought, and acquaintance in relation to some of the cultural projects emerging in the 2010s. We share, for example, the influence of Greil Marcus's book on the Situationists and punk, *Lipstick Traces* (1989),[9] although our theoretical influences are very different: for Fisher, Deleuze and Guattari, while mine is Bataille via Derrida. We also share an interest and fascination with techno music and 1970s weird television. Certainly, however, these commonalities and parallels do not and did not preclude criticism and crucial differences. In fact, the path of Fisher's work is useful in illuminating deficiencies and difficulties that beset the integration of Continental thought in a left framing, which would include my own work and that of many others.

In particular, re-reading from the vantage of the present and reading the work *en bloc*, reveals Nietzschean elements in Fisher's work. This is, according to Fisher, the aristocratic Nietzsche who rejects culturally levelling, an anti-bourgeois Nietzsche, but despite the Fisher's claim that this is not a reactionary Nietzsche it recycles central elements of Nietzsche's reactionary cultural critique.[10] Fisher, I think, is best seen as a cultural critic and as belonging, in a somewhat mutant fashion, to the tradition of cultural criticism identified and analysed by Francis Mulhern (see Chapter 12). Fisher exemplifies the tension of left Nietzschean thought, and a particular attempt to combine a sympathy with popular culture (largely absent in the tradition of cultural criticism, with its mandarin stance) with a revised elitism based on a popular modernist experimentation. The tension of these elements with commitments to a left politics become evident in Fisher's work, but they also indicate broader

---

6   Fisher 2014.
7   Fisher 2016.
8   Fisher, 2018. The fragment on 'Acid Communism', pp. 751–70.
9   Fisher 2018, pp. 40–1, p. 162.
10   Fisher 2018, pp. 135–7, p. 274.

critical tensions. The antinomies of Fisher involve a fracture between conception of capitalist totality, registered as object of horror, and a potential outside,
registered as space of the weird and non-human. This antinomy also, as we
will see, reproduces an antinomy between the thinking of Marx, geared to a
dialectical thought of totality, and that of Nietzsche, in which modernity itself
becomes fatally contaminated.

1   Returning to (Capitalist) Realism

Capitalist Realism, the book, has, in ten years, become a resonant phrase: 'what
Mark Fisher calls "capitalist realism"' or 'as Mark Fisher has described, capitalist realism'. 'Capitalist realism' is, as Fisher suggests, not an aesthetic mode,
but the ideological acceptance that capitalism is the only viable system – an
acceptance accompanied by feelings of depression and resignation. Fisher's
diagnosis is accepted but the risk is that the substance of *Capitalist Realism*
the book is uncannily absent. The success of the title is at the expense of the
book. That is why I want to return to the substance of the book, but in a particular fashion. The substance of the book is not simply the substance of capitalist
realism. Certainly, few could be as devastating as Fisher in making resonant and
felt the 'political phenomenology of late capitalism', in which we experience
'a system that is unresponsive, impersonal, centreless, abstract and fragmentary'.[11] This is, in one way, recorded in the various responses and analyses that
Fisher devoted to contemporary popular culture,[12] but also in the texture of his
own and others' lived experience of work and consumption.[13] There is however,
another substance at work in the book, which is those desires, experiences and
lived moments that call to another collective order not oriented to value.

The dual form of this substance is why it is important to consider the breakdown of capitalist realism. No longer is capitalist realism simply a resonant
phrase capturing our experience of crisis and austerity, of our increasingly apocalyptic present, in which alternatives now seem more likely to take fascist
forms than communist. Capitalism, for Fisher, is consonant if not cotermin-
ous with catastrophe: 'Capitalism is what is left when beliefs have collapsed at
the level of ritual or symbolic elaboration, and all that is left is the consumer-
spectator, trudging through the ruins and the relics'.[14] This melancholic tone,

---

11   Fisher 2010, p. 64.
12   Fisher 2018.
13   Fisher 2018, p. 203.
14   Fisher 2010, p. 4.

which remains resonant, has also to be thought alongside the more utopian moments that mark Fisher's work. The breakdown of capitalist realism as an apocalyptic moment has to be paired with the breakdown of capitalist realism as a breakthrough, to borrow from R.D. Laing.[15] Despite Fisher's mordant skill at capturing the worst of the present moment, he did not cease in thinking the better.

That said, Fisher's writing could often oscillate between elation and despair, apocalypse and utopia. This is reminiscent of the writing of Franco 'Bifo' Berardi, which was an influence on Fisher. In Berardi's work the insurgent power he gives to the newly emergent cognitariat encourages elation, but this turns to despair as they seem to bungle the job. The over-emphasis on creative power ascribed to new political actors results in despair when that power encounters the limits of the conjuncture.[16] In the case of Fisher this oscillation results from a rather different cause. Here the split is caused by the conception of capitalism and capitalist culture as an all-engulfing machine of integration. Treated in such a way, the interiority of capitalist culture takes on the nightmare hues of the paranoid fictions of Philip K. Dick as a 'divine invasion', or as monstrous Lovecraftian cosmic horror. This is the moment of despair, in which each moment of revolt, and especially the moment of punk, which Fisher lauds, is doomed to integration and recuperation. The alternative is, however, the outside, reached in experiences of the weird, which threatens to destroy capitalist realism and the common sense which underpins our ideological integration into the capitalist order. It is the aesthetics of the weird, in a broad sense, that rewrites the capitalist brain and offers a liberation by reprogramming our sensory experiences.[17]

Such a model has a problem with its conception of substance, which is a result of Fisher's peculiar Spinozism, indebted to Deleuze.[18] Instead of Spinoza's understanding of substance as a causally-determinate totality, subject to rational understanding, we instead have the aim to move beyond the sad passions that attach us to capitalist realism by means of a breakout to the weird outside. The problem of elitism emerges here as well, as the breakout to the outside is often only achieved by a minority. This minority is often itself elitist and tied to tropes of antagonism to the masses derived from Nietzsche. In the case of Philip K. Dick, for example, Waite has detailed his extensive debt to Nietzsche,

---

15   Laing 1970, p. 110.
16   Berardi 2015.
17   Fisher 2018, pp. 695–7.
18   Fisher 2018, pp. 695–9.

hostility to Marxism, and self-proclaimed fascism.[19] The dissolution of rational understanding, substance in Spinoza's sense, creates difficulties for Fisher's project. In particular, the division between a fully-saturated capitalist 'inside' and a weird 'outside' is simplistic and creates an oscillation between elation and despair. Certainly, especially in his close critical readings, Fisher is more attentive to the complexities and tensions that model the integrations of contemporary capitalism, but these relations between the 'inside' of capitalism and its 'outside' are not fully mapped.[20] While not inhabiting Dick's politics, Fisher relies on a similar sense of aesthetics and will to depose capitalist reality, leaving his project vulnerable.

Central to Fisher's analysis of capitalist realism are mental health and education. This is one reason for the resonance of the book amongst students, and the insight of the book into how we experience crisis as it runs through self-reproduction. In terms of mental health, the breakdown of capitalist realism is not only a social breakdown, but also a psychic breakdown that condenses the forms and process of the continual series of breakdowns and crises that compose capitalism. Hence the resonance of the reference to R.D. Laing. While 'Capitalist realism insists on treating mental health as if it were a natural fact, like weather (but, then again, weather is no longer a natural fact so much as a political-economic effect)',[21] the effect of crisis is to further estrange and de-naturalise capitalism, mental health, and, of course, with climate crisis, the weather. Overlapping forms of breakdown strike at the very heart of the usual ideological mechanism, central to the analysis of Roland Barthes in *Mythologies* (1957),[22] of treating what is cultural as natural. Now nature is not natural.

The resulting politicisation of mental health that Fisher suggests is not one that simply embraces the anti-psychiatric celebration of the schizophrenic or psychotic, no matter how complex that gesture often was. Despite his debt to the work of Gilles Deleuze and Félix Guattari, Fisher does not embrace this moment of their work.[23] Rather than tracing some signature disorder as a sign of immersion in or exit from capitalism, Fisher preferred to focus on the ambient suffering of stress, tiredness (TATT – Tired All the Time), and anxiety. Fisher's move is deflationary, away from high anti-psychiatry, but at the same time attentive to everyday suffering and its intimate connection to capitalist forms. The psychic landscape of late capitalism is chaotic, and, for Fisher, 'as

---

19   Waite 1996, p. 389.
20   Walker 2013; 2016.
21   Fisher 2010, p. 19.
22   Barthes 1973.
23   Deleuze and Guattari 1983.

production and distribution are restructured, so are nervous systems'.[24] Precarity is a lived psychic experience that fragments the possibilities of the future.

This is, however, not only a negative phenomenology. Staying true to Deleuze and Guattari, Fisher considers capitalism as a 'desire machine'. Adapting Deleuze and Guattari's question about fascism, Fisher asks why do we desire capitalism? Why do we displace our desires to capitalism and 'launder our libidos'?[25] The phenomenology of late capitalism is a phenomenology of our libidinal investment in capitalism. Here is where the problem of education becomes the problem of the education of desire. I am reminded of Fredric Jameson's contention that the problem with desire is not so much good desire versus bad desire, but 'lies in trying to figure out what we really want in the first place'.[26] Utopias are negative lessons, finally, that teach us the limits of our imagination in the face of the addictive culture of capitalism. It is only, Jameson insists, once the utopia has impoverished us, undertaken an act of 'world reduction',[27] that we can undertake a 'desiring to desire, a learning to desire, the invention of the desire called Utopia in the first place'.[28] While Jameson, in the text I am quoting from, sought this experience of impoverishment and the birth of desire in Andrei Platonov's communist modernist novel *Chevengur*, Fisher sought such experiences in popular culture – in the weird and the eerie, in the remnants of 1970s social democracy, and in the inventiveness of dance music culture. In both cases, this is a project of education,[29] of a teaching of the desire to desire out of an act of world reduction.

Fisher argued that 'the most powerful forms of desire are precisely cravings for the strange, the unexpected, the weird'.[30] He saw in the weird and eerie, as detailed in the book of that name, experiences of estrangement that not only registered the forms of late capitalism in their psychic dimensions but that also promised us liberation from them. The breakdown of capitalist realism is not only a breakdown of capitalism but also a breakdown of *realism*. Unlike the various contemporary projects that aim to re-think the possibilities of critical realism, in the wake of Lukács and Jameson,[31] Fisher remained attached to the possibilities of the surreal and, in his unfinished work on 'acid communism', the psychedelic.

---

24   Fisher 2010, p. 34.
25   Fisher 2010, p. 15.
26   Jameson 1994, p. 75.
27   Jameson 2005, pp.
28   Jameson 1994, p. 90.
29   Tally 2014.
30   Fisher 2010, p. 76.
31   Toscano and Kinkle 2015; Cunningham 2010 and 2013; Jameson 2009.

We should note that even these projects of critical realism are articulated to engage with the phantasmagoric and 'irreal' as key constituents of the fabric of capitalism.[32] Fisher, instead, directly engages with the weird as the promise of a liberation from capitalist realism. This brings him into proximity with the work of China Miéville, whose novel *The Last Days of New Paris* (2016) turns to surrealism as an equivocal power of liberation. Miéville's novel details the form of endless conflict that has resulted from the detonation of the S-blast, a surrealist weapon that unleashes their fictional creations into reality.[33] While intended to bring World War Two to an end, the bomb's detonation has left us with a surreal repeating loop, allegorising the stasis of the Cold War, the surreal nature of capitalist culture as perpetual present, and the seemingly endless war on terror. The question becomes one of how to bring an end to the end, in an echo of his earlier novel of perpetually delayed revolution, *Iron Council* (2004). These last days are caught between the sense of the final apocalypse and the sense of a suspended time that remains.[34] While surrealism has the uncanny capacity to dream the twentieth century in advance, as J.G. Ballard contended,[35] the aim of surrealism to liberate us from capitalist life and its limits is both realised and left as unsatisfactory.

In a similar fashion, Fisher's 'hauntological' reconstructions of the weird charge carried by forms of cultural production marked by British social democracy suggest the temporal disruption these unfollowed paths might cause.[36] The sense is that these works, created before the advent of aggressive neoliberal capitalism, offer anachronistic potential to galvanise new futures that have been left in our past. In this way Fisher can coordinate an accelerationist faith in the possibilities of technological liberation with this seemingly nostalgic return to the recent past. The aim of these returns is to reactivate these lost potentials and unleash these latent weird forces. This does suggest a complication of the model of capitalist inside and weird outside, but it also seems to rely on the promise of a return to an outside that was well within post-war capitalism. The link between that past and our present often seems tenuous, and the aim of the liberation of the sensorium is left, ironically, as an almost private matter of concern.

---

32   WReC 2015.
33   Miéville 2016.
34   Agamben 2005.
35   Ballard 1997.
36   Fisher 2014; 2018.

2   The Limits of the Outside

The utopias that Fisher implies are established in the ruins and fragments of
capitalist modernity, which echo something like the prehistoric monument of
Stonehenge: 'For the symbolic structures which made sense of the monuments
have rotted away, and in a sense what we witness here is the unintelligibility and
the inscrutability of the Real itself'.[37] If the prehistoric past lacks an intelligible
Symbolic that can be reconstructed, confronting us with the Real as remnant,
then the 'ruins and relics' of late capitalism in which all is rendered as value,
confronts us with another form of the Real as remnant. The eeriness of the
places of late capitalism needs to be rendered and outbid by the weird opening
to the outside. Again, this is the 'world reduction' that Jameson suggests, a levelling in which we can reconstruct and educate our future desires by educating
us into a desire for the future.

    At the same time, this outside is an equivocal figure of externality, which
serves to deny the closed vision of abstract capitalism as desiring machine.
Here lies a tension or oscillation that is not explicitly confronted or resolved.
There is a split between the interiority of capital that reaches down into the
nervous system and an outside that is another, different, form of liberation
into the inhuman. The substance of capitalist realism remains split between
inside and outside and not articulated. It is in the coordination of the hauntological and the accelerationist moments of Fisher's work that an articulation is
attempted: reaching back to those moments of haunting that can then be activ-
ated and accelerated to realise a 'missed' future.[38] Yet, this articulation remains
often limited and fantasmatic, and here is where the project of the education
of desire might have been fleshed out to think a phenomenology of capital that
could also trace its fractures without supposing a leap into a great outside. The
project of a phenomenology of capitalism needs to be supplemented, in the
Derridean sense of a necessary addition, with a project of education and reconstruction.

    The elaboration of the project of the education of desire remains one of the
losses caused by Mark Fisher's death. It is a project that remains to be reconstructed, from the complete collection of his writings, but also to be collectively
constructed. Fisher's own work as a teacher, both within and without educational institutions, was central to his phenomenology of late capitalism and
to the alternative forms of substance, of desire, that were possible. There is a

---

37   Fisher, 2016.
38   Noys 2014a.

pedagogic project of 'consciousness raising',[39] which is particularly true of the project of acid communism. Earlier in his writing Fisher had identified psychedelia with 'the denial of the existence of the Symbolic order as such', as a 'psychotic' regression that fails to register sociality at all.[40] At this point Fisher remains within the punk moment of 'never trust a hippie', and the dismissal of psychedelia as 'flabby' regression.[41] The fragment of acid communism tries to re-evaluate how experiments in consciousness change, now as visions beyond or outside capitalist realism. The tensions remain, however, between an interior world of capital that is embedded in the nervous system or the unconscious and a psychedelic outside that we can somehow reach.

It is also important to consider Marx's third thesis on Feuerbach, which suggests 'it is essential to educate the educator', and that 'the coincidence of the changing of circumstances and of human activity or self-changing can be conceived and rationally understood only as *revolutionary practice*'.[42] If Fisher is writing largely outside of this revolutionary context, as are we all, then we still have to consider this problem of education and self-education. It is this project that remains before us and is left implied as the true substance of which 'capitalist realism' is the truncated and mutilated form. It is the articulation of the weird outside with the eerie spaces of absence, of the fractures and dialectical tensions of capitalism with its empty appearance that remains to be made, if this is possible. This would also require a more detailed attention to the weird as an articulation of the possibilities and limits of contemporary capitalism, rather than as simple solution and exit. It would entail, I would suggest, the abandonment of this conceptualisation of inside and outside for a more dialectical grasping of the interior limits of capitalism and the articulation of those limits and their possibilities with that interior. It would involve thinking the totality as the whole of which capitalism is a subset and of thinking how Fisher's inside and outside are actually arrayed in this conception of totality.

Amongst the utopian suggestions of Jameson is one that seems resonant to me for Fisher's project: 'a Utopia of misfits and oddballs, in which the constraints for uniformization and conformity have been removed, and human beings grow wild like plants in a state of nature'.[43] This, it seems to me, is something of what Fisher's work implies: a wild substance, a wild desire, which, as *Capitalism Realism* insisted, was not oddly foreign to forms of discipline and

---

39   Fisher 2018, p. 764; Fisher 2018, pp. 421–3.
40   Fisher 2018, p. 83.
41   Fisher 2018, p. 274.
42   Marx, 1975, p. 422.
43   Jameson 1994, p. 99; Isaacson 2016.

organisation. In fact, this tension of chaos and discipline is another repetition of the tensions that animate and problematise Fisher's project, especially as discipline can only seem to be imposed on chaos rather than generated from forms of organisation. The difficulty still remains, however, of articulating that desire in its collective dimension and of dealing with the problematic Nietzschean accents at work in Fisher's writing. The inversion of elitism in the interests of what Badiou called 'proletarian aristocratism' are unconvincing, as they are in Badiou.[44] The inversion merely reverses the elitism and does not deal with the problem of treating the masses as inferior and lacking the requisite insight into the outside. Despite the best intentions of Fisher's project such Nietzschean retentions leave the collective dimension that would escape Nietzsche lacking. Part of the education into liberation that we have argued animates Fisher's project would also require a liberation from these Nietzschean conceptions, if we hope to achieve a utopia of misfits and oddballs.

---

44   Badiou 2006, p. 147; Landa 2013.

Conclusion

How do we understand crisis? This is a more complex question than it might appear, precisely because our understandings are culturally and ideologically shaped. That is why this collection has been framed by the concepts of crisis and criticism. Crisis is not simply given, although it is a reality with which we have to engage, and cultural mediations of crisis are not simply neutral, but ideological and therefore require criticism. To conclude, I want to examine the framing of crisis and, in particular, how many contemporary framings treat crisis as a subjective matter. This might seem strange – after all, what could be more objective than a global capitalist crisis? But while this might be true, our response and understanding of such a crisis can still be one that understands it in subjective terms. Such a subjectivism can and has inflected critical understandings of crisis and the result, I suggest, is often a cycle of appeals to subjective capacities to break with the crisis.[1] If we understand crisis in subjective terms then we may look for subjective solutions. In that sense, such subjective understandings leave us more vulnerable and unable to think the nature of crisis. This is not to say that subjectivity is not important, but it is to stress the issue of how we mediate subjectively the objective experience of crisis. That is also why attention to cultural understandings, which shape the response to crisis, remain vital. If those cultural understandings reinforce subjectivism then they require criticism.

As a first step, we might be advised not to overstate the novelty of our current situation. Lukács had noted that the literary problems of modernism were in continuity with those of the nineteenth century, particularly in the oscillation between boredom and intoxication.[2] That diagnosis, originally made by Baudelaire,[3] continues to remain resonant in contemporary culture, where the forms of culture may have significantly changed, especially with the rise of the internet, but the problems remain remarkably similar. Contemporary theoretical and critical work has continued to work variations on the problems of boredom and intoxication, only slightly updated to reflect on online life.[4] While Lukács focused on the philosophy of existentialism, so prevalent in the 1950s and early 1960s, we remain with many of its themes of absurdity

---

1 Hallward 2009.
2 Lukács 1970, p. 13.
3 Baudelaire 2008. See Benjamin 1976, p. 55 on how the nineteenth-century experience of intoxication is an experience of the intoxication of the commodity.
4 Fisher 2018, pp. 549–50; Preciado 2013.

and anguish, now updated into the worlds of the digital and objects. Lukács' reflection that 'one overcomes ennui as little through intoxication (one is even impelled back into its sphere) as one is liberated by shock from manipulated alienation, for shock merely groups, concentrates and conserves the character-istic moral features of this alienation', remains particularly resonant.[5] As we have seen, with thinkers like Lyotard and Fisher, the desire to shock as mode of liberation remains present, even if, as Lukács suggests, it repeats and conserves the experience of alienation.

While the forms of cultural production may be very different, the cultural experiences that Lukács describes seem, if anything, intensified by online life and the new modes of literary and cultural over-production.[6] It should also be noted that these new conditions of literary and cultural production also echo older modes, such as the industrial production of cheap ('dime') fiction.[7] Cer-tainly, cultural producers today are not prone to invoke the human condition as a fundamental theme, as they did when Lukács was writing, but they do invoke substitute formulations of material density, historical detail, and vari-ous forms of meta-proliferation, which serve the same purpose. Alienation, absurdity, intoxication and boredom, remain resonant, but now tend to res-onate with our experience of the world of objects, including digital objects, as well as with subjective experience. Contemporary cultural producers leave us with detailed descriptions of fragments of our existence, a rendered past that we passively observe, and reflections of the proliferations of value that are themselves inert. It is necessary to see these representations as themselves symptoms, to connect them to historical developments, and to understand our present as one that we can critically grasp. This is what I have called the neces-sity of criticism in response to crisis and why I do not think we should give in to resignation and despair, which, as Lukács notes, merely fuels our experience of manipulated alienation.[8]

In particular, to reinforce this issue of continuity, we can refine further these debts our present theoretical understandings owe to the recent past. Lukács was struggling with the subjectivist forms of existentialism of the 1950s and the nascent forms of postmodern experimentation emerging in the 1960s. As he noted, these forms oscillated between a radical subjectivism, in which fic-tion accessed the interiority and will of the embattled subject, and a natural-ism that rendered the world as inert and passive. These often went together,

---

5   Lukács 1970, p. 13.
6   McGurl 2021.
7   Denning 1998.
8   Lukács 1970, p. 13.

as defending the subject was a defence against this world that threatened to engulf and destroy the subject. It might appear obvious to say that the philosophy of existentialism was a philosophy of subjectivity, as was seen in Sartre, de Beauvoir and Camus. The difficulty is that this only appears to be a brief post-war moment and Lukács' cultural criticism could be regarded as outdated for not grasping the new theoretical tendencies that would abolish the role of subjectivity. Instead, in line with Lukács' arguments concerning Heidegger, I want to suggest that there is more continuity between existentialism and contemporary currents, beyond some direct references,[9] and that this continuity shapes and distorts the contemporary understanding of crisis.

Starting from Heidegger's criticisms of humanism,[10] we are now accustomed to seeing the 1950s and 1960s as the eclipse of existentialism by the new currents of structuralism that displace subjectivity. These set out, in the words of Claude Lévi-Strauss, 'not to constitute, but to dissolve man'.[11] This dissolution was only intensified by what became known as post-structuralism, which would, in the memorable words of Michel Foucault, 'wager that man would be erased, like a face drawn in sand at the edge of the sea'.[12] Instead of the subject we would have structures and then forces or effects. In the field of Marxism, Althusser's anti-humanism would also dissolve the humanist subject into social relations and formations.[13] Finally, we have another series of displacements in theoretical work that have taken place over the last forty years. These include a generalised historicism, especially in literary studies, and the various turns to matter and speculative forms of realism of the twenty-first century. While heterogenous, we could note that the subject is displaced by attention to networks of historical connection and by attention to matter and reality that is not dependent on the subject in any way.[14] What we seem to have witnessed is an almost continual loss of the subject.

I want to dispute this characterisation and suggest a stronger continuity with earlier subjectivist currents. Lukács' analysis of the late nineteenth-century literary mode of naturalism, which tries to represent reality as it is through a scientific objectivity, is key here. Lukács suggested that such naturalism involves the attempt to reproduce reality exactly, which at once involves the labour

---

9   Neyrat 2018.
10   Heidegger 1998, pp. 239–76.
11   Lévi-Strauss 1972, p. 247.
12   Foucault 1970, p. 387.
13   Althusser 1969.
14   Meillassoux 2008.

of the subject and also the seeming absence of the subject. His discussion of Flaubert's historical novel *Salammbô* (1862) is particularly useful.[15] Flaubert's disgust with bourgeois life drives him to this reconstruction of antiquity. The subjective factor, as Lukács points out, is vital, but the result is distance and a 'sterile exoticism'.[16] Flaubert dissolves his own subjectivity into the passivity of being a pure spectator, although this relation disguises his own active role in recording that reality. The result is a novel that records the minute detail of historical Carthage, but this is left as a dead reality. In the effort to maintain a living connection, Lukács argues, Flaubert endows his characters with a modern psychology. The result is 'the ghostly illusion of life', which then 'dissolves the hyper-objective reality of the objects'.[17]

What I am suggesting is that the theoretical currents that criticised or claimed to have surpassed subjectivity remained with the problem of naturalism that faced Flaubert. Such currents often do not mediate between subjectivity and objectivity,[18] but instead attempt to render a hyper-objective reality in which various attempts at subjective understanding then intrude. It is striking that Foucault's response to Flaubert, focusing on the novel *The Temptation of Saint Anthony* (1874), is the opposite of Lukács. For Foucault, Flaubert is not failing to maintain realism, but rather creating a new kind of text that is only mirroring other texts.[19] Foucault praises the archival impulse of Flaubert, which renders reality through texts, in act that might be self-diagnostic. From the position of Lukács, however, such a presentation of reality leaves it dead and leaves the subject trying to insert themselves into this inert archive. In the case of Foucault, we could say the replication of archival material is then given subjective colouring not by modern psychology but as a supposed history of the present, inflected with Nietzschean tropes.[20]

This is evident in the historical works of Foucault that involve a seemingly passive act of describing historical moments that are then intended to represent a major historical shift. Foucault treats the historical past naturalistically, and then uses subjective selection and juxtaposition to achieve a critical effect. So, in *Discipline and Punish* (1975) we have the juxtaposition of the execution by torture of Damiens the regicide in 1757, in all its gory detail, with the rules for young prisoners eighty years later, in all their banal-

15   Lukács 1962, pp. 218–29.
16   Lukács 1962, p. 221.
17   Lukács 1962, p. 224.
18   Rose 2009 and Rose 1984.
19   Foucault 1977a, pp. 87–109.
20   Foucault 1977a, pp. 139–64.

ity.[21] These descriptions obviously serve to introduce Foucault's distinction between the intimate bodily confrontation of sovereign power, visible in the public execution, and the new hidden and lifelong shaping of biopower, in which a series of norms guide and develop a mode of life. In the earlier *Madness and Civilization* (1961) we have a similar contrast between the emptying of the lazar houses, where those suffering from leprosy were confined, and the emergence of the figure of the ship of fools, as a passage in the treatment of madness.[22] In this case the ship of fools is treated as a brief moment of the recognition of madness before a new pattern of confinement for those regarded as mad modelled on the previous treatment of those suffering from leprosy. In both cases, powerful and resonant images are left to do historical work, but these images are treated as if they are found images, when instead they are curated elements of reality. Subjectivity intrudes in the aesthetic shaping of this naturalistic description of the past in which the subject is seemingly absent. We could add that contemporary theoretical trends treat the present in similar fashion, by creating and curating resonant images of objects and reality. Again, subjectivity intrudes in the act of selection and arrangement, but retreats again to simply leave such objects as objects of contemplation.

The failure of mediation is evident in a subjectivism that only apparently presents itself as an objectivism and the dissolution of the subject. In particular, I want to suggest that instead of gaining access to objective reality by dissolving the subject, we find reality turned into subjectivity or into a series of subjectivities. The so-called dissolution of subjectivity does not so much end the problem of the subjective but extend it into reality. While Flaubert tried to bridge between subjectivity and a hyper-objectivity through modern psychology, today Nietzsche's thought of reality and the subject as effects of the will-to-power serves that purpose.[23] While this is designed to downgrade the subject into mere effect it, in fact, subjectivises reality. If the subject is a mere force or effect amongst a reality of teeming forces and effects, then that reality takes on subjective hues as it too is a matter of teeming forces. A Nietzschean metaphysics of forces and effects does the work of Flaubert's projection of modern psychology, creating a living reality, or relation to reality, by treating reality as at once distant from the subject and then endowed with its own sense of activity.

---

21   Foucault 1977b, pp. 3–7.
22   Foucault 1989, pp. 3–13.
23   Nietzsche 2008a, p. 29.

The importance of Nietzsche for the subjectivising of reality becomes evident if we return to the problem of crisis and of crisis as an objective reality. The problem, as I have suggested, is the treatment of capitalist crisis as a crisis of civilisation. The irony is that this inflation of crisis is, at the same time, the treatment of crisis as subjective and so a failure to engage with the objectivity of capitalist crisis. While the crisis might be seen as the result of opaque financial instruments, as non-human agents, such a vision treats these instruments and the crisis as malign and magical. The fact that such instruments were made by humans recedes into invocations of complexity and agency that leave us as spectators. We are now spectators of a haunted world; the world of the phantasmagoria of the commodity.[24] While Marx wanted to explain how such a world is generated and how we might end it, now the spectral nature of this world is treated as an ontological reality.[25] This is due to the inflation of subjectivity, which comes to take over objective reality. In this case, crisis is rendered as a vast subjective theatre and we as the passive spectators.

Nietzsche is important as his thought represents this inflation of subjectivity and this inflation as a mode of crisis. Nietzsche seems to put an end to subjectivity, which is left as a mere fiction or effect.[26] What we have instead is the will-to-power and the world as a competing and clashing of these various expressions of the will-to-power. Yet, this is not so much the refutation of subjectivity but its extension. In his madness Nietzsche would proclaim 'at root every name in history is I'.[27] The fact that this is a statement out of madness (or some equivalent experience) might seem to refute this inflation of subjectivity to the point at which the subject becomes the crisis. In fact, the opposite lesson is drawn, and Nietzsche's experience of madness is seen as unlocking reality through this complete identification with it.[28] Nietzsche becomes the world-historical crisis of civilisation in order to resolve it, at least in thought. The subjectivisation of crisis is complete, in that this identification makes the crisis subjective and makes the solution to crisis subjective.

Nietzsche's crisis is, in fact, a crisis of mediation between subjectivity and objectivity, and his identification of subjectivity with objectivity is a false solution. In this way, the solution to crisis is celebrated as the collapse of mediation. Nietzsche ratifies the ideological understanding of crisis as the absorption of the subject into reality and the transformation of reality into subjectivity. In

---

24   Marx 1990, pp. 163–7; Cohen 1989.
25   Derrida 1994.
26   Nietzsche 2008a, p. 29.
27   Nietzsche 1996, p. 347.
28   Deleuze and Guattari 1983, p. 21; Foucault 1989, p. 288.

that case the resolution of crisis becomes a subjective experience, a matter of will, to 'break the history of mankind in two'.[29] Nietzsche casts crisis as a matter of civilisation and of the singular subject who embodies that civilisation, even if they are all the names in history. In doing so he treats crisis as a matter of the subject and the resolution of crisis as subjective. It will be the new subject, the *übermensch*, who supposedly solves the crisis by transcending the limits of the usual forms of the subject. These claims mystify the reality of crisis. Nietzsche was living through an experience of recurrent capitalist crisis and, in the commune, the most significant proletarian response of the nineteenth century.[30] Nietzsche recognised the significance of the commune, but only as something to be rejected and anathematised. This exclusion of reality left Nietzschean thought with fantasmatic solutions that themselves would feed into future experiences of crisis.[31]

The current experience of crisis has rarely taken on the pathos and pain of Nietzsche's identification, but the tendency to subjectivism remains. Instead of the drama of Nietzsche's self-presentation we tend to have a softer and more liberal mode of Nietzschean pluralism. In this case, reality and crisis is recognised and given independence from the subject, but this independence comes by treating reality and crisis as a series of actors not subject to human intervention or understanding. One significant form of this contemporary subjectivism is the rehabilitation of animism, in which the world becomes a set of subjectivities, even if those are non-human.[32] The aim of the new animism might be the humbling of human ambition and dominance, which is especially resonant due to the damage of human-initiated climate change, but the risk is that we have a world that is mirror of a series of dispersed subjectivities. While Flaubert projected modern psychology onto the past to create a living relation, now the ontology of animism is projected into reality itself to create a living relation with a hyper-objective reality. We displace the resolution of crisis to these non-human agencies as well, or to our interaction with them as equals. In such a way our profoundly significant role in causing the crisis is left obscured.[33]

The aim of such theoretical tendencies might be to hold on to the objectivity of the world and to endow it with more power, but the risk is that objectivity disappears into a generalised subjectivism. While we might apparently be con-

---

29   Nietzsche 1996, p. 330.
30   Lenin 1970.
31   Lukács 2021, pp. 7–8.
32   Mattar 2012. For a reading which tries to integrate animism and historical materialism, see Durrant 2022.
33   Malm 2017b.

tent to be passive spectators of a reality that is beyond the human, in fact we are entering into and shaping that reality as co-creators or curators (see Chapter 1). We engage with reality in a mode of selecting out and identifying its particular forms, in caring for moments of reality, or in organising and presenting them. In this way reality is supposedly given its full weight as beyond the subject, but the subjective actions of creation and curation of that reality, which shape its representation, are left obscure.

This mystification of our powers to shape reality is particularly problematic as it has been those powers, our anthropogenic intervention into nature, which has resulted in climate crisis. Marx wrote that 'it can be seen how the history of *industry* and the *objective* existence of industry as it has developed is the *open* book of the essential powers of man'.[34] Instead of the task of reading this book, of understanding how our alienated powers have shaped and altered the objective world, in this case in disastrous ways, we instead leave ourselves contemplating this world with wonder or horror. Again, the striking nature of the images that Foucault selects is something to be critically considered. Such shocking images may not simply spur us into thought, as they were intended, but leave us further alienated from the historical past and contemporary reality.

This is not only a matter of understanding the historical past, but also the present, and the nature of matter. Lukács describes how the twentieth-century economist Stuart Chase writes of a pencil as a 'mad dance of electrons'.[35] Such a description, reminiscent of our new animists and speculative realists, is 'a completely irrational subjectifying, anthropologizing and mythicizing of natural phenomena'.[36] Lukács points out that the description denies the objective reality of the pencil as an object in a set of relations, and that the choice to describe its existence at the sub-atomic level as a 'mad dance' is a subjective impression; physicists aim to describe and analyse such phenomena rationally. It is not difficult to find contemporary parallels to Chase. Franco 'Bifo' Berardi treats the Coronavirus as a 'chaotic concretion of matter' that 'has shattered any control that the capitalist abstraction had on the world'.[37] While claiming that matter as chaos escapes control, Berardi also leaves the virus beyond rational apprehension, which is particularly ironic considering the global scientific effort to analyse the virus and produce a vaccine. This is not to absolve

---

34   Marx 1975, p. 354.
35   In Lukács 2021, p. 781.
36   Lukács 2021, p. 781.
37   Berardi 2021, p. 17.

that effort from critical interrogation, but rendering the virus as chaotic matter is of little help in analysing the various successes, failures, and disasters of the attempts to deal with the pandemic.

An even closer parallel, in terms of subject matter, can be found in Graham Harman, the leading exponent of object-oriented philosophy. Harman, discussing the work of Alphonso Lingis, says we do not encounter a pen as a black cylindrical object, but as 'the condensation of a somber power'.[38] According to Harman, this idol-worship of the pen reveals its ominous force – a force that is lost when it is used for everyday tasks. The pen is explicitly removed from social relations to reveal an 'inner channel of horizontal thrust'.[39] While this revelation is claimed for a phenomenological reduction, this time on the side of the object and not of the human, which brackets science, such a subjectivism explicitly denies the pen its place in a series of relations as well as our capacity to rationally analyse it. We are left with an object ascribed capacities of force and thrust that, as with Berardi's chaos, echo Nietzsche's chaotic concept of reality.[40]

If we use Lukács to read these contemporary proponents of matter as site of force or chaos then we can see them as combining the attempt at a naturalist reading of the world without the subject combined with a romantic reading of the world as an array of chaotic powers. The evacuation of the subject leads to its return with a vengeance, precisely in terms of a failure to grasp mediation. While claiming some deeper objectivity, what we find is a mad dance of subjective perceptions detached from reality. We can see, especially in Berardi, a desire to resist capitalist abstraction and the dominance of exchange value over objects by invoking the powers of objects against control. This gives such thinking its anti-capitalist edge and resonates in a world in which our actions have produced a remarkably malignant object world.[41] The difficulty is that our own role in producing this world ends up being denied such that we cannot grasp the world as a book of our objectified powers and the world of nature. What I am suggesting is that while contemporary thought tries to do justice to contemporary reality supposedly against human hubris, its own descriptions and approach are hubristic human projections that also mystify our relationship to capitalism, crisis, and reality.[42]

---

38   Harman 2010, p. 19.
39   Harman 2010, p. 19.
40   Granier 1985.
41   Williams 2011.
42   Fluss and Frim 2021.

These difficulties also beset many critical or left responses to crisis as well. We have already seen, in Chapter 3, how currents of Autonomist and Post-Autonomist thought treat the productive forces as subjective expressions. While trying to recognise Marx's point that these powers are our alienated powers, such a bending of the stick ends up treating the productive forces as entirely subjective. As we have seen, this position is driven to an extreme in Berardi's recent work, in which reality takes on a chaotic and wilful form.[43] Reality is subjectivised down to the level of the Coronavirus, which takes on the insurgent and mutant forms usually ascribed to human resistance. Crisis then becomes a matter of will, induced by the activities of the cognitariat or multitude, and has less to do with the objective developments and crises of capitalism as a mode of production. The resolution is also another matter of will, in forms of refusal or flight that are supposed to resolve the crisis to the benefit of a latent communism somehow present and yet not realised.[44] This is not to deny forms of emergent agency or contestation, but it is to dispute the failure to integrate or understand the subjective mediation of objective crisis.

Communisation would appear to be the inverse position. In this case, we have a 'proletarian structuralism' in which the changing objective forms of capitalism only now permit the emergence of a proletarian struggle able to introduce a rupture with labour as a capitalist category.[45] This would appear to be a strict objectivism – one that is problematic in its denial of subjective and collective mediation. Yet the definition of proletarian identity as purely negative and as rupture is close to the Post-Autonomist focus on flight and exodus. We seem to have an oscillation or a turn from an extreme objectivism to a sudden breakout of subjectivism in the emergence of subjective capacities that had been previously overlooked. What is missing, as before, is the mediation of the subjective and objective. This difficulty of mediation remains present in the traces of consideration of class consciousness within communisation, which is a concept that haunts communisation without being fully developed as a mode of mediation.

The Nietzschean accents might be less present in these left currents, although they are not absent from the formation of Autonomia in its emphasis on subjective capacities and will.[46] This is a fact recognised even by the adherents

---

43   Berardi 2021.
44   Badiou 2012, p. 10.
45   Dauvé 2008, p. 40.
46   Tronti 2019.

of Autonomia, although this does not lead to a fundamental self-criticism.[47] Berardi, as we have seen, embraces these Nietzschean elements as they are transmitted by Deleuze and Guattari. That said, insofar that they remain close to the Marxist tradition, there are remnants in these currents of the discussion of objective reality and the mediations of class consciousness – and this is what makes them important still. We can see that Autonomia errs on the side of explicit subjectivism, while communisation errs on the side of objectivism, but both converge in the failure of mediation. While questions of mediation and consciousness do appear, they remain undeveloped, and that is why I have identified and focused on the problematic tendencies to subjectivism and objectivism in these left currents. My aim here is to stress such continuities in ways that might then allow us to develop a better critical understanding, not simply as an act of dismissal.

It might appear ironic to turn to objectivity, as so much discussion in the twentieth-century has argued that the problem with Marxism, and with philosophy, was its objectivism.[48] This is not to say that there were no such problems or modes of thought that were Stalinist and made use of claims to objectivity. Of course, as Lukács points out, Stalinism could also be understood as a form of subjectivism, by its denying of actual reality in the name of so-called objective reality.[49] Stalinist currents made appeals to the objective form of reality, but in ways that were shaped by subjective demands and illusions. This is evident in the disastrous forms of economic and social planning that Stalinism undertook, which regularly led to sudden reversals as reality took its revenge on subjective illusions. Such a critical analysis could also be used to grasp Lukács' own problematic concessions to Stalinism, which overestimate the objectivity of Stalinism as an existing mode of socialism. Once again, subjective projections can take on objective forms. The story here is complex, but what we can establish is that there remains a pressing problem of mediation between subjectivity and objectivity. This problem is rendered even more pressing by a subjectivism that mystifies objective reality, and this subjectivism is heavily indebted to Nietzschean modes of thought.

That is why, writing in retrospect, I regard the essays here as attempts to engage and develop the cultural mediations of crisis. They do not always escape the problems of subjectivism and the notes of despair that Lukács identifies with this ideological form. The aim, however, was to engage critically with exist-

---

47   Negri 2005, pp. 257–8.
48   Cleaver 2000.
49   Lukács 1963, p. 128.

ing forms of mediation and to draw attention to how we might move away from the Nietzschean naturalism I have described. The treatment of crisis in a subjective mode at once naturalises it and inflates its subjective possibilities of resolution. In contrast, we have traced a critical movement that pays close attention to cultural forms and does not abandon them as hopelessly tainted by ideology. The sympathetic nature of my readings is always intended to draw out possibilities, and my attention to thinkers and cultural forms is never entirely negative. That said, we must know our enemies and engage in the ruthless criticism, including the self-criticism, which Marx recommended.

Bibliography

Abu-Manneh, Bashir 2015, 'Tonalities of Defeat and Palestinian Modernism', *Minnesota Review*, 85: 56–79.

Achcar, Gilbert 2000, 'The 'Historical Pessimism' of Perry Anderson', *International Socialism* 88, available at: http://pubs.socialistreviewindex.org.uk/isj88/achcar.htm.

Adams, Jason 2012, 'Occupy Time', *Radical Philosophy*, 171: 15–18.

Adorno, Theodor 1973 [1966], *Negative Dialectics*, trans. E.B. Ashton, London: Routledge & Kegan Paul.

Adorno, Theodor 1992, 'On Dickens', in *Notes to Literature Volume 2*, ed. Rolf Tiedemann, trans. Shierry Weber Nicholsen, New York: Columbia University Press.

Adorno, Theodor 2002 [1964], *The Jargon of Authenticity*, London: Routledge.

Agamben, Giorgio 1998 [1995], *Homo Sacer: Sovereign Power and Bare Life*, trans. Daniel Heller-Roazen, Stanford: Stanford University Press.

Agamben, Giorgio 1999 [1970], *The Man without Content*, trans. Georgia Albert, Stanford: Stanford University Press.

Agamben, Giorgio 2005 [2000], *The Time That Remains: A Commentary on the Letter to the Romans*, trans. Patricia Dailey, Stanford: Stanford University Press.

Alderman, Nigel 2000, 'Introduction: Pocket Epics: British Poetry after Modernism', *The Yale Journal of Criticism*, 13, 1: 1–2.

Alexievich, Svetlana 2016, *Second-Hand Time*, trans. Bela Shayevich, London: Fitzcarraldo.

Allison, David (ed.) 1985, *The New Nietzsche: Contemporary Styles of Interpretation*, Cambridge, MA: The MIT Press.

Althusser, Louis 1969 [1965], *For Marx*, trans. Ben Brewster, Harmondsworth: Penguin.

Althusser, Louis 1971 [1968], *Lenin and Philosophy and Other Essays*, trans. Ben Brewster, London: New Left Books.

Althusser, Louis 1978 [1976], *Essays in Self-Criticism*, trans. Graham Lock, London: Verso.

Althusser, Louis 1990 [1974], *Philosophy and the Spontaneous Ideology of the Scientists*, trans. Gregory Elliott, London: Verso.

Althusser, Louis 2006, *Philosophy of the Encounter: Later Writings, 1978–1987*, ed. Oliver Corpet and François Matheron, trans. G.M. Goshgarian, London: Verso.

Althusser, Louis 2020, *On Ideology*, trans. Ben Brewster, London: Verso.

Althusser, Louis and Balibar, Étienne 2009 [1965], *Reading Capital*, trans. Ben Brewster, London: Verso.

Anderson, Benedict 2016, *Imagined Communities: Reflections on the Origin and Spread of Nationalism*, London: Verso.

Anderson, Perry 1976, *Considerations on Western Marxism*, London: Verso.

Anderson, Perry 1980, *Arguments within English Marxism*, London: Verso.

Anderson, Perry 1983, *In the Tracks of Historical Materialism*, London: Verso.

Anderson, Perry 1992a, *English Questions*, London: Verso.

Anderson, Perry 1992b, *A Zone of Engagement*, London: Verso.

Anderson, Perry, 1998, *The Origins of Postmodernity*, London: Verso.

Anderson, Perry 2000, 'Renewals', *New Left Review*, 1: 5–24.

Anderson, Perry 2005, *Spectrum: From Right to Left in the World of Ideas*, London: Verso.

Anderson, Perry 2007, 'Jottings on the Conjuncture', *New Left Review*, 48: 5–37.

Anderson, Perry 2009, *The New Old World*, London: Verso.

Anderson, Perry 2012, *The Indian Ideology*, New Delhi: Three Essays Collective.

Anderson, Perry 2019, *Brazil Apart: 1964–2019*, London: Verso.

Anon. 2011, 'Peru's Vargas Llosa: Economic Crisis Spurs Literature, Predicts Good Cultural Times Coming', *Latin American Herald Tribune*, 25, 4: 55–73.

Apter, Emily 1997, 'Out of Character: Camus's French Algerian Subjects', *MLN* 112, 4: 499–516.

Badiou, Alain 1999 [1989], *Manifesto for Philosophy*, trans., ed. and intro. Norman Madarasz, Albany: State University of New York Press.

Badiou, Alain 2005 [1988], *Being and Event*, trans. Oliver Feltham, London: Bloomsbury.

Badiou, Alain 2006, *Polemics*, trans. and intro. Steve Corcoran, London: Verso.

Badiou, Alain 2007 [2005], *The Century*, trans., with commentary and notes, Alberto Toscano, Cambridge: Polity.

Badiou, Alain 2009a [1982], *Theory of the Subject*, trans. and intro. Bruno Bosteels, London: Continuum.

Badiou, Alain 2009b [2006], *Logics of Worlds*, trans. Alberto Toscano, London: Continuum.

Badiou, Alain 2010, *The Communist Hypothesis*, trans. David Macey and Steve Corcoran, London: Verso.

Badiou, Alain 2012, *The Rebirth of History: Times of Riots and Uprisings*, trans. Gregory Elliott, London: Verso.

Badiou, Alain 2013, 'Our Contemporary Impotence', *Radical Philosophy* 181: 43–7.

Badiou, Alain 2014, *The Age of the Poets*, ed. and trans. Bruno Bosteels, intro. Emily Apter and Bruno Bosteels, London: Verso.

Bakhtin, Mikhail 1984 [1965], *Rabelais and His World*, Bloomington: Indiana University Press.

Balibar, Étienne 1989, 'Spinoza, the Anti-Orwell: The Fear of the Masses', *Rethinking Marxism*, 2, 3: 104–39.

Balibar, Étienne 2007 [1994], *The Philosophy of Marx*, trans. Chris Turner, London: Verso.

Ballard, J.G. 1997, *A User's Guide to the Millennium: Essays and Reviews*, London: Flamingo.

Barragan, Yesenia 2014, *Selling Our Death Masks: Cash-For-Gold in the Age of Austerity*, Winchester, UK: Zero Books.

Barry, Andrew 2011, 'Networks', *Radical Philosophy*, 165: 35–40.

Barthelme, Fredric 2009a, 'Interview with Frederick Barthelme', Fictionaut Blog, available at: http://blog.fictionaut.com/2009/04/11/an-interview-with-frederick-barthelme/.

Barthelme, Fredric 2009b, *Waveland*, New York: Doubleday.

Barthes, Roland 1970 [1953], *Writing Degree Zero*, trans. Annette Lavers and Colin Smith, Boston: Beacon Press.

Barthes, Roland 1973 [1957], *Mythologies*, trans. Annette Lavers, London: Paladin.

Barthes, Roland 1977, *Image-Music-Text*, trans. Stephen Heath, London: Paladin.

Bataille, Georges 1985, *Visions of Excess: Selected Writings 1927–1939*, ed. and intro. Allan Stoekl, trans. Allan Stoekl et al, Minneapolis: University of Minnesota Press.

Bataille, Georges 2022, *Critical Essays Vol. 1: 1944–1948*, ed. Benjamin Noys and Alberto Toscano, trans. Chris Turner, London: Seagull Books.

Baudelaire, Charles 2008, *The Flowers of Evil*, trans. James McGowan, intro. Jonathan Culler, Oxford: Oxford University Press.

Baudrillard, Jean 1975, *The Mirror of Production*, trans. Mark Poster, New York: Telos.

Baudrillard, Jean 1987, *Forget Foucault*, trans. Nicole Dufresne, New York: Semiotext(e).

Benjamin, Walter 1968, *Illuminations*, New York: Shocken Books.

Benjamin, Walter 1976, *Charles Baudelaire: A Lyric Poet in the Era of High Capitalism*, trans. Harry Zohn, London: Verso.

Benjamin, Walter 1996, 'Capitalism as Religion', trans. Rodney Livingstone, in *Selected Writings Vol. 1*, Cambridge, MA: Belknap Harvard Press.

Benjamin, Walter 2019, *The Storyteller Essays*, intro. Samuel Titan, trans. Tess Lewis, New York: NYRB books.

Bennett, Jane 2010, *Vibrant Matter: A Political Ecology of Things*, Durham, NC: Duke University Press.

Bennington, Geoffrey 1988, *Lyotard: Writing the Event*, Manchester: Manchester University Press.

Berardi, Franco 'Bifo' 2009, 'Communism is back but we should call it the therapy of singularisation', *Generation Online*, available at: http://www.generation-online.org/p/fp_bifo6.htm.

Berardi, Franco 'Bifo' 2012, *The Uprising: On Poetry and Finance*, Los Angeles: Semiotext(e).

Berardi, Franco 'Bifo' 2015, *Heroes: Mass Murder and Suicide*, London: Verso.

Berardi, Franco 'Bifo' 2017, 'After the European Union', Verso Blog, available at: https://www.versobooks.com/blogs/3129-after-the-european-union.

Berardi, Franco 'Bifo' 2021, *The Third Unconscious*, London: Verso.

Berardi, Franco 'Bifo', Chantal Mouffe, Wilhelm Heimeyer, G.M. Tamás 2018, *A New Fascism?*, ed. Susanne Pfeffer, London: Koenig Books.

Berger, John 1992, *Pig Earth*, London: Vintage.

Berlant, Lauren 2008, 'Intuitionists: History and the Affective Event', *American Literary History*, 20, 4: 845–60.

Bernes, Jasper 2017, *The Work of Art in the Age of Deindustrialization*, Stanford: Stanford University Press.

Bernes, Jasper 2020, 'Rifts and Swerves', Nilpotencies substack, available at: https://jasperbernes.substack.com/p/rifts-and-swerves.

Best, Sharon and Marcus, Steven 2009, 'Surface Reading: An Introduction', *Representations*, 108, 1: 1–21.

Bishop, Claire 2012, *Artificial Hells: Participatory Art and the Politics of Spectatorship*, London: Verso.

Blanton, C.D. 2015, *Epic Negation: The Dialectical Poetics of Late Modernism*, Oxford: Oxford University Press.

Blissett, Luther 2004, *Q*, London: Arrow.

Bonney, Sean 2015, *Letters against the Firmament*, London: Enitharmon Press.

Borges, Jorge Luis 1999, *Collected Fictions*, trans. Andrew Hurley, London: Penguin.

Bourriaud, Nicholas 2002, *Relational Aesthetics*, trans. Simon Pleasance and Fronza Woods with the participation of Mathieu Copeland, les presses du réel.

Bourriaud, Nicholas 2005, *Postproduction*, trans. Jeanine Herman, London: Steenberg Press.

Brecht, Bertolt 1978, *Brecht on Theatre*, ed. and trans. John Willett, London: Methuen.

Brecht, Bertolt 2007, 'Against Georg Lukács', in *Aesthetics and Politics*, Adorno et al. London: Verso.

Brecht, Bertolt 2016, *Me-Ti: Book of Interventions in the Flow of Things*, London: Bloomsbury.

Brennan, Timothy 2014, *Borrowed Light: Vico, Hegel, and the Colonies*, Stanford: Stanford University Press.

Brenner, Robert 1976, 'Agrarian Class Structure and Economic Development in Pre-Industrial Europe', *Past & Present*, 70, 1: 30–75.

Brenner, Robert 1982, 'The Agrarian Roots of European Capitalism', *Past & Present*, 97, 1: 16–113.

Breuer, Joseph and Sigmund Freud 1974, *Studies on Hysteria*, trans. James and Alix Strachey, ed. Angela Richards, London: Penguin.

Bromberg, Svenja 2013, 'The Anti-Political Aesthetics of Objects and Worlds Beyond', *Mute Magazine*, available at: http://www.metamute.org/editorial/articles/anti-political-aesthetics-objects-and-worlds-beyond.

Brouillette, Sarah 2014, *Literature and the Creative Economy*, Stanford: Stanford University Press.

Brouillette, Sarah 2017, 'On the African Literary Hustle', *Blindfield: A Journal of Cultural Inquiry*, available at: https://blindfieldjournal.com/2017/08/14/on-the-african-literary-hustle/.

Brown, Bill 2001, 'Thing Theory', *Critical Inquiry*, 28, 1: 1–22.

Brown, Ian 2009, 'The 18th Brumaire of Barack Obama', *The Globe and Mail*, available at: https://www.theglobeandmail.com/opinion/the-18th-brumaire-of-barack-obama/article1198981/.

Brown, Nathan 2011, 'Red Years: Althusser's Lesson, Rancière's Error and the Real Movement of History', *Radical Philosophy*, 170: 16–24.

Build the Party, 2013 'A Fine Hell', build the party blog, available at: http://umfnyc.wordpress.com/2013/01/18/a-fine-hell/.

Bull, Malcolm 2011, *Anti-Nietzsche*, London: Verso.

Bull, Malcolm 2014, 'Pure Mediterranean', *London Review of Books* 36, 4, available at: https://www.lrb.co.uk/the-paper/v36/n04/malcolm-bull/pure-mediterranean.

Bürger, Peter 1984, *Theory of the Avant-Garde*, trans. Michael Shaw, Minneapolis: University of Minnesota Press.

Calabrese, Omar 1992, *Neo-Baroque: A Sign of the Times*, trans. Charles Lambert. Princeton: Princeton University Press.

Calder Williams, Evan 2010, *Combined and Uneven Apocalypse*, Winchester, UK: Zero Books.

Camatte, Jacques 1995, *This World We Must Leave and Other Essays*, ed. Alex Trotter, New York: Autonomedia.

Camus, Albert 2013 [1947], *The Plague*, trans. Robin Buss, afterword by Tony Judt, London: Penguin.

Carey, John 1992, *The Intellectuals and the Masses*, London: Faber and Faber.

Caudwell, Christopher 2017, *The Crisis in Physics*, London: Verso.

Caudwell, Christopher 2018, *Culture as Politics: Selected Writings of Christopher Caudwell*, ed. David Margolies, London: Pluto.

Caygill, Howard 2012, 'Also Sprach Zapata: Philosophy and Resistance', *Radical Philosophy*, 171: 19–26.

Caygill, Howard 2013, *On Resistance: A Philosophy of Defiance*, London: Bloomsbury.

Ciccariello-Maher, George 2016, *Building the Commune: Radical Democracy in Venezuela*, London: Verso.

Clark, T.J. 1999, *Farewell to an Idea*, New Haven: Yale University Press.

Clark, T.J. 2012, 'For a Left with No Future', *New Left Review*, 74: 53–75.

Clark, T.J. 2016, 'Where are we now? Responses to the Referendum', *London Review of Books*, 38, 14, available at: https://www.lrb.co.uk/v38/n14/on-brexit/where-are-we-now#clark.

Clark, T.J. 2018, *Heaven on Earth: Painting and the Life to Come*, London: Thames & Hudson.

Cleaver, Harry 2000, *Reading Capital Politically*, Leeds: Anti/Theses.

Clover, Joshua 2010, 'Remarks on Method', *Film Quarterly*, 63, 4: 7–9.

Clover, Joshua 2011, 'Autumn of the System: Poetry and Financial Capital', *Journal of Narrative Theory*, 41, 1: 34–52.

Clover, Joshua 2015, *Red Epic*, Oakland: Commune Editions.

Clover, Joshua 2016, *Riot. Strike. Riot: The New Era of Uprisings*, London: Verso.

Cohen, Margaret 1989, 'Walter Benjamin's Phantasmagoria', *New German Critique*, 48: 87–107

Cohn, Norman 1970, *The Pursuit of the Millennium*, London: Paladin.

Colquhoun, Matt 2020, *Egress: On Mourning, Melancholy and Mark Fisher: On Mourning, Melancholy and the Fisher-Function*, London: Repeater.

Connolly, William E. 2011, *A World of Becoming*, Durham, NC: Duke University Press.

Conway, Daniel 2009, 'Whither the 'Good Europeans'? Nietzsche's New World Order', *South Central Review*, 26, 3: 40–60.

Critchley, Simon 2001, *Continental Philosophy: A Very Short Introduction*, Oxford: Oxford University Press.

Cunningham, David 2010, 'Capitalist Epics: Abstraction, Totality, and the Theory of the Novel', *Radical Philosophy*, 163: 11–23.

Cunningham, David 2013, 'Here Comes the New: *Deadwood* and the Historiography of Capitalism', *Radical Philosophy*, 180: 8–24.

Cusset, François 2008, *French Theory: How Foucault, Derrida, Deleuze, and Co. Transformed the Intellectual Life of the Unites States*, trans. Jeff Fort, Minneapolis: University of Minnesota Press.

Dainotto, Roberto 2020, 'Historical Immanence and the Problem of the New: On the "Necessary Anachronism" of György Lukács', *Diacritics*, 48, 2: 18–35.

Dauvé, Gilles 2008, 'Human, All Too Human?', *Endnotes* 1: 39–43.

Dauvé, Gilles and Karl Nesic 2008, 'Love of Labour? Love of Labour Lost ...', *Endnotes* 1: 104–52.

Davidson, Neil 2004, 'The Prophet, his Biographer and the Watchtower', *International Socialism* 104, available at: http://pubs.socialistreviewindex.org.uk/isj104/davidson.htm.

Davis, Mike 2000, *Late Victorian Holocausts*, London: Verso.

Day, Gail 2011, 'Realism, Totality and the Militant *Citoyen*: Or, What Does Lukács Have to Do with Contemporary Art?', in *Georg Lukács: The Fundamental Dissonance of Existence*, ed. Timothy Bewes and Timothy Hall, London: Continuum.

Dean, Jodi 2018, *Crowds and Party*, London: Verso.

Debord, Guy 1992, *Panegyric Volume One*, trans. James Brook, London: Verso.

Debord, Guy 2003, *Complete Cinematic Works*, trans. and ed. Ken Knabb, Oakland: AK Press.

Deleuze, Gilles 1983 [1962], *Nietzsche and Philosophy*, trans. Hugh Tomlinson, London: Athlone.

Deleuze, Gilles 1988 [1986], *Foucault*, trans. and ed. Seán Hand, Foreword by Paul Bové, Minneapolis: University of Minnesota Press.

Deleuze, Gilles 1989 [1985], *Cinema 2: The Time-Image*, trans. Hugh Tomlinson and Robert Galeta, London: The Athlone Press.

Deleuze, Gilles 1992, 'Postscript on the Societies of Control', *October*, 59: 3–7.

Deleuze, Gilles 1993 [1988], *The Fold: Leibniz and the Baroque*, trans. Tom Conley. London: Athlone Press.

Deleuze, Gilles 1994 [1968], *Difference and Repetition*, trans. Paul Patton, London: The Athlone Press.

Deleuze, Gilles 1998 [1993], *Essays Critical and Clinical*, trans. Daniel W. Smith and Michael A. Greco, London: Verso.

Deleuze Gilles and Félix Guattari 1983 [1972], *Anti-Oedipus*, trans. Robert Hurley, Mark Seem and Helen R. Lane. Minneapolis: University of Minnesota Press.

Deleuze, Gilles and Félix Guattari 1986 [1975], *Kafka: Towards a Minor Literature*, trans. Dana Polan, Minneapolis: University of Minnesota Press.

Deleuze, Gilles and Félix Guattari 1998 [1980], *A Thousand Plateaus*, trans. and intro. Brian Massumi, London: Athlone.

DeLillo, Don 2003, *Cosmopolis*, New York: Scribner.

Demmers, Jolle, and Lauren Gould 2018, 'An Assemblage Approach to Liquid Warfare: AFRICOM and the 'Hunt' for Joseph Kony', *Security Dialogue*, 49, 5: 364–81.

Denning, Michael 1998, *Mechanic Accents: Dime Novels and Working-Class Culture in America*, London: Verso.

Derrida, Jacques 1978 [1967], *Writing and Difference*, trans. Alan Bass, Chicago: University of Chicago Press.

Derrida, Jacques 1984, 'Of an Apocalyptic Tone Recently Adopted in Philosophy', trans. John P. Leavey Jr., *Oxford Literary Review* 6, 2: 3–37.

Derrida, Jacques 1989 [1987], *Of Spirit: Heidegger and the Question*, trans. Geoffrey Bennington and Rachel Bowlby, Chicago: The University of Chicago Press.

Derrida, Jacques 1992, *The Other Heading: Reflections on Today's Europe*, trans. Pascale-Anne Brault and Michael B. Naas, intro. Michael B. Naas, Bloomington: Indiana University Press.

Derrida, Jacques 1994 [1993], *Specters of Marx*, trans. Peggy Kamuf, London: Routledge.

Deutscher, Isaac 1969, *Heretics and Renegades and Other Essays*, intro. E.H. Carr, London: Jonathan Cape.

Dews, Peter 2007, *Logics of Disintegration: Post-structuralist Thought and the Claims of Critical Theory*, London: Verso.

Dickens, Charles 1997 [1865], *Our Mutual Friend*, London: Penguin.

Dollimore, Jonathan and Alan Sinfield (eds.) 1985, *Political Shakespeare: Essays in Cultural Materialism*, Manchester: Manchester University Press.

Dombowsky, Don 2014, *Nietzsche and Napoleon: The Dionysian Conspiracy*, Cardiff: University of Wales Press.

Duncan, Dennis (ed.) 2015, *Theory of the Great Game*, London: Atlas.

Durrant, Sam 2022, 'Critical Spirits: New Animism as Historical Materialism', *New Formations*, 104–105: 50–76.

Eagleton, Terry 1996, *Literary Theory: An Introduction Second Edition*, Oxford: Blackwell.

Eagleton, Terry 2009, *Walter Benjamin, or Towards a Revolutionary Criticism*, London: Verso.

Easthope, Antony 1991, *British Post-Structuralism Since 1968*, London: Routledge.

Edwards, Steve 2020, 'Making a Case: Daguerreotypes', British Art Studies, 18, available at: https://www.britishartstudies.ac.uk/issues/issue-index/issue-18/making-a-case.

Eliot, T.S. 1974, *Collected Poems, 1909–1962*, London: Faber and Faber.

Elliott, Gregory 1993, *Labourism and the English Genius: The Strange Death of Labour England?*, London: Verso.

Elliott, Gregory 1998, *Perry Anderson: The Merciless Laboratory of History*, Minneapolis: University of Minnesota Press.

Elliott, Gregory 2006a, *Althusser: The Detour of Theory*, Leiden: Brill.

Elliott, Gregory 2006b, 'Parisian Impostures', *New Left Review*, 41: 139–45.

Elliott, Gregory 2008, *Ends in Sight: Marx/Fukuyama/Hobsbawm/Anderson*, London: Pluto Press.

Endnotes 2010, 'The History of Subsumption', *Endnotes*, 2: 130–52, available at: http://endnotes.org.uk/articles/6.

Engels, Friedrich 1976 [1877], *Anti-Dühring*, Beijing: Foreign Languages Press.

Felski, Rita. 2011a, ' "Context Stinks!"', *New Literary History*, 42, 4: 573–91.

Felski, Rita. 2011b, 'Suspicious Minds', *Poetics Today*, 32, 2: 215–34.

Felski, Rita 2015, *The Limits of Critique*, Chicago: The University of Chicago Press.

Finlayson, Alan 2018, 'The Metaphysics of Brexit', *Third Text*, 32, 5–6: 598–604.

Fisher, Mark 2010, *Capitalist Realism: Is There No Alternative?*, Winchester, UK: Zero Books.

Fisher, Mark 2014, *Ghosts of My Life: Writings on Depression, Hauntology and Lost Futures*, Winchester, UK: Zero Books.

Fisher, Mark 2016, *The Weird and the Eerie*, London: Repeater.

Fisher, Mark 2018, *K-Punk: The Collected and Unpublished Writings of Mark Fisher (2004–2016)*, ed. Darren Ambrose, London: Repeater. Fluss, Harrison and Landon Frim 2022, *Prometheus and Gaia: Technology, Ecology and Anti-Humanism*, London: Anthem Press.

Fontaine, Claire 2013, *Human Strike has Already Begun and Other Writings*, Lünberg: PML Books.

Fortini, Franco 2013, *The Dogs of Sinai*, trans. Alberto Toscano, London: Seagull Books.

Foster, Hal 2014, 'Jeff Koons', *London Review of Books*, 36, 15, available at: https://www.lrb.co.uk/the-paper/v36/n15/hal-foster/at-the-whitney.

Foster, Hal 2017, *Bad New Days: Art, Criticism, Emergency*, London: Verso.

Foucault, Michel 1970 [1966], *The Order of Things: An Archaeology of the Human Sciences*, trans. Alan Sheridan. London and New York: Tavistock / Routledge.

Foucault, Michel 1973 [1963], *The Birth of the Clinic: An Archaeology of Medical Perception*, trans. A.M. Sheridan, London: Routledge.

Foucault, Michel 1977a, *Language, Counter-Memory, Practice*, ed. and intro. Donald F. Bouchard, trans. Donald F. Bouchard and Sherry Simon. Ithaca: Cornell University Press.

Foucault, Michel 1977b [1975], *Discipline and Punish: The Birth of the Prison*, trans. Alan Sheridan, New York: Vintage.

Foucault, Michel 1989 [1961], *Madness and Civilization: A History of Insanity in the Age of Reason*, trans. Richard Howard, London: Routledge.

Foucault, Michel 2003, *Abnormal*, trans. Graham Burchell, London: Verso.

Foucault, Michel 2008, *The Birth of Biopolitics: Lectures at the Collège de France, 1978–79*, trans. Graham Burchell, Basingstoke: Palgrave.

Frank, Thomas 1997, *The Conquest of Cool*, Chicago: University of Chicago Press.

Freud, Sigmund 1977, *On Sexuality*, ed. Angela Richards, London: Penguin.

Freud, Sigmund 2002, *Civilization and Its Discontents*, trans. David McLintock, intro. Leo Bersani, London: Penguin.

Fukuyama, Francis 1992, *The End of History and the Last Man*, London: Hamish Hamilton.

Fuller, Matthew, and Eyal Weizman 2021, *Investigative Aesthetics: Conflicts and Commons in the Politics of Truth*, London: Verso.

Galloway, Alexander R. 2004, *Protocol: How Control Exists after Decentralization*, Cambridge, MA: The MIT Press.

Galloway, Alexander R. 2013a, 'The Poverty of Philosophy: Realism and Post-Fordism', *Critical Inquiry*, 39: 347–66.

Galloway Alexander R. 2013b, 'Everything is Computational', *Los Angeles Review of Books*, available at: http://lareviewofbooks.org/essay/franco-morettis-distant-reading-a-symposium

Galloway, Alexander R. 2019, 'Mathification', *Diacritics*, 47, 1: 96–115.

Galloway, Alexander R. and Eugene Thacker 2007, *The Exploit: A Theory of Networks*, Minneapolis: University of Minnesota Press.

Gasché, Rodolphe 2009, *Europe, or the Infinite Task: A Study of a Philosophical Concept*, Stanford: Stanford University Press.

Gasché, Rodolphe 2017, 'Patočka on Europe in the aftermath of Europe', *European Journal of Social Theory*, xx, x: 1–16.

Geras, Norman 2016, *Marx and Human Nature: Refutation of a Legend*, London: Verso.

Gibson, William 1986, *Neuromancer*, London: Grafton.

Gibson, William 2008, *Spook Country*, London: Penguin.

Gibson, William 2010, *Zero History*, London: Viking.

Gilroy, Paul 1992, *There Ain't No Black in the Union Jack*, London: Routledge.

Ginzburg, Carlo 1980, *The Cheese and the Worms: The Cosmos of a Sixteenth-Century Miller*, trans. John and Anne Tedeschi, London: Routledge & Kegan Paul.

Glenn, Paul F. 2001, 'Nietzsche's Napoleon: The Higher Man as Political Actor', *The Review of Politics*, 63, 1: 129–58.

Godwin, William 2009 [1794], *Caleb Williams*, ed. Pamela Clemit, Oxford: Oxford University Press.

Goldmann, Lucien 2016 [1964], *The Hidden God: A Study of Tragic Vision in the* Pensées *of Pascal and the Tragedies of Racine*, trans. Philip Thody, London: Verso.

Gordillo, Gastón R. 2011, 'The Speed of Revolutionary Resonance', *Space and Politics Blog*, available at: http://spaceandpolitics.blogspot.co.uk/2011/03/speed-of-revoluti onary-resonance.html.

Gramsci, Antonio 1957, *The Modern Prince and Other Writings*, New York: International Publishers.

Gramsci, Antonio 1971, *Selections from Prison Notebooks*, ed. and trans. Quintin Hoare and Geoffrey Nowell Smith, London: Lawrence and Wishart.

Granier, Jean 1985, 'Nietzsche Conception of Chaos', in *The New Nietzsche*, ed. David B. Allison.

Hallward, Peter 2001, *Absolutely Postcolonial: Writing Between the Singular and the Specific*, Manchester: Manchester University Press.

Hallward, Peter 2009, 'The Will of the People: Notes Toward a Dialectical Voluntarism', *Radical Philosophy*, 155: 17–29.

Halpin, Harry 2012, 'The Philosophy of Anonymous: Ontological Politics Without Identity', *Radical Philosophy*, 176: 19–28.

Hamacher, Werner 2008, '*Lingua Amissa*: The Messianism of Commodity-Language and Derrida's *Specters of Marx*', in *Ghostly Demarcations: A Symposium on Jacques Derrida's* Specters of Marx, ed. Michael Sprinker, London: Verso.

Hammond, Simon, 2019, 'K-Punk at Large', *New Left Review*, 118: 37–66.

Hardt, Michael, and Antonio Negri 2000, *Empire*, Cambridge, MA: Harvard University Press.

Hardt, Michael, and Antonio Negri 2005, *Multitude*, London: Hamish Hamilton.

Harman, Graham 2009, *Prince of Networks: Bruno Latour and Metaphysics*, Melbourne: re.press.

Harman, Graham 2010, *Towards Speculative Realism: Essays and Lectures*, Winchester, UK: Zero Books.

Harman, Graham 2012a, 'The Well-Wrought Broken Hammer: Object-Oriented Literary Criticism', *New Literary History*, 43: 183–203.

Harman, Graham 2012b, *Weird Realism: Lovecraft and Philosophy*, Winchester: Zero Books.

Harman, Graham, 2016, *Dante's Broken Hammer*, London: Repeater.

Harman, Graham 2020, *Art and Objects*, Cambridge: Polity.

Hartley, Daniel 2017, 'Radical Schiller and the Young Marx', in *Aesthetic Marx*, ed. Samir Gandesha and Johan Hartle, London: London: Bloomsbury.

Hatherley, Owen 2016, *Ministry of Nostalgia*, London: Verso.

Hawkes, Terence 1986, *That Shakespeherian Rag: Essays on a Critical Process*, London: Methuen.

Hegel, G.W.F. 1977 [1807], *The Phenomenology of Spirit*, trans. A.V. Miller, Oxford: Oxford University Press.

Hegel, G.W.F. 2010 [1812], *The Science of Logic*, trans. George di Giovanni, Cambridge: Cambridge University Press.

Heidegger, Martin 1998, *Pathmarks*, ed. William McNeill, Cambridge: Cambridge University Press.

Heinrich, Michael 2012, *An Introduction to the Three Volumes of Marx's* Capital, trans. Alexander Locascio, New York: Monthly Review Press.

Henry, Michel 2014, *From Communism to Capitalism: Theory of a Catastrophe*, trans. Scott Davidson, London: Bloomsbury.

Heron, Kai, and Jodi Dean 2022, 'Climate Leninism and Revolutionary Transition: Organization and Anti-Imperialism in Catastrophic Times', *Spectre*, available at: https://spectrejournal.com/climate-leninism-and-revolutionary-transition/.

Hester, Diarmuid 2015, 'Revisiting Pierre Guyotat's *Éden, Éden, Éden*: Splanchnology, Writing, Matter, and the Devastation of Ethics', *French Forum*, 40, 1: 31–45.

Hobsbawm, 1994, *Age of Extremes: The Short Twentieth Century, 1914–1991*, London: Abacus.

Hochschild, Adam 1998, *King Leopold's Ghost: A Story of Greed, Terror, and Heroism in Colonial Africa*, Boston: Mariner Books.

Hoggart, Richard 1958, *The Uses of Literacy*, Harmondsworth: Penguin.

Horkheimer, Max 2012, *Critique of Instrumental Reason*, London: Verso.

Houellebecq, Michel 1991, *H.P. Lovecraft: Against the World, Against Life*, trans. Donna Khazeni, San Francisco: Believer Books.

Hulme, Alison 2015, *On the Commodity Trail: The Journey of a Bargain Store Product from East to West*, London: Bloomsbury.

Husserl, Edmund 1965, *Phenomenology and the Crisis of Philosophy*, trans. and intro. Quentin Lauer, New York: Harper & Row.

Husserl, Edmund 1977 [1931], *Cartesian Meditations*, trans. Dorion Cairns, The Hague: Martinus Nijhoff.

Invisible Committee 2009, *The Coming Insurrection*, Los Angeles: Semiotext(e).

Invisible Committee 2016, *Call*, Ill Will Editions, available at: https://illwilleditions .noblogs.org/files/2016/11/Invisible-Committee-The-Call-IWE-READ.pdf

Isaacson, Johanna 2011, 'From Riot Grrrl to CrimethInc: A Lineage of Expressive Nega-
    tion in Feminist Punk and Queercore', *Liminalities: A Journal of Performance Studies*,
    7, 4, available at: http://liminalities.net/7-4/expressivenegation.pdf.
Isaacson, Johanna 2014, 'The Transfenestrational Imaginary: Periodizing *Vineland*'s Six-
    ties', *Reconstruction: Studies in Contemporary Culture*, 14, 4, [Last accessed 15 March
    2015]
Isaacson, Johanna 2016, *The Ballerina and the Bull: Anarchist Utopias in the Age of Fin-
    ance*, London: Repeater.
Jameson, Fredric 1991, *Postmodernism, or, The Cultural Logic of Late Capitalism*, Dur-
    ham, NC: Duke University Press.
Jameson, Fredric 1994, *The Seeds of Time*, New York: Columbia University Press.
Jameson, Fredric 1995, *The Geopolitical Aesthetic: Cinema and Space in the World System*,
    Bloomington: Indiana University Press.
Jameson, Fredric 2000, *Brecht and Method*, London: Verso.
Jameson, Fredric 2002 [1981], *The Political Unconscious: Narrative as a Socially Symbolic
    Act*, London: Routledge.
Jameson. Fredric, 2003 'Fear and Loathing in Globalization', *New Left Review* 23: 105–14.
Jameson, Frederic 2006, *Archaeologies of the Future: The Desire Called Utopia and Other
    Science Fictions*, London: Verso.
Jameson, Frederic 2007, *The Modernist Papers*, London: Verso.
Jameson, Fredric 2008 [1979], *Fables of Aggression: Wyndham Lewis, the Modernist as
    Fascist*, London: Verso.
Jameson, Frederic 2009a, *The Cultural Turn: Selected Writings on the Postmodern, 1983–
    1998*, London: Verso.
Jameson, Fredric 2009b, 'Marx and Montage', *New Left Review* 58: 109–17.
Jameson, Frederic 2009c, *Valences of the Dialectic*, London: Verso.
Jameson, Frederic 2013a, *The Antinomies of Realism*, London: Verso.
Jameson, Frederic 2013b, *A Singular Modernity*, London: Verso.
Jameson, Frederic 2016, *Raymond Chandler: The Detections of Totality*, London: Verso.
Jameson, Frederic 2019, *Allegory and Ideology*, London: Verso.
Johnson, Walter 2013, *River of Dark Dreams: Slavery and Empire in the Cotton Kingdom*,
    Cambridge, MA: The Belknap Press of Harvard University Press.
Jones, Donna v. 2010, 'The End of Europe: Pessimistic Historiography in the Interwar
    Years and the Paradox of Universalism', *Clio*, 39, 2: 1–27.
Jones, Owen 2016, *Chavs: The Demonization of the Working Class*, London: Verso.
Jünger, Ernst 2003 [1920], *Storm of Steel*, trans. Michael Hofmann, London: Penguin.
Jünger, Ernst 2018 [1932], *The Worker: Dominion and Form*, ed. Laurence Paul Hemming,
    trans. Bogdan Costea and Laurence Paul Hemming, Evanston: Northwestern Uni-
    versity Press.
Kagarlitsky, Boris, 2000, 'The Suicide of the New Left Review', *International Socialism*
    88, available at: http://pubs.socialistreviewindex.org.uk/isj88/kagarlitsky.htm.

Karatani, Kojin 2017, *Isonomia and the Origins of Philosophy*, Durham, NC: Duke University Press.

Katz, Daniel 2017, ''I did not walk here all the way from prose': Ben Lerner's Virtual Poetics', *Textual Practice* 31, 2: 315–37.

Keiller, Patrick 2014, *The View from the Train*, London: Verso.

Kinkle, Jeff and Alberto Toscano 2011, 'Filming the Crisis: A Survey', *Film Quarterly*, 65, 1: 39–51.

Klein, Naomi 2007, *The Shock Doctrine: The Rise of Disaster Capitalism*, London: Allen Lane.

Klossowski, Pierre 2007 [1963], *Such a Deathly Desire*, trans. Russell Ford, New York: State University of New York Press.

Knorr Cetina, Karin and Urs Breugger 2000, 'The Market as an Object of Attachment: Exploring Postsocial Relations in Financial Markets', *Canadian Journal of Sociology*, 25, 2: 141–68.

Knowles, Caroline 2015, 'The Flip-Flop Trail and Fragile Globalization', *Theory, Culture & Society*, 32, 7–8: 231–44.

Kofman, Sarah 2014 [1975], *Camera Obscura: Of Ideology*, trans. Will Straw, Ithaca: Cornell University Press.

Kornbluh, Anna 2014, *Realizing Capital: Financial and Psychic Economies in Victorian Form*, New York: Fordham University Press.

Kornbluh, Anna 2017, 'We Have Never Been Critical: Toward the Novel as Critique', *Novel: A Forum on Fiction*, 50, 3: 397–408.

Kornbluh, Anna 2019, *The Order of Forms: Realism, Formalism and Social Space*, Chicago: The University of Chicago Press.

Kraniauskas, John 2009, 'Elasticity of Demand: Reflections on *The Wire*', *Radical Philosophy*, 154: 25–34.

Kraus, Chris 2011, *Where Art Belongs*, Los Angeles, CA: Semiotext(e).

Kurz, Robert 2011, 'A World Without Money', *Exit Online*, available at: https://www.exit-online.org/textanz1.php?tabelle=transnationales&index=1&posnr=87&backtext1=text1.php.

Laing, R.D. 1970, *The Politics of Experience* and *The Bird of Paradise*, Harmondsworth: Penguin.

Lakatos, Imre and Alan Musgrave (ed.) 2008, *Criticism and the Growth of Knowledge*, Cambridge: Cambridge University Press.

Land, Nick 2013, *Fanged Noumena: Collected Writings 1987–2007*, ed. Robin Mackay and Ray Brassier, Falmouth: Urbanomic.

Landa, Ishay 2007, *The Overman in the Marketplace: Nietzschean Heroism in Popular Culture*, Washington, DC: Lexington Books.

Landa, Ishay 2013, 'True Requirements or the Requirements of Truth? The Nietzschean Communism of Alain Badiou', *International Critical Thought*, 3, 4: 424–443

Laruelle, François 2013, *Anti-Badiou: On the Introduction of Maoism into Philosophy*, trans. Robin Mackay, London: Bloomsbury.

Latour, Bruno 1988, *The Pasteurization of France*, trans. Alan Sheridan and John Law, Cambridge, MA: Harvard University Press.

Latour, Bruno 2004, 'Why has Critique Run Out of Steam? From Matters of Fact to Matters of Concern', *Critical Inquiry*, 30: 225–48.

Latour, Bruno 2005, *Reassembling the Social*, Oxford: Oxford University Press.

Latour, Bruno 2010, 'An Attempt at a 'Compositionist Manifesto'. *New Literary History*, 41: 471–90.

Latour, Bruno 2013, *An Inquiry into Modes of Existence: An Anthropology of the Moderns*, trans. Catherine Porter, Cambridge, MA: Harvard University Press.

Lears, Jackson 2010, 'Mad Monkey. Review of *Matterhorn* by Karl Marlantes', *London Review of Books*, 32,18, 15–17, available at: http://www.lrb.co.uk/v32/n18/jackson-lears/mad-monkey.

Lenin, Vladimir Ilyich 1970, *On the Paris Commune*, Moscow: Progress Publishers.

Lenin, Vladimir Ilyich 2008, 'The Military Programme of the Proletarian Revolution', *Marxists Internet Archive*, available at: https://www.marxists.org/archive/lenin/works/1916/miliprog/index.htm#ii.

Lerner, Ben 2014, *10.04*, London: Granta.

Leslie, Esther 2015, 'Introduction: Walter Benjamin and the Birth of Photography', in Walter Benjamin, *On Photography*, ed. and trans. Esther Leslie, London: Reaktion Books.

Levine, Carol 2015, *Forms: Whole, Rhythm, Hierarchy*, Network, Princeton: Princeton University Press.

Lévi-Strauss, Claude 1972 [1962], *The Savage Mind*, London: Weidenfeld and Nicolson.

Linebaugh, Peter 1986, 'In the Flight Path of Perry Anderson', *History Workshop Journal*, 21: 141–6.

Lish, Gordon 2013, *Peru*, Champaign: Dalkey Archive Press.

Losurdo, Domenico 2019 [2002], *Nietzsche, the Aristocratic Rebel: Intellectual Biography and Critical Balance-Sheet*, intro. Harrison Fluss, trans. Gregor Benton, Leiden: Brill.

Love, Heather 2010, 'Close but not Deep: Literary Ethics and the Descriptive Turn', *New Literary History*, 41: 371–91.

Luisetti, Federico 2011, 'Nietzsche's Orientalist Biopolitics', *BioPolítica*, last accessed 12.10.2011.

Lukács, Georg 1962 [1955], *The Historical Novel*, trans. Hannah and Stanley Mitchell, London: Merlin.

Lukács, Georg 1963, *The Meaning of Contemporary Realism*, trans. John and Necke Mander, London: Merlin Press.

Lukács, Georg 1970, *Writer and Critic and Other Essays*, trans. Arthur D. Kahn, London: Merlin.

Lukács, Georg 1971a [1916], *The Theory of the Novel: A Historico-Philosophical Essay on the Forms of Great Epic Literature*, trans. Anna Bostock, London: Merlin.

Lukács, Georg 1971b [1923], *History and Class Consciousness*, trans. Rodney Livingstone, London: Merlin.

Lukács, Georg 2007, 'Realism in the Balance', in *Aesthetics and Politics*, Adorno et al. London: Verso.

Lukács, Georg 2021 [1952], *The Destruction of Reason*, intro. Enzo Traverso, trans. Peter Palmer, London: Verso.

Lupton, Christina 2008, 'Theorizing Surfaces and Depths: Gaskell's *Cranford*', *Criticism*, 50, 2: 235–54.

Lupton, Christina 2011, 'Giving Power to the Medium: Recovering the 1750s', *The Eighteenth Century*, 52, 3: 289–302.

Lustig, Kfir Cohen 2019, *Makers of Worlds, Readers of Signs: Israeli and Palestinian Literature of the Global Contemporary*, London: Verso.

Lutz, Garry 2009, 'The Sentence is a Lonely Place', *The Believer*, available at: http://www.believermag.com/issues/200901/?read=article_lutz.

Lyotard, Jean-François 1984 [1979], *The Postmodern Condition*, trans. Geoff Bennington and Brian Massumi, Minneapolis: University of Minnesota Press.

Lyotard, Jean-François 1988, *Peregrinations: Law, Form, Event*, New York: Columbia University Press.

Lyotard, Jean-François 1989, 'Beyond Representation', in *The Lyotard Reader*, ed. Andrew Benjamin, Oxford: Blackwell, pp. 155–168.

Lyotard, Jean-François 1993 [1974], *Libidinal Economy*, trans. Iain Hamilton Grant. London: Athlone.

Lyotard, Jean-François 2003 [1996], *Postmodern Fables*, trans. Georges Van Den Abbeele, Minneapolis: University of Minnesota Press.

Lyotard, Jean-François, and Jean-Loup Thébaud 1985 [1979], *Just Gaming*, trans. Wlad Godzich, Minneapolis: University of Minnesota Press.

MacCabe, Colin 1974, 'Realism and the Cinema: Notes on some Brechtian theses', *Screen*, 15, 2: 7–27.

McClanahan, Annie 2016, *Dead Pledges: Debt, Crisis, and Twenty-First Century Culture*, Stanford: Stanford University Press.

McGurl, Mark 2009, *The Program Era: Postwar fiction and the Rise of Creative Writing*, Cambridge, MA: Harvard University Press.

McGurl, Mark 2021, *Everything and Less: The Novel in the Age of Amazon*, London: Verso.

McNally, David 2012, *Monsters of the Market: Zombies, Vampires, and Global Capitalism*, Chicago: Haymarket Books.

Malm, Andreas 2016, *Fossil Capital: The Rise of Steam Power and the Roots of Global Warming*, London: Verso.

Malm, Andreas 2017a, 'The Walls of the Tank: On Palestinian Resistance', *Salvage*, available at: https://salvage.zone/the-walls-of-the-tank-on-palestinian-resistance/.

Malm, Andreas 2017b, *The Progress of this Storm: Nature and Society in a Warming World*, London: Verso.

Malm, Andreas 2020, *Corona, Climate, Chronic Emergency: War Communism in the Twenty-First Century*, London: Verso.

Mansoor, Jaleh 2016, *Marshall Plan Modernism: Italian Postwar Abstraction and the Beginning of Autonomia*, Durham, NC: Duke University Press.

Mansoor, Jaleh, Daniel Marcus, and Daniel Spaulding 2012, 'Response to Occupy', *October*, 142: 48–50.

Marcus, Greil 2011, *Lipstick Traces: A Secret History of the Twentieth Century*, London: Faber and Faber.

Marcuse, Herbert 1972 [1955], *Eros and Civilisation: A Philosophical Inquiry into Freud*, London: Abacus.

Marcuse, Herbert 2002 [1964], *One-Dimensional Man: Studies in the Ideology of Advanced Industrial Society*, London: Routledge.

Martin, Nicholas 1995, ' 'We Good Europeans': Nietzsche's New Europe in Beyond Good and Evil', *History of European Ideas*, 20, 1–3: 141–4.

Martin, Stewart 2009, 'Artistic Communism – a Sketch', *Third Text* 23, 4: 481–94.

Marx, Karl 1973, *Grundrisse*, trans. Martin Nicolaus, Harmondsworth: Penguin.

Marx, Karl 1975, *Early Writings*, intro. Lucio Colletti, trans. Rodney Livingstone and Gregor Benton, Harmondsworth: Penguin.

Marx, Karl 1990 [1867], *Capital vol. 1*, intro. Ernest Mandel, trans. Ben Fowkes, London: Penguin.

Marx, Karl 1992 [1894], *Capital. Vol. 3*, intro. Ernest Mandel, trans. David Fernbach, London: Penguin.

Marx, Karl 2000, *Selected Writings*, ed. David McLellan, Oxford: Oxford University Press.
Marx, Karl 2019, *The Political Writings*, foreword by Tariq Ali, intro. David Fernbach, London: Verso.

Marx, Karl and Friedrich Engels 2011, *The German Ideology: Parts I and III*, Mansfield Centre: Martino Publishing.

Mattar, Sinéad Garrigan 2012, 'Yeats, Fairies, and the New Animism', *New Literary History* 43, 1: 137–57.

Mattis, Leon de 2011, 'Reflections on the *Call*', in *Communization and its Discontents: Contestation, Critique, and Contemporary Struggles*, ed. Benjamin Noys, Brooklyn, NY: Autonomedia / Minor Compositions.

Meiksins Wood, Ellen 1991, *The Pristine Culture of Capitalism: A Historical Essay on Old Regimes and Modern States*, London: Verso.

Meillassoux, Quentin 2008, *After Finitude: An Essay on the Necessity of Contingency*, trans. Ray Brassier, London: Continuum.

Miéville, China 2005, 'Introduction', in H.P. Lovecraft, *At the Mountains of Madness*, New York: The Modern Library.

Miéville, China 2016, *Last Days of the New Paris*, New York: Del Ray Books.

Mirowski, Philip 2014, *Never Let a Good Crisis Go to Waste: How Neoliberalism Survived the Financial Meltdown*, London: Verso.

Mitchell, Timothy 2011, *Carbon Democracy: Political Power in the Age of Oil*, London: Verso.

Mitropolous Angela, and Melinda Cooper 2009, 'In Praise of Ursura', *Mute*, 2, 13: 92–107.

Montag, Warren 1994, *The Unthinkable Swift: The Spontaneous Philosophy of a Church of England Man*, London: Verso.

Moore, Jason 2015, *Capitalism in the Web of Life*, London: Verso.

Moretti, Franco 1996, *Modern Epic: The World System from Goethe to Garcia Marquez*, trans. Quintin Hoare, London: Verso.

Moretti, Franco 2005, *Distant Reading*, London: Verso.

Mulhern, Francis 1974, 'The Marxist Aesthetics of Christopher Caudwell', *New Left Review*, I, 85: 37–58.

Mulhern, Francis 1979, *The Moment of 'Scrutiny'*, London: New Left Books.

Mulhern, Francis 1998, *The Present Lasts a Long Time: Essays in Cultural Politics*, Cork: Cork University Press.

Mulhern, Francis 2000, *Culture / Metaculture*, London: Routledge.

Mulhern, Francis 2015, 'Afterlives of the Commune', *New Left Review*, 96: 129–37.

Mulhern, Francis 2016, *Figures of Catastrophe: The Condition of Culture Novel*, London: Verso.

Müntzer, Thomas 2010, *Sermon to the Princes*, intro. Wu Ming, London: Verso.

Nain, Tom 1964, 'The British Political Elite', *New Left Review*, I, 23: 19–25.

Nairn, Tom 1988, *The Enchanted Glass: Britain and Its Monarchy*, London: Radius.

Nancy, Jean-Luc 1991, *The Inoperative Community*, ed. Peter Connor, trans. Peter Connor et al, Minneapolis: The University of Minnesota Press.

Nealon, Christopher 2011, *The Matter of Capital: Poetry and Crisis in the American Century*, Cambridge, MA: Harvard University Press.

Neel, Phil A. 2018, *Hinterland: America's New Landscape of Class and Conflict*, London: Reaktion Books.

Negarestani, Reza 2008, *Cyclonopedia: Complicity with Anonymous Materials*, Melbourne: re.press.

Négation 2007, 'Lip and the Self-Managed Counter-Revolution', trans. Peter Rachleff and Alan Wallach, *Lib.com*, available at: http://libcom.org/library/lip-and-the-self-managed-counter-revolution-negation.

Negri, Antonio 2003, *Time for Revolution*, trans. Matteo Mandarini, London: Continuum.

Negri, Antonio 2005, *Books for Burning: Between Civil War and Democracy in 1970s Italy*, ed. Timothy S. Murphy, trans. Arianna Bove et al, London: Verso.

Negri, Antonio 2009, 'No New Deal is possible', trans. Arianna Bove, *Radical Philosophy*, 155: 2–5.

Neyrat, Frédéric 2018, *Atopias: Manifesto for a Radical Existentialism*, trans. Walt Hunter and Lindsay Turner, New York: Fordham University Press.

Niblett, Michael 2012, 'World-Economy, World-Ecology, World Literature', *Green Letters*, 16, 1: 15–30.

Nietzsche, Friedrich 1968, *The Will to Power*, trans. Walter Kaufmann and R.J. Hollingdale, ed. Walter Kaufmann, New York: Vintage.

Nietzsche, Friedrich 1973 [1886], *Beyond Good and Evil*, trans. R.J. Hollingdale, London: Penguin.

Nietzsche, Friedrich 1983 [1873], *Untimely Meditations*, trans. R.J. Hollingdale, Cambridge: Cambridge University Press.

Nietzsche, Friedrich 1996, *Selected Letters of Friedrich Nietzsche*, ed. and trans. Christopher Middleton, Indianapolis: Hackett Publishing Company.

Nietzsche, Friedrich 2001 [1882], *The Gay Science*, ed. Bernard Williams, Cambridge: Cambridge University Press.

Nietzsche, Friedrich 2005, *The Anti-Christ, Ecce Homo, Twilight of the Idols, and Other Writings*, ed. Aaron Ridley and Judith Norman, trans. Judith Norman, Cambridge: Cambridge University Press.

Nietzsche, Friedrich 2008a [1887], *On the Genealogy of Morals*, trans. Douglas Smith, Oxford: Oxford University Press.

Nietzsche, Friedrich 2008b [1872], *The Birth of Tragedy*, trans. Douglas Smith, Oxford: Oxford University Press.

Nordau, Max 1993 [1892], *Degeneration*, Lincoln, NE: University of Nebraska Press.

Not Bored! 1999, 'Norman Cohn's *The Pursuit of the Millennium*', available at: http://www.notbored.org/cohn.html

Noys, Benjamin 2000, *Georges Bataille: A Critical Introduction*, London: Pluto.

Noys, Benjamin 2009, ''Monumental Construction': Badiou and the Politics of Aesthetics', *Third Text*, 23, 4: 383–92.

Noys, Benjamin 2010, *The Persistence of the Negative: A Critique of Contemporary Continental Theory*, Edinburgh: Edinburgh University Press.

Noys, Benjamin 2014, *Malign Velocities: Accelerationism & Capitalism*, Winchester, UK: Zero Books.

Noys, Benjamin 2015a, ''Love and Napalm: Export USA': Schizoanalysis, Acceleration, and Contemporary American Literature', in *Deleuze and the Schizoanalysis of Literature*, ed. Ian Buchanan, Tim Matts, and Aidan Tynan. London: Bloomsbury Academic.

Noys, Benjamin 2015b, 'Drone Metaphysics', 'Drone Culture' Special Issue, ed. Rob Coley and Dean Lockwood, *Culture Machine*, 16, available at: https://culturemachine.net/vol-16-drone-cultures/drone-methaphysics/.

Noys, Benjamin 2019, 'The Art of Capital: Artistic Identity and the Paradox of Valorisation', in *In the Mind but Not from There: Real Abstraction and Contemporary Art*, ed. Gean Moreno, London: Verso.

Noys, Benjamin 2023, *The Matter of Language: Poetry and Abstraction*, Calcutta: Seagull Books.

Nunes, Rodrigo 2012, 'The Lessons of 2011: Three Theses on Organisation', *Mute*, available at: http://www.metamute.org/editorial/articles/lessons-2011-three-theses-orga nisation.

Nunes, Rodrigo 2021, *Neither Vertical nor Horizontal: A Theory of Political Organization*, London: Verso.

Osborne, Peter 2013, *Anywhere or Not at All: Philosophy of Contemporary Art*, London: Verso.

Perlman, Fredy 1983, *Against His-story, Against Leviathan!*, Detroit: Black & Red.

Polanyi, Karl 1980 [1944], *The Great Transformation: The Political and Economic Origins of Our Time*, Boston, MA: Beacon Press.

Popper, Karl 2002 [1963], *Conjectures and Refutations: The Growth of Scientific Knowledge*, London: Routledge.

Postone, Moishe 1993, *Time, Labor, and Social Domination*, Cambridge: Cambridge University Press.

Preciado, Paul B. 2013, *Testo Junkie: Sex, Drugs and Biopolitics in the Pharmacopornographic Era*, trans. Bruce Benderson, New York: The Feminist Press.

Pynchon, Thomas 1975, *Gravity's Rainbow*, London: Picador.

Pynchon, Thomas 2007, *Against the Day*, London: Penguin.

Rancière, Jacques 2004 [1995], *Disagreement: Politics and Philosophy*, Minneapolis: University of Minnesota Press.

Rancière, Jacques 2007, 'Art of the possible: Fluvia Carnevale and John Kelsey in conversation with Jacques Rancière', *Artforum*, XLV, 256–9, 261–4, 266–7, 269.

Rancière, Jacques 2009, *The Emancipated Spectator*, trans. Gregory Elliott, London: Verso.

Rancière, Jacques 2010 [2005], *Chronicles of Consensual Times*, trans. Steve Corcoran, London: Continuum.

Rancière, Jacques 2011 [1974], *Althusser's Lesson*, trans. Emiliano Battista, London: Continuum.

Reid, Donald 2018, *Opening the Gates: The Lip Affair, 1968–1981*, London: Verso.

Retort 2005, *Afflicted Powers: Capital and Spectacle in a New Age of Art*, London: Verso.

Ricoeur, Paul 1977, *Freud and Philosophy: An Essay on Interpretation*, trans. D. Savage, New Haven: Yale University Press.

Roberts, John 2010, 'Revolutionary Pathos, Negation, and the Suspensive Avant-Garde', *New Literary History*, 41, 4: 717–30.

Roberts, John 2015, *Revolutionary Time and the Avant-Garde*, London: Verso.

Robinson, Kim Stanley 2012, 'Terraforming Earth', *Slate*, available at: https://slate.com/technology/2012/12/geoengineering-science-fiction-and-fact-kim-stanley-robinson-on-how-we-are-already-terraforming-earth.html.

Rocamadur / Blaumachen 2012, 'The Feral Underclass Hits the Streets: On the English Riots and other Ordeals', *sic: International Journal for Communization*, available at: http://sic.communisation.net/en/the-feral-underclass-hits-the-streets?DokuWiki=e19764affecb034401ae1fc9df032fbb.

Rose, Gillian 1984, *Dialectic of Nihilism: Post-Structuralism and Law*, Oxford: Blackwell.

Rose, Gillian 2009 [1981], *Hegel Contra Sociology*, London: Verso.

Rose, Gillian 2017 [1993], *Judaism and Modernity: Philosophical Essays*, London: Verso.

Rose, Jacqueline 2020, 'Pointing the Finger', *London Review of Books*, 42, 9, available at: https://www.lrb.co.uk/the-paper/v42/n09/jacqueline-rose/pointing-the-finger.

Rosenberg, Jordy 2014, 'The Molecularization of Sexuality: On Some Primitivisms of the Present', *Theory and Event*, 17, 2, available at: http://muse.jhu.edu/journals/theory_and_event/v017/17.2.rosenberg.html.

Ross, Kirsten 2016, *Communal Luxury: The Political Imaginary of the Paris Commune*, London: Verso.

Roth, Marco 2009, 'Rise of the Neuro-Novel', *n+1*, 8, available at: https://nplusonemag.com/issue-8/essays/the-rise-of-the-neuronovel/.

Sartre, Jean-Paul 2000, *Nausea*, trans. Robert Baldick. London: Penguin.

Schebera, Jürgen 1995, *Kurt Weill: An Illustrated Life*, New Haven: Yale University Press.

Schmidgen, Henning 2013, 'The Materiality of Things? Bruno Latour, Charles Péguy and the History of Science', *History of the Human Sciences* 26, 1: 3–28.

Schmidgen, Henning 2015, *Bruno Latour in Pieces: An Intellectual Biography*, trans. Gloria Custance, New York: Fordham University Press.

Schmitt, Carl 2007 [1963], *Theory of the Partisan*, trans. G.L. Ulmen, New York: Telos Publishing.

Sedgwick, Peter 1964, 'The Two New Lefts', *International Socialism* (1st series) 17, *Marxists Internet Archive*, available at: http://www.marxists.org/archive/sedgwick/1964/08/2newlefts.htm.

Seymour, Benedict 2006, 'Drowning by Numbers: The Non-Reproduction of New Orleans', *Mute Magazine*, available at: https://www.metamute.org/editorial/articles/drowning-numbers-non-reproduction-new-orleans.

Sharpe, Matthew 2021, 'Golden Calf: Deleuze's Nietzsche in the Time of Trump', *Thesis Eleven*, 163, 1: 77–88.

Shaviro, Steven 2015, *No Speed Limit: Three Essays on Accelerationism*, Minneapolis: University of Minnesota Press.

Silver, Beverly J. 2003, *Forces of Labour*, Cambridge: Cambridge University Press.

Simon, Roland 2011, 'The Present Moment', *SIC: International Journal for Communiz-ation* 1: 95–144, available at: http://riff-raff.se/en/sic1/sic-1-07-the-present-moment .pdf.

Simon, Roland and Collectif 2009, *Histoire Critique de l'Ultragauche: Trajectoire d'une Balle dans le Pied*, Avignon: Editions Senonevero.

Simon, Roland & riff-raff 2006, 'Interview with Roland Simon', *Riff-Raff* 8, available at: http://www.riff-raff.se/en/8/interview_roland.php.

Situationist International 1989, *Situationist International Anthology*, ed. and trans. Ken Knabb, Berkeley: Bureau of Public Secrets.

Slaton-Cox, Glynn 2013, 'Literary Praxis Beyond the Melodrama of Commitment: Edward Upward, Soviet Aesthetics, and Leftist Self-Fashioning', *Comparative Literature*, 65: 408–28.

Sohn-Rethel, Alfred 1978 [1970], *Intellectual and Manual Labour: A Critique of Epistemology*, London: Macmillan.

Sontag, Susan 2009, *Against Interpretation and Other Essays*, London: Penguin.

Sotiris, Panagiotis, and Spyros Sakellaropoulos 2018, 'European Union as Class Project and Imperialist Strategy', *Viewpoint Magazine* 6: Imperialism, available at: https://viewpointmag.com/2018/02/01/european-union-class-project-imperialist-st rategy/.

Starr, Peter 1995, *Logics of Failed Revolt: French Theory after May '68*, Stanford: Stanford University Press.

Tally, Robert T. 2014, *Fredric Jameson: The Project of Dialectical Criticism*, London: Pluto Books.

Tally, Robert T. 2022, *For a Ruthless Critique of All that Exists: Literature in an Age of Capitalism Realism*. Winchester, UK: Zero Books.

Taussig, Michael 1999, *Defacement: Public Secrecy and the Labor of the Negative*, Stanford: Stanford University Press.

Théorie Communiste 2008, 'Much Ado About Nothing?', *Endnotes* 1: 154–206, available at: http://endnotes.org.uk/articles/13.

Théorie Communiste 2009, 'The Glass Floor', riff-raff, available at: http://www.riff-raff .se/wiki/en/theorie_communiste/the_glass_floor.

Theorié Communiste 2011, 'Communization in the Present Tense', trans. Endnotes, in *Communization and its Discontents*, ed. Benjamin Noys, Brooklyn: Autonomedia / Minor Compositions.

Thompson, E.P. 1965, 'The Peculiarities of the English', *Socialist Register Vol. 2*, pp. 311–61.

Thompson, E.P. 1978, *The Poverty of Theory and Other Essays*, London: Merlin Press.

Thompson, E.P. 2013 [1963], *The Making of the English Working Class*, London: Penguin.

Tiqqun 2010, *Introduction to Civil War*, trans. Alexander R. Galloway and Jason Smith, Los Angeles: Semiotext(e).

Toscano, Alberto 2008a, 'The Culture of Abstraction', *Theory, Culture & Society*, 25, 4: 57–75.

Toscano, Alberto 2008b, 'The Open Secret of Real Abstraction', *Rethinking Marxism*, 20, 2: 273–87.

Toscano, Alberto 2013, 'Gaming the Plumbing: High-Frequency Trading and the Spaces of Capital', *Mute*, 3, 4, available at: https://www.metamute.org/editorial/articles/gaming-plumbing-high-frequency-trading-and-spaces-capital.

Toscano, Alberto 2014, 'Transition Deprogrammed', *South Atlantic Quarterly*, 113, 4: 761–775.

Toscano, Alberto 2017, *Fanaticism: On the Uses of an Idea*, London: Verso.

Toscano, Alberto 2021, 'The Tragic Festival', *Nineteenth-Century French Studies*, 49, 3: 657–81.

Toscano, Alberto, and Jeff Kinkle 2015, *Cartographies of the Absolute*, Winchester, UK: Zero Books.

Tronti, Mario 2019 [1966], *Workers and Capital*, trans. David Broder, London: Verso.

Tronti, Mario 2020, *The Weapon of Organization: Mario Tronti's Political Revolution in Marxism*, ed. and trans. Andrew Anastasi, New York: Common Notions.

Urpeth, Jim 2014, 'Religious Immanence: A Critique of Meillassoux's 'Virtual' God', *Angelaki: Journal of the Theoretical Humanities*, 19, 1: 49–64.

Vesser, H. Aram (ed.) 1989, *The New Historicism*, London: Routledge.

Virilio, Paul 1990 [1978], *Popular Defense and Ecological Struggles*, trans. Mark Polizzotti, New York: Semiotext(e).

Virilio, Paul 2006 [1977], *Speed and Politics*, trans. Marc Polizzotti, New York: Semiotext(e).

Virilio Paul, and Sylvère Lotringer 1983, *Pure War*, trans. Mark Polizzotti, New York: Semiotext(e).

Virno, Paolo 2005 [2001], *A Grammar of the Multitude: For an Analysis of Contemporary Forms of Life*, trans. Isabella Bertolleti et al, foreword by Sylvère Lotringer, Los Angeles: Semiotext(e).

Wade, Robert 2008, 'Financial Regime Change?', *New Left Review*, 53: 5–21.

Waite, Geoff 1996, *Nietzsche Corps/e: Aesthetics, Politics, Prophecy, or, The Spectacular Technoculture of Everyday Life*, Durham, NC: Duke University Press.

Walker, Gavin 2013, 'The Absent Body of Labour Power: Uno Kōzō's Logic of Capital', *Historical Materialism*, 21, 4: 201–34.

Walker, Gavin 2016, *The Sublime Perversion of Capital: Marxist Theory and the Politics of History in Japan*, Durham, NC: Duke University Press.

Wark, Mackenzie 2011, *The Beach Beneath the Street*, London: Verso.

Wark, Mackenzie 2015, *Molecular Red: Theory for the Anthropocene*, London: Verso.

Weber, Max 1989 [1905], *The Protestant Ethic and the Spirit of Capitalism*, London: Unwin Hyman.

Weber, Max 2020, *Charisma and Disenchantment: The Vocation Lectures*, ed. Paul Reitter and Chad Wellmon, New York: NYRB.

Weber, Samuel 2009, 'Europe and Its Others: Some Preliminary Reflections on the Relation of Reflexivity and Violence in Rodolphe Gasché's *Europe, or the Infinite Task*', CR: *The New Centennial Review*, 8, 3: 71–83.

Wenzel, Jennifer 2006, 'Petro-Magic-Realism: Toward a Political Ecology of Nigerian Literature', *Postcolonial Studies*, 9, 4: 449–64.

WReC (Warwick Research Collective) 2015, *Combined and Uneven Development: Towards a New Theory of World-Literature*, Liverpool: Liverpool University Press.

White, Hylton 2013, 'Materiality, Form, and Context: Marx contra Latour', *Victorian Studies*, 55, 4: 667–82.

Williams, Evan Calder 2011, 'Hostile Object Theory', *Mute Magazine*, available at: https://www.metamute.org/editorial/articles/hostile-object-theory.

Williams, Raymond 1958, *Culture and Society: 1780–1950*, Harmondsworth: Penguin.

Williams, Raymond 1977, *Marxism and Literature*, Oxford: Oxford University Press.

Williams, Raymond 1991, *Orwell*, London: Fontana.

Winters, David 2013, 'Truth, Force, Composition', *3AM Magazine*, available at: http://www.3ammagazine.com/3am/truth-force-composition/.

Wright, Patrick 1985, *On Living in an Old Country: The National Past in Contemporary Britain*, London: Verso.

Zerzan, John 1998, *Elements of Refusal*, Columbia: C.A.L. Press.

Žižek, Slavoj 1989, *The Sublime Object of Ideology*, London: Verso.

Index

www.ingramcontent.com/pod-product-compliance
Lightning Source LLC
Chambersburg PA
CBHW061725120626
46550CB00005B/1708